STUDY GUIDE

TO ACCOMPANY

MICROECONOMICS:
THEORY AND APPLICATIONS
Seventh Edition

EDGAR K. BROWNING
Texas A&M University

MARK A. ZUPAN
University of Arizona

Prepared by

JOHN LUNN
Hope College

JOHN WILEY & SONS, INC.

To order books or for customer service call 1-800-CALL-WILEY (225-5945).

ISBN 0-471-11160-0

Printed in the United States of America

10 9 8 7 6 5 4 3 2

Printed and bound by Courier Kendallville, Inc.

Table of Contents

CHAPTER 1 *An Introduction to Microeconomics*

CHAPTER ANALYSIS

1.1 Individuals make choices based on their own desires and the opportunities they face. **Microeconomics** is a body of theory that attempts to explain the choices individuals make given the opportunities and constraints in their environments.

1.2-1.4 Here the subject of microeconomics is discussed by focusing on the purpose of theory. On any given day, countless millions of economic decisions are made by millions of individuals, and it would be an impossible task to determine and understand every factor that influences each decision. A theory, then, enables an economist to distinguish facts that are important in explaining economic behavior from those that are trivial or irrelevant. The authors emphasize that a good theory is one that explains and predicts the phenomena that it is intended to explain and predict.

Economics is often used to evaluate public policy. Three steps are involved—(1) determine the effects of the policy, (2) determine the size of the effects, and (3) evaluate whether the effects are desirable or not. The first two steps are examples of **positive analysis** since they involve objective analysis. The third step involves a value judgment and is an example of **normative analysis**. (See illustration "Policy Evaluation" below.)

Markets play an important role in microeconomic theory. Markets include local farmers' markets where people come to a common location in a town a few days a week to buy and sell vegetables, the New York Stock Exchange where shares of stock of large corporations are bought and sold, and labor markets where people search for jobs and firms search for workers. Economists focus on the role of prices in affecting the behavior of buyers and sellers in a market. The absolute price of a good is the money price of the good, but this price is not very useful because the absolute price changes over time due to inflation. Economists concentrate on the **relative price** (or real price) of a good, which is the nominal (or absolute) price relative to the nominal prices of other goods. In this book, unless specifically told otherwise, the price of a good refers to its real price.

1.5-1.6 To develop theories, some common starting ground is needed. In microeconomics, we begin with three assumptions about participants in markets. First, market participants are assumed to be **goal-oriented**. That is, people set goals and try to achieve their goals. Noneconomists often take this assumption to mean that economists assume people are selfish. However, goal-oriented behavior does not imply selfishness, although certainly many people do behave selfishly. A parent who works long hours and refrains from buying many goods and services in order to save for the child's college education is engaging in goal-oriented behavior. Individuals determine their goals. The second assumption is that people pursue their goals **rationally**. That is, they make plans and deliberately seek to attain their goals. The third assumption is that people confront **scarce resources**. We cannot have everything we want because of scarcity. In order to attain some of the goals a person sets, that person must rationally make choices that take into consideration the fact that resources are scarce. Microeconomics is concerned with the way people make choices subject to scarcity.

An implication of scarcity is that people must make choices. To make a choice is to choose one thing instead of something else. Suppose you and a friend go to a movie and each pays $7 to see the movie. Suppose further that if you had not spent the seven dollars on the movie you would have bought a book, while your friend would have rented two videos. The **opportunity cost** of the movie for you is the book you didn't buy while the opportunity cost of the movie for your friend is the two videos that were not rented. There is a cost to any choice that a person makes, and the cost is the value of the next best alternative.

Costs can be classified as explicit and implicit costs. **Explicit costs** are the dollars spent on the goods and services we choose to have. **Implicit costs** are associated with the alternative uses of resources owned by the person, including the use of the person's time. For implicit costs, there is not an explicit payment made, but something of value is given up. People take into consideration both explicit and implicit costs when they rationally make choices in pursuit of the goals they have set.

Accountants and economists do not measure costs in the same way. Implicit costs are difficult to objectively measure and are usually ignored by accountants. Further, they generally rely on the price paid for something as a measure of its cost even when the value of the good has increased or decreased. The relevant cost for making rational decisions is the opportunity cost, which may or may not be related to the price paid for the good at some time in the past.

There is a difference between opportunity costs and **sunk costs** that must be noted. Sunk costs are costs that have already been incurred and cannot be recovered. In making economic decisions, sunk costs should be ignored. If you go to a restaurant, order a large meal, and then are full before the food is gone, should you continue eating the food because you're paying for it? The economic answer is no, since you must pay for the food whether you eat it or not. The price of the meal is a sunk cost since you can't alter it by either eating or not eating the rest of the food. If you will make yourself uncomfortable by finishing the meal, you would be better off not doing so. The sunk cost is irrelevant in making the decision.

1.7 A **production possibility frontier (PPF)** illustrates the basic assumptions we have made about market participants, as well as the idea of opportunity cost. A production possibility frontier shows the different combinations of two goods that a person can attain with a given amount of resources. For example, suppose a rancher with a certain amount of land, workers, and other resources can raise cattle or sheep on the ranch. The rancher can either raise only cattle, or only sheep, or different combinations of cattle and sheep.

Figure 1-1 illustrates the rancher's situation. By devoting all the resources to raising cattle, the rancher can raise 10,000 cattle (Point A); by devoting all the resources to raising sheep, the rancher can raise 15,000 sheep (Point F). The curve shows all the possible combinations of cattle and sheep that the rancher can choose from, assuming that the rancher is using all the resources as efficiently as possible.

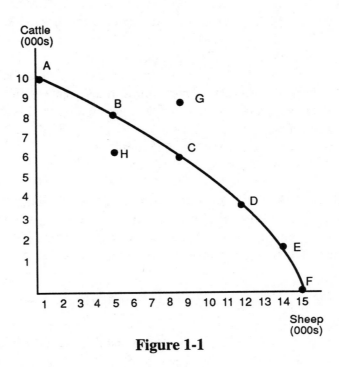

Figure 1-1

Point G shows a combination of cattle and sheep that the rancher cannot attain, given the resources owned by the rancher. The rancher would prefer to be at Point G rather than many of the points on the PPF but cannot. The goal of the goal-oriented rancher is to have as many cattle and sheep as possible. But scarcity impinges on these goals. Scarcity is shown by the curve. Rational behavior presumes the rancher will be on the curve rather than inside it. At Point H, the rancher can get more cattle by moving to B, or can get more sheep by moving to C, or more of both by moving to the PPF between Points B and C. A rational, goal-oriented person will be on the PPF. Finally, the curve illustrates the idea of opportunity cost, since the only way the rancher can raise more cattle is by raising fewer sheep. The opportunity cost of more cattle is less sheep, and vice-versa.

ILLUSTRATIONS

Policy Evaluation

Capital punishment is a controversial subject that can be used to illustrate the evaluation of policy. Although there are many things to consider in evaluating the desirability or undesirability of capital punishment, we will focus on one question: Is capital punishment a deterrent to crime?

The first step is to determine the effect of capital punishment on the crime rate. Proponents of capital punishment believe that it will reduce the crime rate. This can be tested by comparing crime rates in areas with capital punishment with crime rates in areas that do not allow capital punishment (Note that other factors could affect crime rates-gun control laws, poverty, number of police, and the like-and these factors must be accounted for too.) The second step is to determine the magnitude of the deterrent effect of capital punishment. Is the reduction in the crime rate large or small? These two steps are in the realm of positive analysis because they deal with propositions that can be tested objectively.

Suppose we perform these tests and determine that capital punishment will cause a 10 percent reduction in the crime rate. Should capital punishment be used in our society? To answer this question requires a value judgment; some people will answer affirmatively and others negatively, depending on their values. Thus, this last question is in the realm of normative economics.

Goal-Oriented Behavior

The assumption that people are goal-oriented is controversial to many noneconomists. It is often presumed that economists are saying that everyone is selfish. As noted above, goal-orientation is not equivalent to selfishness. People also counter that people behave on whim or don't know what they really want.

Psychologists have tried to determine whether people engage in self-interested behavior or sometimes behave altruistically. There is disagreement among psychologists—some think all altruistic behavior is actually a disguised form of self-interest, while others think genuine altruism occurs. Does a person give blood in a blood drive to feel good about themselves or out of concern for others? It is difficult to distinguish since even if one is acting out of concern for others, he or she is likely to feel good about him- or herself afterwards.

[For further discussion, see David Myers, Social Psychology (New York: McGraw Hill, 1993).]

KEY CONCEPTS

microeconomics

macroeconomics

price theory

positive analysis

normative analysis

markets

nominal or absolute price

real price

relative price

goal-oriented behavior

rational behavior

scarce resources

explicit costs

implicit costs

economic cost

opportunity cost

accounting cost

sunk costs

production possibility frontier (PPF)

REVIEW QUESTIONS

True/False

_____ 1. A theory must simplify and abstract from reality.

_____ 2. An economist is a better judge than a noneconomist of whether the effects of minimum wage are desirable.

_____ 3. The term *price* as used in microeconomics refers to the nominal price of a good.

_____ 4. The behavior of buyers and sellers depends on the nominal price of a good.

_____ 5. Market participants engage in goal-oriented, which is the same thing as selfish behavior.

_____ 6. A person who gives money to a charity that supplies food to the poor in other parts of the world is engaging in goal-oriented behavior.

_____ 7. Because of scarcity, an individual must decide which goals to pursue and to what extent.

_____ 8. Explicit costs are opportunity costs but implicit costs are not.

_____ 9. Sunk costs are opportunity costs.

_____ 10. If the production possibility curve is a straight line, then costs are constant per unit.

Multiple Choice/Short Answer

1. A good theory is one that
   a. has assumptions that mirror reality.
   b. describes the real world as closely as possible.
   c. incorporates as many facts as possible.
   d. explains or predicts what it is designed to explain or predict.

2. Policy analysis involves
   a. positive economics alone.
   b. normative economics alone.
   c. scientific criteria alone.
   d. both positive and normative analysis.

3. Identify the following statements as positive (P) or normative (N).
   a. Monopolies are more innovative than other firms. P N
   b. Monopolies charge higher prices than competitive firms. P N
   c. Monopolies should be controlled by the government. P N
   d. High interest rates discourage investment spending. P N
   e. The tax burden in the U.S. is too great. P N
   f. If tariffs on imported steel are raised, sales of U.S. automakers will fall. P N
   g. Government should subsidize the arts because the arts benefit everybody. P N

4. In microeconomics, markets refer to
   a. the interaction of buyers and sellers of a particular good.
   b. formal markets only, such as the New York Stock Exchange.
   c. grocery stores and farmers' markets.
   d. the coming together of buyers and sellers at a specific location.

5. The term *price*, as used in microeconomics, always refers to
   a. the absolute price of the good.
   b. the nominal price of the good.
   c. the real price of the good.
   d. any of the above.

6. If the price of a gallon of gasoline was 28 cents in 1965 and 32 cents in 1969, then the
   a. nominal price increased but we can't tell the real price unless we know what happened to the prices of other goods.
   b. nominal price increased but the real price decreased.
   c. absolute price increased but the real price decreased.
   d. absolute and relative price increased.

7. Which of the following is an example of goal-oriented behavior? (More than one answer may be correct.)
   a. A new Ph.D. in accounting accepts a job teaching in a college that pays $50,000 a year instead of a job with a firm paying $75,000 a year.
   b. A family gives ten percent of its income to its place of worship.
   c. A physician leaves her practice in New York City to practice medicine in Rwanda.
   d. A student turns down an opportunity to attend a rock concert in order to study for his math test.
   e. A person gambles in Las Vegas even though the odds are in favor of the casino.

8. Which of the following is an example of a resource that is not scarce?
   a. Air.
   b. Fresh water.
   c. Unskilled labor.
   d. Friends.

9. Explicit costs differ from implicit costs in that explicit costs
   a. are greater than implicit costs.
   b. involve actual expenditures and implicit costs don't.
   c. are opportunity costs and implicit costs are not.
   d. involve materials and equipment and implicit costs involve labor.

10. The economic cost of a resource equals
    a. explicit costs minus implicit costs.
    b. implicit costs minus explicit costs.
    c. explicit costs plus implicit costs.
    d. explicit costs.

11. Given the difference between accounting costs and economic costs, it is generally true that
    a. accounting profits understate the real profitability of a firm.
    b. accounting costs are greater than economic costs.
    c. accounting profits overstate the real profitability of a firm.
    d. better decision making is achieved by ignoring implicit costs.

12. In constructing a production possibility frontier,
    a. resources are assumed to be fixed.
    b. the endpoints of the frontier are determined by the goals set by the rational actor.
    c. sunk costs are measured along the frontier.
    d. the frontier reflects an ideal that is actually unattainable.

13.   Which of the three assumptions about market actors determines the best position on the PPF?
a. Individuals are goal-oriented.
b. Individuals are rational.
c. Market actors are confronted by scarcity.
d. None of these since the three assumptions only place an actor on the PPF boundary.

Questions 14 and 15 use Figure 1-2.

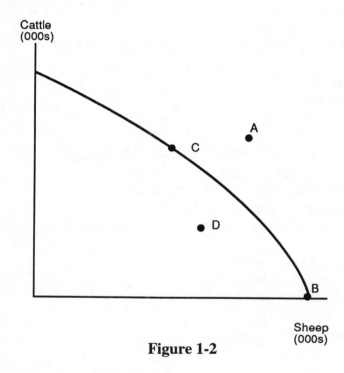

Figure 1-2

14.   An irrational person would be at Point
a. A.
b. B.
c. C.
d. D.

15.   The curved shape of the PPF indicates that
a. people are not rational.
b. opportunity costs are constant as fewer sheep and more cattle are raised.
c. some of the resources are better suited for raising cattle than for raising sheep.
d. cattle are scarcer than sheep.

Discussion Questions and Problems

1. What is the difference between microeconomics and macroeconomics? Why is microeconomics also called price theory?

2. Economists generally assume that firms attempt to maximize profits. Business people often protest that they do not just seek profits but also have other goals for their firms.

   a. Is the assumption of profit maximization realistic?

   b. What might be the goals of managers of firms?

   c. Assume for now that not all business people seek to maximize profits. Does this mean the assumption of profit maximization should be discarded? Why or why not?

3. How is microeconomic theory an example of positive analysis?

4. Explain why True/False question #2 is false.

5.   Suppose we have the following price information:

	Gasoline	*Dozen donuts*
January 1, 2000	$1.00	$4.00
January 1, 2001	$1.50	$4.50

a. What is the real price of gasoline in 2000?

b. Did the real price of gasoline increase or decrease from 2000 to 2001? By how much?

c. What could have caused the change?

d. What happened to the real price of donuts between 2000 and 2001?

6.   Explain how each of the choices in Multiple Choice question #7 can be examples of goal-oriented behavior.

7.   The authors state that the most important assumption economists make about market participants is that they face scarce resources. Can you give a reason for the claim that this is the most important assumption?

8.   Explain how a martyr could be acting in a goal-oriented manner.

9.   Distinguish between an explicit cost and an implicit cost.

10.   Suppose a friend of yours paid $20,000 a year tuition to attend a private college. A few years after graduation, your friend quits a $50,000 a year job to go to graduate school at a public university. The friend comments that the tuition of $5000 a year meant it was cheaper to go to graduate school than to go to college. What economic advice can you give your friend?

11.   Shopping carts are about 50 percent larger today than they were 30 years ago. Give an economic explanation for this.

12.   What are sunk costs? Are sunk costs opportunity costs? Explain.

13. Explain why the three basic assumptions about the behavior of market participants imply that a person will be on the boundary of their PPF.

14. What is the difference between a PPF that characterizes constant costs and a PPF that characterizes increasing costs?

15. Suppose you have a farm that has two types of land—Type A land is great for growing rice and Type B land is great for growing soybeans. What will the PPF look like? Why?

ANSWERS

Review Questions

True/False

1. True
2. False
3. False. Real prices.
4. False. Real prices.
5. False
6. True
7. True
8. False
9. False
10. True

Multiple Choice/Short Answer

1. d
2. d
3. a. P
   b. P
   c. N
   d. P
   e. N
   f. P
   g. N
4. a
5. c
6. a
7. All are examples of goal-oriented behavior.
8. a. Note—clean air may be scarce though.
9. b
10. c
11. c
12. a
13. d
14. d
15. c

Discussion Questions and Problems

1. Microeconomics analyzes the behavior of small units such as consumers, workers, business owners, and individual markets. Macroeconomics is concerned with aggregates such as the total production of the economy and inflation. Because economists consider prices to be an important determinant of individual decision making, microeconomics is also referred to as price theory.

2. a. It is probably not completely realistic since other goals will influence business people.
    b. Possibilities suggested by some economists include sales maximization, growth of sales, maximization of utility, making some minimally accepted profit target. You may think of some others.
    c. No. The assumption simplifies reality. Business people may not seek to maximize profits, but they are striving to make some profits. The assumption allows us to predict the behavior of firms. So long as these predictions tend to coincide with behavior the assumption is useful.

3. Microeconomic theory attempts to explain and predict the behavior of market participants. It tries to determine what the qualitative and quantitative effects of changes in some variable are. It does not enable economists to determine whether a particular change is desirable or not.

4. Economists can determine the qualitative and quantitative effects of the minimum wage law, but the desirability of the law is not determined by these effects. Two people can agree on the effects of the law and still disagree on whether the law is desirable or not. The latter is a value judgment that cannot be evaluated by scientific criteria. Hence, an economist is better able to determine the effects, but the expertise as an economist does not imply that the economist's value judgments are better.

5. a. (P_{gas}/P_{donuts}) 2000 = 1/4 or 1 gal. of gas = 3 donuts
    b. Increase. (P_{gas}/P_{donuts}) 2001 = 1.50/4.50 = 1/3 or 1 gal. of gas = 4 donuts
    c. Many possible explanations, such as an increase in demand for gas, a decrease in demand for donuts, a decrease in supply of gas, an increase in supply of donuts, or some combination.
    d. The real price of donuts fell 4 gallons of gasoline per dozen donuts in 2000 to 3 gallons of gasoline per dozen donuts in 2001. Note that if the real price of gasoline increased, the real price of donuts had to decrease.

6. The accountant may prefer an academic career to a business career and is willing to receive a lower salary to teach. The family that gives a tenth of its income to its place of worship values the beliefs and benefits they receive from the place of worship enough to pay the money. They may believe this is God's will for them, and they want to be obedient. The family sees itself as better off by acting in this way. The physician may want to serve others more than earn a large salary and is better off by her decision. The student may have enjoyed the rock concert more, but he has other goals, including wanting to do well in math. So, he is making himself better off by studying. The gambler may receive enough enjoyment in the act of gambling or the possibility of winning to warrant spending the money at the casino.

7. One way to think about this is to assume one of the assumptions doesn't hold and see what the changes in analysis would be. If resources were not scarce, then people wouldn't have to make choices because they could have everything they want. Suppose people don't care about themselves at all, and only want to do things for others. With scarce resources, they still have to make choices about whether to get food for someone else or to get them clothing. If people aren't rational but resources are scarce, they still would have to make decisions in some way. Relaxing the assumption of scarcity has the greatest effect.

8. A martyr may adhere to a belief so strongly that he or she is willing to die rather than give up the belief. In the case of a religious martyr, a belief in an after-life may also support the person's willingness to die. Again the idea of goal setting is one in which the person decides what makes the person better or worse off.

9. An explicit cost exists when specific payments are made for something while an implicit cost exists when someone uses a resource they own in one activity rather than another. Both are opportunity costs.

10. Perhaps the friend should have had some economics in college. The cost of graduate school is not only the explicit costs of $5000 for tuition, but also the implicit cost of $50,000 since the foregone salary is relevant too. Since most college-age people don't have jobs making $50,000 a year, the implicit cost associated with going to college would be much less than $50,000 in most cases.

11. The opportunity cost of shoppers' time has increased with the increase in incomes and two-wage earner families. The larger carts enable people to make fewer shopping trips and economize on their time.

12. Sunk costs are expenditures that have already been made and cannot be recovered. Sunk costs are not opportunity costs because they are in the past. Nothing can be done about sunk costs, so there are no alternatives to be concerned with.

13. The boundary of the PPF represents the fact that resources are scarce, so there are limits to what can be produced. Assuming the person wants to be as far towards the northeast as possible, then a rational person will choose a point on the boundary rather than one inside the boundary.

14. A constant-cost PPF would be a downward-sloping straight line since the amount of one good given up to produce an additional unit of the other good would be constant. An increasing-cost PPF is concave-shaped (bowed-out from the origin).

15. The PPF will be concave. If the farm produces only rice, then land that is better suited for soybeans is used to produce rice. If the farmer decides to grow some soybeans, he will use the land best suited for soybeans first. Since this land is not very suitable for rice, the opportunity cost is low, i.e., not very many bushels of rice are given up. But, once all the good soybean land is used to raise soybeans, then further production of soybeans requires the use of land better suited for rice. Hence, the number of bushels of rice given up increases, so the opportunity cost of an additional bushel of soybeans has increased.

CHAPTER 2 *Supply and Demand*

CHAPTER ANALYSIS

2.1-2.3 Demand and supply analysis is the workhorse of economics, and the ability to correctly use the demand-supply model is essential to success in this course. The demand curve is derived and developed in Chapters 3-4 and the supply curve is derived and developed in Chapters 7-9.

It is imperative that you understand the difference between a shift in demand and a change in the quantity demanded. Although the terms are similar, the concepts are different. A **shift in demand** refers to movement of the entire demand curve. A **change in the quantity demanded** refers to a movement along a specific demand curve. Figure 2-1 illustrates the difference. There are four demand curves drawn (D_1-D_4). A shift in demand occurs when we move from one demand curve to another, for example, from D_2 to D_3 or D_4 to D_1. In each of these examples, the location and/or shape of the demand curve have changed. A change in the quantity demanded is a movement along a demand curve. For example, moving from point A to point B on demand curve D_2 involves a change in quantity demanded.

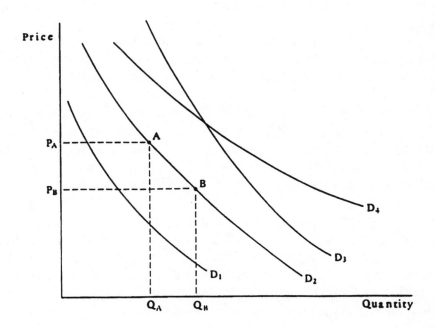

Figure 2-1

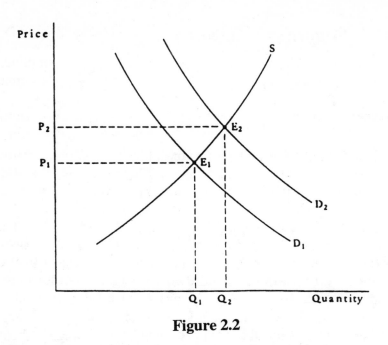

Figure 2.2

Three of the factors that determine the shape and location of a demand curve are: income of consumers, prices of closely related goods, and tastes or preferences of consumers. Whenever one of these three factors changes, there is a shift in demand. If we are on demand curve D_1 and consumers' income increases, we will move to D_2. *There is an increase in demand.*

Only one factor determines our location along a given demand curve--the price of the good itself. At point A on demand curve D_2, the price is P_A, and the quantity demanded is Q_A. If price falls to P_B, the quantity demanded increases to Q_B as we move along the demand curve.

It is also important to distinguish between a **shift in supply** and a **change in the quantity supplied**. The shape and location of a supply curve are determined by the state of technological knowledge and the conditions of the supply of inputs such as the prices of inputs. A change in either of these conditions will cause the supply curve to shift. The sole determinant of our location along a particular supply curve is the price of the good itself.

The equilibrium price and quantity are found by combining the demand curve and the supply curve into one graph. Refer to Figure 2-2. Quantity demanded equals quantity supplied where the demand curve and the supply curve intersect at point E_1. P_1 is the equilibrium price and Q_1 is the equilibrium quantity. If a consumer's income increases, the demand curve shifts to D_2. The new equilibrium is E_2 with a price of P_2 and quantity of Q_2. But note: the change in demand resulted in a change in quantity supplied. The movement from E_1 to E_2 is a movement along the supply curve.

2.4 Markets tend to be self-regulating. That is, any change of behavior leads to other changes of behavior by the market participants. For example, an increase in demand leads to an increase in price, which induces suppliers to increase production and quantity supplied. But, what if the price cannot change? Then the increase in demand would lead to an excess demand, or shortage.

Governments sometimes intervene into markets and set a maximum or minimum price for a good. Examples in the United States include some agricultural products, labor (minimum wage), interest rates (usury laws in some states), and rents in some cities. In the text, note the effects of rent controls. Are some of these results unintended by the governments that generated the rent-control legislation?

2.5 In studying demand and supply, it is often useful to have a measure of how responsive one economic variable is to changes in another economic variable. Such a measure is called **elasticity**. If there are two variables, X and Y, and changes in X cause changes in Y, then the elasticity of Y with respect to X is defined as the percentage change in Y divided by the percentage change in X.

Elasticity can be defined for each of the factors that affect demand-price, income, prices of related goods, and tastes (although tastes are not included because tastes are hard to quantify).

1. **Price elasticity of demand** = $(\Delta Q_d/Q_d)/(\Delta P/P)$

2. **Income elasticity of demand** = $(\Delta Q_d/(\Delta I)$

3. **Cross-price elasticity of demand** = $(\Delta Q_{dx}/Q_{dx})/(\Delta P_y/P_y)$

The price elasticity of demand is the most important of these, and there are two formulas for calculating it. The first is given above. The second is the arc elasticity formula:

Arc elasticity = $[\Delta Q_d/(1/2)(Q_{d1}+Q_{d2})] / [\Delta P/(1/2)(P_1+P_2)]$

The price elasticity of demand is a negative number because demand curves slope down. However, economists generally take the absolute value (drop the negative sign). If the value of the elasticity of demand is greater than one, demand is **elastic**; if it is less than one, demand is **inelastic**, and if it equals one, demand is **unit elastic**. Demand for a good is relatively more elastic the more suitable substitutes there are for the good, and the longer the time period over which consumers can make adjustments to their behavior.

Note the relationship between the price elasticity of demand and the total expenditures on a good. A price increase leads to an increase in expenditures on the good when demand is inelastic, but to a decrease in expenditures when demand is elastic. On the other hand, when price decreases, total expenditures increase when demand is elastic and decrease when demand is inelastic.

The other two elasticities can be positive or negative. For most goods, an increase in income leads to an increase in demand. These goods are called **normal goods**, and a normal good has a positive income elasticity of demand. There are some goods that people consume less when their incomes increase, and these goods are known as **inferior goods**. An inferior good has a negative income elasticity of demand, which indicates that an increase in income causes a decrease in demand.

There are two types of related goods. Two goods are **complements** if an increase in the price of one good leads to a decrease in demand for the other good. Complements are goods that are consumed together, so the price increase in one good causes quantity demanded of the good to fall, which causes the demand for the other good to fall. As the name implies, two goods are **substitutes** when either good can replace the other in consumption. If the cross-price elasticity of demand is positive, the goods are substitutes, and if it is negative they are complements.

The price elasticity of supply measures the responsiveness of quantity supplied to a change in the price of the good. It is found by the formula:

Price elasticity of supply $= (\Delta Q_s/Q_s)/(\Delta P/P)$

Like the price elasticity of demand, the elasticity of supply is elastic when the value is greater than one, inelastic when the value is less than one, and unit elastic when the value equals one.

ILLUSTRATIONS

The California Electricity Crisis in 2001

The winter of 2000-2001 saw an electricity crisis in California. Many blamed deregulation in the industry for the crisis. At the most basic level, the problem in California was that demand grew over time and supply did not. Electric generating plants take a long time to build, and they often face many environmental obstacles. Figure 2-3 illustrates the change in the electricity market in California between 1991 and 2001. The demand for electricity increased substantially over the decade because of higher incomes and increased population. The supply curve is shown as unchanged. Its shape reflects the idea that the supply of electricity is relatively elastic when firms are not close to capacity, but much more inelastic when they are operating at capacity. The result is a substantial increase in price. But, the price consumers pay is still controlled and is not free to rise to level P_2. Consequently, shortages occurred. The state tried to reduce the impact of the shortages through buying electricity from other states and establishing planned power outages that affected different geographic areas at different times. In the long run, supply must increase or prices will go only higher.

[This section drew from Hal R. Varian, "Economic Scene: California must control demand for power while supply slowly catches up." *The New York Times*, January 11, 2001.]

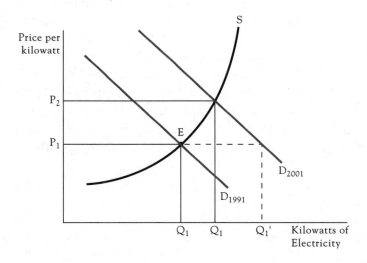

Figure 2-3

21

The Cellophane Case

The question of how close a substitute one good is for another is important for several related reasons. Whether two goods are close substitutes determines if they are in the same industry and also determines the price elasticity of demand. The question of substitution is also important in defining a monopoly--for monopoly to exist, the good must have no close substitutes.

In the 1950s, all these factors played a role in the antitrust lawsuit against DuPont, which was accused of monopolizing the cellophane market. If the government could have proved that the correct definition of the industry was cellophane production alone, DuPont would have been found guilty because the firm produced 75 percent of all cellophane sold. DuPont argued that cellophane competed with other flexible wrapping materials (such as aluminum foil and wax paper) and that the definition of the industry should be broadened to include flexible packaging materials. By this broader definition of the market, DuPont's market share was 20 percent.

The writer of the majority opinion of the Supreme Court, Justice Reed, summarized the issues:

> The Government [Justice Department] asserts that cellophane and other wrapping material are neither substantially [interchangeable] nor liked priced. For these reasons, it argues that the market for other wrappings is distinct from the market for cellophane and that the competition afforded by cellophane by other wrappings is not strong enough to be considered in determining whether DuPont had monopoly power. The ultimate consideration in such a determination is whether the defendants [DuPont] control the price and competition in market for such part of trade or commerce as they are charged with monopolizing. Every manufacturer is the sole producer of the particular commodity it makes but its control in the above sense of the relevant market depends upon the availability of alternative commodities for buyers; i.e., whether there is a cross-elasticity of demand between cellophane and other wrappings. The interchangeability is largely gauged by the purchase of competing products for similar use considering the price, characteristics and adaptability of the competing commodities. The court must determine whether the trial court erred in its estimate of the competition afforded cellophane by other materials. [351 U.S. 377, 381 (1956)].

Justice Reed continued:

> The "market" which one must study to determine when a producer has monopoly power will vary with the part of commerce under consideration. The tests are constant. That market is composed of products that have reasonable interchangeability for the purposes for which they are produced-price, use and qualities considered. [*Ibid.*, p. 404].

[For further discussion of this case, see Donald F. Turner, "Antitrust Policy and the Cellophane Case," *Harvard Law Review,* 70 (1956)].

KEY CONCEPTS

law of demand

normal good

inferior good

complements

substitutes

tastes or preferences

shift in demand v. movement along
     a given demand curve

law of supply

shift in supply v. movement along a
     given supply curve

equilibrium

disequilibrium

shortage

surplus

price ceiling

price floor

rent control

black markets

elasticity

price elasticity of demand

elastic

inelastic

unit elastic

point elasticity formula

arc elasticity formula

income elasticity of demand

cross-price elasticity of demand

price elasticity of supply

REVIEW QUESTIONS

True/False

____   1. According to the law of demand, a price decrease leads to an increase in demand.

____   2. Demand curves slope down because of the presence of more consumers at lower prices.

____   3. A change in income will induce a shift in the demand curve.

____   4. An excess supply occurs when the market price exceeds the equilibrium price.

____   5. Price is determined by production costs.

_____ 6. If two goods are substitutes, an increase in the price of one leads to an increased demand for the other.

_____ 7. Slope and elasticity are the same thing.

_____ 8. The price elasticity of demand will frequently vary from one point on the demand curve to another.

_____ 9. The larger the time period over which consumers can adjust, the more elastic the demand.

_____ 10. A negative cross-price elasticity indicates the two goods are substitutes.

Multiple Choice/Short Answer

Questions 1 to 5 refer to Figure 2-4.

1. Which of the following could cause a movement from point A to point B? (More than one is correct)
    a. A change in the price of the good itself.
    b. A shift in demand.
    c. A change in the technological knowledge used in producing the good.
    d. A change in the price of an input.
    e. A change in consumers' income.
    f. A shift in supply.

2. A movement from point B to point A is called
    a. a decrease in quantity demanded.
    b. a decrease in demand.
    c. a shift in demand.
    d. an increase in quantity supplied.

3. A movement from D_1 to D_2 is called
    a. an increase in quantity demanded.
    b. an increase in demand.
    c. a change in quantity demanded.
    d. an increase in supply.

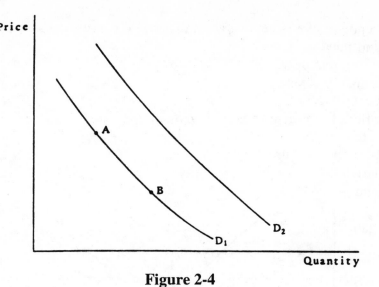

Figure 2-4

4. A movement from D_1 to D_2 could be caused by
   a. a change in price.
   b. a shift in supply.
   c. a change in the price of a closely related good.
   d. a change in the conditions of input supply.

5. For an inferior good, an increase in income would cause
   a. a movement from D_2 to D_1.
   b. a movement from D_1 to D_2.
   c. a movement from point A to point B.
   d. a movement from point B to point A.

6. An increase in demand causes
   a. a decrease in quantity demanded.
   b. a decrease in quantity supplied.
   c. an increase in quantity supplied.
   d. a decrease in price.

7.   If the supply curve is vertical and the demand curve slopes down, what will happen to price if demand increases?
     a. No change in price.
     b. Price will increase.
     c. Price will decrease.
     d. Can't tell from the information given.

Questions 8 to 10 refer to Figure 2-5.

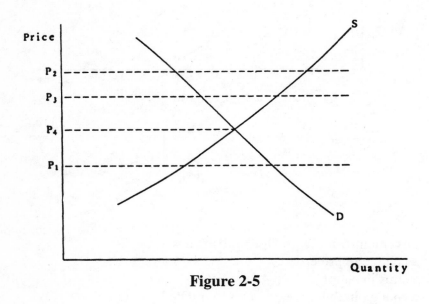

Figure 2-5

8.   At P_1 there is a
     a. shortage or excess demand.
     b. shortage or excess supply.
     c. surplus or excess demand.
     d. surplus or excess supply.

9.   If price is currently at P_3, over time price will
     a. increase to P_2 because sellers have been successful at raising price and will continue to raise price.
     b. stay at P_3 unless the government intervenes.
     c. drop to P_1 because people will alter their behavior too much when they discover the excess supply.
     d. drop to P_4, because the excess supply puts downward pressure on price.

26

10. If P_2 is the highest price that can be set for gasoline due to price controls, what price will gasoline sell for?
    a. P_1.
    b. P_2.
    c. P_3.
    d. P_4.

11. Which of the following might be observed in a community with rent control laws? (There may be more than correct answer.)
    a. Conversion of rental units into condominiums.
    b. Shortage of rental units.
    c. Reduction in the quality of rental units.
    d. Nonprice rationing becomes more prevalent.

12. One reason for the popularity of rent control laws by renters is that
    a. all renters always benefit by rent control laws.
    b. the short-run effects tend to benefit renters, while the long-run effects tend to be ignored.
    c. the short-run effects tend to be negative, but renters know the long-run effects are positive.
    d. the short-run effects benefit renters and the long-run effects benefit landlords, and renters see this as equitable.

13. Indicate whether the following pairs of goods are substitutes, complements, or unrelated.
    a. Coffee and tea.
    b. Coffee and cream.
    c. Automobiles and tires.
    d. Milk and cereal.
    e. Movies and popcorn.
    f. Baseballs and footballs.
    g. Electricity and natural gas.
    h. Fishing poles and golf clubs.
    i. Coffee and baseballs.

14. Some goods are not closely related to each other and are neither substitutes nor complements. For such goods, the cross-price elasticity of demand would be
    a. positive
    b. negative.
    c. zero.
    d. Can't tell without more information.

15. If the price elasticity of demand is 0.5, then
    a. a 10 percent increase in price will increase quantity demanded by 5 percent.
    b. a 10 percent increase in price will decrease quantity demanded by 50 percent.
    c. a 10 percent increase in price will decrease quantity demanded by 0.5 units.
    d. a 10 percent increase in price will decrease quantity demanded by 5 percent.

16. If the income elasticity of demand is 1.0, then
    a. a 10 percent increase in income will induce a 1 percent increase in purchases of the good.
    b. a 10 percent decrease in income will induce a 10 percent decrease in purchases of the good.
    c. a 10 percent increase in income will induce a 10 percent decrease in purchases of the good.
    d. a 10 percent increase in income will induce a 10 percent increase in purchases of a complement.

Questions 17 through 20 refer to the following information.
(Note that this is not a demand schedule.)

Price of X	Quantity of X	Income	Price of Y
$10	5	$20,000	$10
10	7	30,000	10
10	7	20,000	8
8	7	20,000	10

17. Which of the following is a true statement?
    a. X and Y are substitutes and X is a normal good.
    b. X and Y are complements and X is a normal good.
    c. X and Y are substitutes and X is an inferior good.
    d. X and Y are complements and X is an inferior good.

18.   The price elasticity of demand for X is
        a. 0.67.
        b. 1.50.
        c. 1.00.
        d. 1.95.

19.   The income elasticity of demand is
        a. greater than 1.
        b. between 0 and 1.
        c. less than 0.
        d. 0.

20.   The cross-price elasticity of demand is
        a. 0.67.
        b. 1.50.
        c. 1.00.
        d. 1.95.

Discussion Questions and Problems

1. In December of 1981, Mexico's government-owned oil company increased the price for regular gasoline from 38 cents a gallon to 82 cents a gallon. The stated purpose for the price increase was to reduce the rising rate of domestic consumption of gasoline, which had been rising at an annual rate of 14 percent.

   a. Figure 2-6 shows an equilibrium price of 38 cents. Show how Mexico could raise the price to 82 cents.

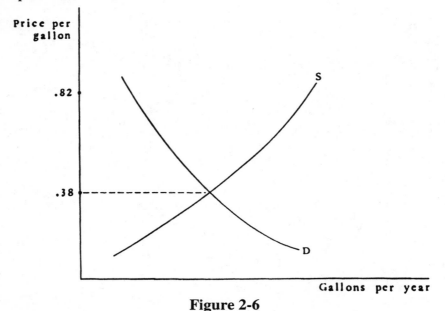

Figure 2-6

   b. Is this a decrease in demand or a decrease in quantity demanded? Explain.

   c. What could have caused the increase in gasoline consumption prior to the price increase? From the information given, can we tell what caused the increase?

d. Americans in cities near the Mexican border often traveled to Mexico to buy gasoline because it was cheaper than gasoline in the U.S. Assume that the price of gasoline in the U.S. is $1.00 a gallon when Mexico raises the price from 38 cents to 82 cents. What would be the effect of Mexico's price increase on the gasoline market in U.S. cities near Mexico?

2. Explain why True/False question #5 is false.

3. Suppose a freeze in Brazil damages Brazil's coffee crop. Show the effects on (a) the coffee market, (b) the tea market, and (c) the cream market.

4. The quality of stereo components has increased dramatically in recent years while the absolute price has stayed the same.
   a. Explain what must have been happening in recent years in the market for CD players.

   b. What would be happening in the market for CDs during this time period?

Questions 5 and 6 utilize Figure 2-7.

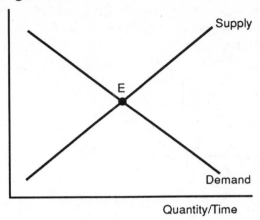

Figure 2-7

5. Let E be the original equilibrium. Shift either the demand curve or the supply curve (but not both) to show how the following equilibriums can be achieved. (Always start from point E.)

    a. Higher price and greater quantity sold. (Label new equilibrium A.)

    b. Higher price and smaller quantity sold. (Label new equilibrium B.)

    c. Lower price and greater quantity sold. (Label new equilibrium C.)

    d. Lower price and smaller quantity sold. (Label new equilibrium D.)

6. It's possible for both supply and demand to change at the same time in actual market situations. Suppose both demand and supply increases and the new equilibrium price is greater than E. What has happened? Suppose both supply and demand decrease and price increases. What has happened?

7. The government sets a legal minimum wage that covers most workers. Suppose an unregulated market for unskilled workers would be in equilibrium at a wage rate of $3.50 an hour and the minimum wage is set at $4.00 an hour.
   a. Does the minimum wage cause an excess demand or excess supply of unskilled labor?

   b. Suppose the inflation rate is very high and the minimum wage is constant at $4.00 an hour. What will happen in the market for unskilled labor over time?

   c. Some people believe the minimum wage should be "indexed," that is, raised automatically to keep pace with inflation. If the minimum wage was indexed, how would you change your answer to part b?

8. During the energy crisis of the 1970s, many predicted severe shortages in oil and other natural resources. These projections were based on trends that existed at the time. These projections showed consumption of oil increasing much faster than production, and indicated severe shortages by the mid-1990s. These shortages have not occurred. Explain why the projected shortages did not take place.

9.   Suppose there are 10,000 tickets available to a rock concert, each with a price of $45. At a price of $45, 15,000 people want to purchase tickets.

    a. Is $45 an equilibrium price?

    b. All 10,000 tickets are to be sold through a ticket office. How will it be decided which of the 15,000 will get the tickets?

    c. Suppose you didn't get a ticket but desperately want to go to the concert. What can you do?

10.   From the tools you have acquired in this chapter, offer a brief explanation for each of the following:

    a. Many firms advertise their products.

    b. The price of shrimp is lower in New Orleans than in Chicago.

    c. There are more telephones per capita in Los Angeles than in Mexico City.

    d. The price of coffee increases immediately after a freeze in Brazil even though the freeze doesn't reduce the amount of coffee beans that exist at the time.

11.

Price	Quantity Demanded (Y= $20,000)	Quantity Demanded (Y= $25,000)	Quantity Supplied
$10	0	1/2	16
9	1/2	2	15
8	1	5	14
7	4	8	12
6	6	10	10
5	8	12	8
4	10	14	5
3	11	15	3
2	12	16	1
1	13	17	0

Use the data above and Figure 2-8 below. Draw the demand curve when income (Y) is $20,000. Label it D_1. Draw the supply curve and label it S. What is the equilibrium price and output? What happens if income increases to $25,000? (Show on the graph.) What happens to quantity supplied?

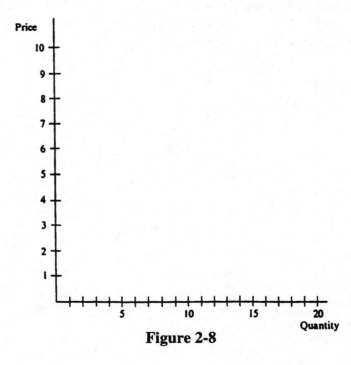

Figure 2-8

12. Suppose you are part of a management team that is considering a change in the price your firm charges for its product. One member of the team believes the price elasticity of demand for the product is 0.5, another member believes it is 1.5, and a third argues it is 1.0. Does it matter which is correct? If so, why?

13. Why is the long-run demand curve more elastic than the short-run demand curve?

14. Suppose a city starts to control rents and establishes a maximum allowed rent that is below the market-clearing rent. In the short run, the elasticity of demand for housing and the elasticity of supply are likely to be small, i.e., inelastic. Show the effects of the new law. In the long run, both demand and supply are much more elastic. What are the long-run effects of the policy?

15.   a. Why is the demand for a particular brand of a product more elastic than the demand for all brands taken together?

       b. The cross-price elasticity of two brands of a product is greater than the cross-price elasticity of all brands taken together and a substitute brand? Why?

       c. Do your answers suggest anything about a relationship between price elasticity of demand and cross-price elasticity of demand?

16.   You are given the following information: P = $10; Q = 1 million units per year; price elasticity of demand = 2.0; income elasticity of demand = 0.5. If income increases by 10 percent and price falls by 10 percent, what will be the new rate of consumption?

17.   a. Suppose David never looks at the menu when he enters his favorite restaurant and always orders 2 eggs for breakfast. What is his price elasticity of demand for eggs? Explain.

       b. Suppose Shelley enters a candy store daily and orders $2 worth of licorice. What is her price elasticity of demand for licorice? Explain.

18.   Figure 2-9 below presents two demand curves for gasoline.

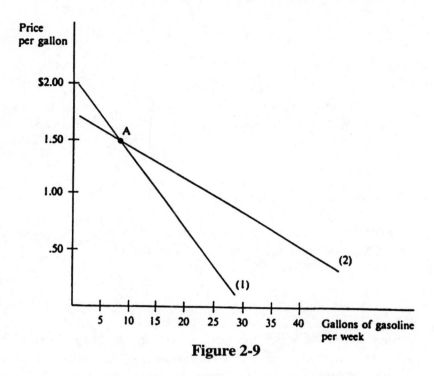

Figure 2-9

a. If price falls from $1.50 per gallon to $ 1.00 per gallon, which demand curve is more elastic?

b. It is possible for both demand curves to apply to a specific individual. How can this be?

ANSWERS

Review Questions

True/False

1. False. A price decrease leads to an increase in quantity demanded.
2. False. Demand curves slope down because of greater consumption by consumers who were buying the good already as well as because of the presence of additional consumers.
3. True
4. True
5. False
6. True
7. False
8. True
9. True
10. False

Multiple Choice/Short Answer

1. a,c,d,f
2. a
3. b
4. c
5. a
6. c
7. b
8. a
9. d
10. d
11. all of them will be observed
12. b
13. a, f, g, and h are substitutes; b, c, d and e are complements; and i is neither since the goods are not closely related
14. c
15. d
16. b
17. b
18. b
19. b
20. b

Discussion Questions and Problems

1.   a. Mexico reduces supply (shift supply curve to left) such that the new equilibrium
          price is 82 cents. See Figure 2-10 below.
      b. Decrease in quantity demanded (moved along demand curve).
      c. Supply could have been increasing, or demand could have been increasing, or both
          supply and demand could have been increasing. We cannot tell what happened
          without knowing what had been happening to price in recent years.
      d. Demand will increase because the price of a related good (Mexican gas) increased.

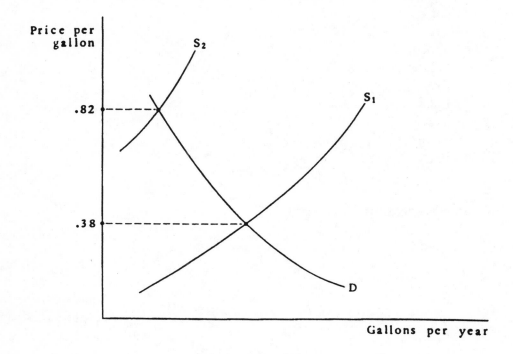

Figure 2-10

2.   Price is determined by the interaction of supply and demand. Costs of production
      affect supply only.

40

3.   a. Figure 2-11(a) illustrates. The freeze caused a reduction in supply of coffee which caused the price of coffee to increase.
     b. Figure 2-11(b) illustrates. Coffee and tea are substitutes, so the increased price of coffee causes the demand curve for tea to increase (shift out). The price of tea will increase and there will be an increased quantity supplied of tea.
     c. Figure 2-11(c) illustrates. Coffee and cream are complements, so the increased price of coffee causes the demand curve for cream to decrease. The price of cream will decrease.

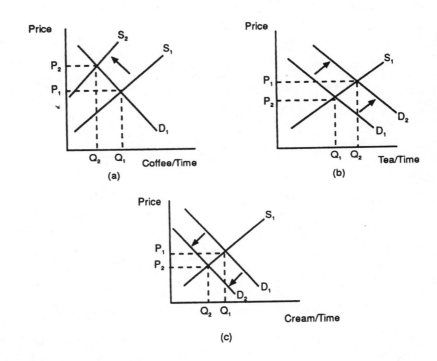

Figure 2-11

4.   a. Demand increased since the CD players are of a higher quality. Supply must have increased even more since the relative price actually decreased (absolute price stayed the same even though there was inflation).
     b. There would be an increase in demand for CDs because of the increased sales of CD players.

5.   See Figure 2-12. The points are labeled.

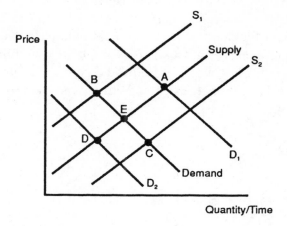

Figure 2-12

6.   If both demand and supply increase but price also increases, then the increase in demand must have been greater than the increase in supply. If both demand and supply decreases but price increases, then the reduction in supply must have been greater than the reduction in demand. (Demonstrate this to yourself using graphs. Try other combinations as well).

7.   a. Excess supply. We call this unemployment.
     b. Excess supply will decrease since a constant absolute wage of $4.00 will decline relatively with inflation.
     c. Excess supply will remain constant since the relative wage does not change with indexing.

42

8. The projections ignored price. The excess demand disappeared as price increases reduced quantity demanded and increased quantity supplied.

9. a. No. There is an excess demand since the quantity demanded at $15 is greater than the quantity supplied.
    b. First come, first served, or by knowing the ticket agent.
    c. Buy one from a person who got a ticket. You will pay more than $15, though. This is called "scalping."

10. a. Advertising is an attempt to increase demand for one's product by changing consumers' tastes.
    b. The supply of shrimp relative to demand is greater in New Orleans than in Chicago.
    c. Per capita income is greater in Los Angeles than in Mexico City, so the demand for telephones in Los Angeles is greater than the demand for telephones in Mexico City.
    d. People know that a freeze in Brazil will cause the supply of coffee to decrease in the future. The higher price of coffee in the future induces speculators to purchase coffee today and hold it off the market for the higher future price. This action results in an increase in current demand for coffee and causes the current price of coffee to increase.

11. See Figure 2-13. Equilibrium price is $5 and output is 8 units per time period. Demand increases after income increases to $25,000. The new equilibrium price is $6 with an output of 10 units per time period. Quantity supplied increased from 8 to 10 units. With a price ceiling of $5, an excess demand is created after income increases. Quantity demanded at $5 is 12 units and quantity supplied is 8 units, so the excess demand is 4 units.

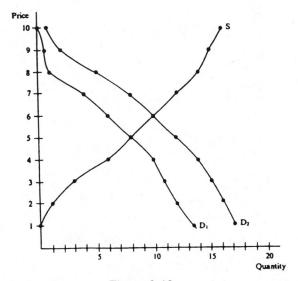

Figure 2-13

12. Yes. If demand is inelastic, then total receipts (expenditures) will increase if we raise price, but fall if we lower price; if demand is elastic, total receipts will decrease if we raise price and increase if we lower price. If demand is unit elastic, total receipts will not change if we lower or raise price.

13. Any adjustment that can be made by consumers in the short run can also be made in the long run, but consumers can make adjustments in the long run that cannot be made in the short run.

14. In Figure 2-14, the short-run demand and supply curves fare D_{sr} and S_{sr}. Equilibrium is originally at E, but rent controls lower rents to R_2, and a shortage of Q_d-Q_s develops. In the long run, both demand and supply are more elastic (D_{lr} and S_{lr}), so the shortage gets much greater (Q_d' - Q_s'). All of the other effects of rent control (such as deterioration of quality, conversion to condos, fraud) would also be more prevalent in the long run.

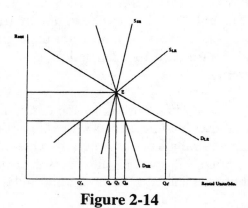

Figure 2-14

15.   a. An important determinant of price elasticity is the number and closeness of substitutes. Any good that is a substitute of the product is a substitute for any specific brand. Further, a specific brand has other close substitutes--the other brands. Therefore, a specific brand has more substitutes and better substitutes than the product as a whole.

      b. The cross-price elasticity of demand is greater when two goods are close substitutes. Different brands of the same product are closer substitutes than other products are to the product as a whole. For example, Coke and Pepsi are closer substitutes to each other than beer and soft drinks are to each other.

      c. The availability of good substitutes affects both elasticities.

16.   A fall in price of 10 percent increases consumption by 20 percent to 1,200,000 units. An increase in income of 10 percent increases consumption by 5 percent to 1,260,000 units.

17.   a. David's price elasticity of demand for eggs is 0. He has the same quantity regardless of the price so he is not responsive at all to (small) changes in price.

      b. Shelley's price elasticity of demand for licorice is one. She spends the same amount of money on licorice regardless of price, indicating a unitary elasticity of demand.

18.   a. Demand curve 2 yields a larger increase in quantity demanded so is more elastic at point A.

      b. Yes. Demand curve 1 could be a short-run demand curve and 2 could be a long-run demand curve.

CHAPTER 3 *The Theory of Consumer Choice*

CHAPTER ANALYSIS

The demand side of most markets is made up of consumers. This chapter develops the theory of consumer choice, which is the foundation of demand analysis. A thorough understanding of the material presented in this chapter is necessary.

3.1-3.2 Every consumer faces thousands of choices every week. The purpose of the theory of consumer choice is to explain how consumers decide which goods they will choose and in what quantities. The interaction of two factors determines the choices an individual consumer makes: the tastes or preferences of the consumer and the ability of the consumer to acquire goods. The former is represented by indifference curves and the latter by a budget line. We will examine indifference curves first.

Indifference curves reflect the tastes or preferences of the consumer. In using consumer choice theory, we make three assumptions about a consumer's preferences:

1. The consumer can rank all market baskets.
2. The consumer's preference ranking is transitive.
3. The consumer prefers more of a good to less.

The first assumption means that a consumer can always make a choice when confronted with two different market baskets of goods, i.e., consumer preferences are complete. Comparing market basket A with market basket B, the consumer will either prefer A to B, prefer B to A, or be indifferent between A and B. The second assumption indicates that the choices are consistent. The third assumption states that a consumer will always choose to have more of a good than less of it when the quantities of other goods are held constant, as long as the commodity is an economic "good" as opposed to an economic "bad".

A consumer's preferences can be represented graphically with **indifference curves**. Figure 3-1 shows several indifference curves for a typical consumer. Indifference curves are downward sloping and nonintersecting. Indifference curves provide an ordinal ranking of market baskets-- market baskets on higher indifference curves are preferred to baskets on lower indifference curves. Thus, any market basket on U_3 is preferred to any basket on U_2, and any market basket on U_2 is preferred to any basket on U_1. Further, indifference curves are convex to the origin. This last characteristic of indifference curves is not an implication of the assumptions but is attributed to the property of diminishing marginal rate of substitution along an indifference curve. The

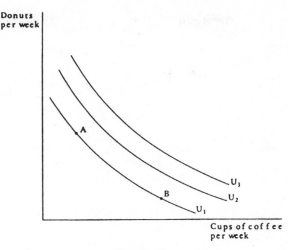

Figure 3-1

marginal rate of substitution is the maximum amount of one good that a consumer will give up to obtain an additional unit of another good and is equal to (minus) the slope of the indifference curve. In Figure 3-1, let the consumer move along indifference curve U_1 from point A to point B. In doing so, the consumer obtains more and more coffee while giving up donuts. At point A the consumer is willing to give up more donuts to get an additional cup of coffee than at point B because the consumer has more coffee and fewer donuts at point B than at point A.

There are several types of indifference curve mappings that represent special cases you should be familiar with. Figure 3-2 presents four such special cases. The top-left figure shows indifference curves for a **"good"**(return) and a **"bad"** (risk). To see why these curves have the shape they do, start at Point A. If we take a unit of the good away from the consumer, he or she is worse off. In order to make the consumer as well off as before, we must take away some of the bad. The top-right figure presents indifference curves for a good and a **"neuter"**. In this case, Frank does not know Bill and has no interest in the number of CDs Bill owns. Frank's utility only increases if his own number of CDs increases. (What would happen if Frank and Bill knew each other or if Frank was jealous of Bill's CD collection?) The bottom-left figure shows indifference curves for a consumer who considers Pepsi and Coca-Cola to be **perfect substitutes**. Since Pepsi and Coca-Cola are perfect substitutes, the marginal rate of substitution is constant. If the units of Pepsi and Coca-Cola are the same, the marginal rate of substitution will equal one. The bottom-right figure shows perfect complements. For most people, a right-hand glove is not useful unless the consumer also had a left-hand glove. If we have two goods that are **perfect complements**, it often is the case that we have misclassified the goods. With respect to the gloves, the actual good is "pairs of gloves".

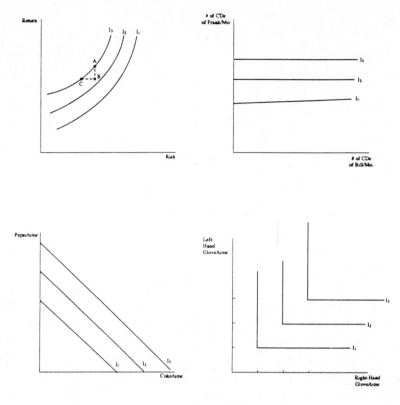

Figure 3-2

The second factor that determines the choice of a consumer is the consumer's **budget constraint**. Two factors determine a consumer's budget line: income and the real prices of goods. Figure 3-3 illustrates the geometry of a budget line. Line AB represents the budget line of a consumer with an income of $5 a week, allocated between coffee and donuts. The price of a cup of coffee (P_c) is 50 cents and the price of a donut (P_d) is 25 cents. Point A shows the number of donuts that could be purchased if the entire $5 was spent on donuts, and point B shows the number of cups of coffee that could be purchased if the entire $5 was spent on coffee.

The slope of the budget line AB equals -2 and is determined by the **price ratio** (P_c/P_d) of the two goods. (The slope is negative because the budget line slopes down and to the right.) Since the ratio of the prices is equivalent to a relative price, the slope of the budget line equals the relative price of coffee, that is, the price of coffee in terms of donuts. The price of a cup of coffee is two donuts (1c=2d).

Line AB in Figure 3-4 reproduces the budget line from Figure 3-3. If the price of a donut rises to 50 cents, the real or relative price of coffee falls, even though the nominal price of a cup of coffee is constant. The new budget line is A'B with a slope of -1, and the price of a cup of coffee is now 1 donut (1c=1d).

48

Let's return to the original budget line, AB, and see the effects of a change in income. If the consumer's income falls to $2.50 a week, the consumer can purchase either 10 donuts and no cups of coffee or 5 cups of coffee and no donuts, so the new budget line is A'B'. The slope of A'B' is equal to -2, which is the same as the slope of budget line AB. Since prices have not changed, neither relative prices nor the slope of the budget line has changed. The slope of the budget line changes only when the price ratio changes.

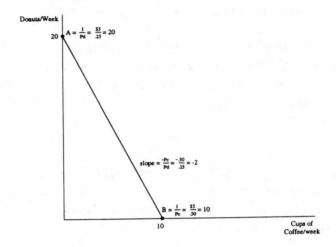

Figure 3-3

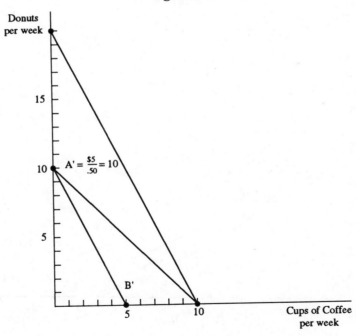

Figure 3-4

49

3.3 The market basket the consumer will choose to consume can be found by combining indifference curves and the budget line, as seen in Figure 3-5. Line AB is the budget line and represents what the consumer is able to spend. The indifference curves U_1, U_2, and U_3 represent the consumer's preferences. The consumer would like to be on indifference curve U_3 but cannot because U_3 lies above the budget line. The consumer is able to be on U_1 between the points C and D or on U_2 at point E. Since U_2 is located above U_1, any point on U_2 is preferred to any point on U_1, and the consumer will choose point E over points C or D. In fact, point E is the market basket the consumer will choose because any point on a higher indifference curve is not attainable while any point on a lower indifference curve is less desirable than point E.

It is important to note that indifference curve U_2 is tangent to the budget line at point E. This tangency characterizes all interior solutions, that is, all equilibriums in which the consumer selects a positive amount of both goods. At the tangency the slope of the indifference curve (marginal rate of substitution) and the slope of the budget line (relative price) are equal:

$$MRS_{cd} = P_c/P_d$$

At point E, the tangency between the indifference curve and the budget line, the rate at which the consumer is willing to trade donuts for coffee equals the rate at which the market will allow donuts to be given up in exchange for coffee. The consumer's subjective marginal evaluation of coffee equals the objective cost of coffee.

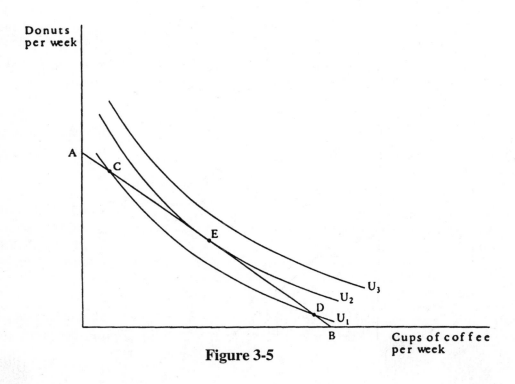

Figure 3-5

A **corner solution** occurs when the consumer chooses zero units of one of the goods. Corner solutions occur when the cost of one good exceeds the consumer's subjective marginal valuation of the good. In these cases the marginal rate of substitution does not equal the ratio of the prices.

Economists often use the **composite good** convention in analyzing economic markets. The good that is to be analyzed is on the horizontal axis and the composite good is on the vertical axis. The composite good is a collection of all goods and services other than the good on the horizontal axis. The quantity consumed of the composite good is measured by the outlays on it, that is, total outlays on all goods other than the good on the horizontal axis. The composite good convention will be used often in the textbook to analyze markets.

3.4-3.5 An increase in income increases the choices of a consumer and is shown as a parallel outward shift of the budget line. The new equilibrium is represented by a tangency between the new budget line and a new, higher indifference curve. An **income-consumption** curve is found by connecting the original equilibrium and the new equilibrium. Under normal circumstances, the consumer will consume larger quantities of both goods when income increases. If consumption of a good increases when income increases, it is called a **normal good**. If consumption of a good decreases when income increases, it is an **inferior good**. Note the following points about normal and inferior goods:

1. A specific good can be inferior for some consumers and normal for others.
2. For a specific consumer, a good may be a normal good at some incomes and an inferior good at other incomes.
3. An inferior good is a good and not an economic "bad", since more is preferred to less, other things held constant.
4. Inferior goods are generally narrowly defined goods such as low-priced brands or inexpensive substitutes for higher-quality goods. For many people steak is a normal good and hamburger is an inferior good.

Keep in mind that economic analysis does not presume people are selfish. The tools developed in this chapter can be used to analyze charitable activity as well. Review Figure 3.19 on page 73 of the textbook to ensure you are familiar with the analysis.

3.6 Another approach to consumer theory is the concept of **utility**. Utility is a measure of the satisfaction that results from consumption of a basket of goods as determined by the consumer. We can think of a "util" as a unit of utility. We assume that a consumer wants to maximize utility, i.e., select the market basket that yields the most utility given the consumer's income and the prices of the goods.

Marginal utility is the increase in **total utility** when a person consumes an extra unit of a good. We assume that as a person consumes more and more units of a good, the extra utility from consuming an extra unit gets smaller. That is, **diminishing marginal utility** prevails. Two points should be kept in mind. First, diminishing marginal utility applies for a given time period. A person may not want a fifth donut right now, but a week later an extra donut may be greatly desired. Second, all other things are held constant, including consumption of other goods.

A consumer maximizes utility by consuming quantities of goods such that the marginal utility obtained from the last dollar spent on each good are equal. That is, where the marginal utility of a good divided by its price is the same for all goods:

$$MU_x/P_x = MU_y/P_y = MU_z/P_z$$

Utility theory and indifference curve theory are similar. This can be seen by referring to Figure 3-5. If a consumer is indifferent between two market baskets of goods, C and D for example, then the two market baskets must yield identical levels of utility to the consumer. Thus, all market baskets on U_1, yield the same level of utility. The utility provided by any market basket on U_2 is greater than that of any basket on U_1, and so on. Of the market baskets that are attainable, E yields the most utility to the consumer and will be chosen.

At point E we know that $MRS_{cd} = P_c/P_d$. The utility-maximizing market basket is the one such that the marginal utility of coffee divided by the price of coffee equals the marginal utility of donuts divided by the price of donuts:

$$MU_c/P_c = MU_d/P_d \text{ or } MU_c/MU_d = P_c/P_d$$

Thus $P_c/P_d = MU_c/MU_d = MRS_{cd}$. The two theories are different ways of examining consumer choice.

ILLUSTRATIONS

The Formation of Preferences

Because economists do not have an adequate theory to explain the determination of preferences, consumer preferences are generally assumed to be given and constant when examining consumer choice. Since preferences seem to change slowly, they can be treated as constant for most problems. Assuming preferences are constant, changes in consumer behavior must therefore be due to either relative price changes or income changes.

We can, however, make some observations about the formation of preferences. The environment in which a person lives affects the individual's preferences. People from different cultures, religions, and families have different tastes. Preferences also differ with age— children often dislike some foods that they like later as adults and musical taste often changes with age.

Information about goods affects preferences as well. Many people's preference for cigarettes changed when they learned that cigarette smoking and lung cancer were linked. Advertisers seek to alter preferences by informing and persuading consumers. While we will generally assume preferences are constant, there will be cases when we will identify a factor that caused preferences to change.

Consumer Choice and Religiosity

The theory of consumer choice can be used to analyze religious activity. Dennis Sullivan examined household decisions concerning two religious activities, church attendance and weekly contributions of money. He used two factors to determine differences in preferences. People in the sample were asked whether they believed that participating in the sacraments was necessary for "salvation" and whether tithing (giving one-tenth of one's income) was necessary for "salvation." Professor Sullivan expected that those who believe sacramental participation is necessary would have a taste for church attendance and those who believe tithing is necessary would have a taste for contributing money, and the results of the study showed just that--those who believed sacramental participation was necessary for salvation attended church more often, while those who believed tithing was necessary gave more money. Further, he found that the taste for church attendance increased with age.

Professor Sullivan also had data pertinent to a budget line. The price of giving $1 to a church is $1 (ignoring taxes). The price of attending church is the other activities a person could do instead of attending church. Since one such activity is work, the price of church attendance increases as income increases. Professor Sullivan found that people attended church less often as their income increased, but gave more money to their church.

In a later study, Lunn, Klay and Douglass used survey data from the Presbyterian Church (U.S.A.) to examine giving, church attendance and theological belief. Like Sullivan, they found that people attend church less often as their income increased and they gave more money to their church as their income increased. They also found that those who classified themselves as theologically conservative gave more to their local churches than did those who classified themselves as theologically liberal, but those who said they were theologically liberal gave more to non-religious charities than those who said they were more theologically conservative.

(See Dennis H. Sullivan, "Simultaneous Determination of Church Attendance and Contributions," *Economic Inquiry,* 24 (April 1985), pp. 309-320, and John Lunn, Robin Klay and Andrea Douglass, "Relationships Among Giving, Church Attendance, and Religious Belief: The Case of the Presbyterian Church (U.S.A.), *The Journal for the Scientific Study of Religion*, forthcoming.)

KEY CONCEPTS

consumer preferences
market baskets
indifference curve
indifference map
marginal rate of substitution (MRS)
diminishing marginal rate of substitution
economic goods
economic bads
economic neuter
perfect substitutes
perfect complements

budget constraint
budget line
marginal benefit
marginal cost
corner solution
composite good
income-consumption curve
normal good
inferior good
total utility
marginal utility
diminishing marginal utility

REVIEW QUESTIONS

True/False

____ 1. If a person prefers steak to hamburger and hamburger to pork, we still cannot conclude that the person prefers steak to pork because steak and pork are so different.

____ 2. A consumer's indifference curves can never intersect.

____ 3. The marginal rate of substitution is constant along an indifference curve.

____ 4. Perfect substitutes are indicated by L-shaped indifference curves.

____ 5. A change in income produces a parallel shift in the budget line.

____ 6. The slope of the budget line is determined by the prices of the two goods.

____ 7. A change in the price of one of the goods produces a parallel shift in the budget line.

____ 8. A 10% increase in the price of both goods causes the budget line's slope to change.

____ 9. A consumer will choose a market basket that is on the indifference curve farthest from the origin.

____ 10. The consumer's equilibrium is characterized by $MRS_{xy} = P_x / P_y$.

____ 11. A corner equilibrium is characterized by $MRS_{xy} = P_x/P_y$.

____ 12. Consumers prefer less of an inferior good to more of it.

____ 13. Under the Food Stamp Program, a family's consumption of food increases by the amount of the subsidy.

____ 14. "Diminishing marginal rate of substitution" and "diminishing marginal utility" are different ways of viewing the same thing.

____ 15. In deciding whether to buy an extra unit of one good or another, a rational consumer selects the good that provides the greatest marginal utility.

Multiple Choice/Short Answer

1. The two factors that determine consumer behavior are
    a. supply and demand.
    b. the prices of each good and income.
    c. the objective ability of the consumer to buy goods and the tastes of the consumer.
    d. the marginal rate of substitution and marginal utility.

2. A consumer has market basket A, which contains 10 cups of coffee and 15 donuts a week. The consumer's marginal rate of substitution (MRS_{cd}) between coffee and donuts is 3 at A. Market basket B contains 12 donuts and 11 cups of coffee. The consumer
    a. prefers A to B.
    b. prefers B to A.
    c. is indifferent between A and B.
    d. cannot tell which basket is preferred without knowing prices.

3. A consumer has four market baskets to choose from. The consumer prefers A to B, is indifferent between B and C, and prefers C to F. How does the consumer rank A and F?
    a. The consumer prefers F to A.
    b. The consumer prefers A to F.
    c. The consumer is indifferent between A and F.
    d. We can't tell from the information given.

4. Indifference curves are convex if
    a. the marginal rate of substitution declines along an indifference curve.
    b. the marginal rate of substitution increases along an indifference curve.
    c. the marginal rate of substitution is constant along an indifference curve.
    d. none of the above.

5. A consumer's marginal rate of substitution between coffee and donuts (MRS_{cd}) is 3. Then the consumer's marginal rate of substitution between donuts and coffee (MRS_{dc}) is
    a. 1/3.
    b. 3.
    c. -3.
    d. uncertain.

6. Suppose an individual has a monthly income of $100 to spend on tapes and books. The price of a book is $12 and the price of a tape is $6.
   a. How many books can the consumer buy if no tapes are bought?
   b. How many tapes can be bought if no books are bought?
   c. What is the relative price of a book?
   d. What is the relative price of a tape?
   e. What is the slope of the budget line if books are on the vertical axis and tapes are on the horizontal axis?
   f. What is the slope of the budget line if income falls to $50 a month?
   g. What is the slope of the budget line if the price of books is $9?
   h. Has the relative price of tapes increased or decreased?
   i. How many books can be bought a month at the new income and price?

7. In Figure 3-6, the slope of budget line AB is
   a. -10.
   b. -1/4.
   c. -1.
   d. -4.

8. In Figure 3-6. the shift from budget line AB to budget line A'B' can be explained by
   a. the price of coffee decreased, the price of a donut increased and income remained constant.
   b. the price of coffee decreased and income decreased.
   c. the price of donuts increased and income increased.
   d. All of the above are possible explanations.

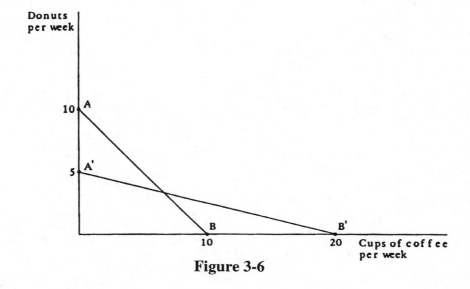

Figure 3-6

Questions 9 to 11 refer to Figure 3-7.

9.   a. Which market basket is the equilibrium basket?
        b. Which market basket(s) is (are) unattainable?
        c. The consumer is indifferent between market basket D and market basket __.
        d. Which market basket costs the same amount of money as market basket D?

10.   Suppose coffee's price is 60 cents a cup.
        a. What is the consumer's income?
        b. What is the price of a donut?
        c. What is the slope of the budget line?
        d. What is the slope of the indifference curve at B?
        e. What is the consumer's marginal rate of substitution at point B?

11.   At point B, the consumer's marginal rate of substitution is equal to
        a. 2/3, which means the consumer will give up 2/3 of a donut to get an extra cup of coffee.
        b. 2/3, which means the consumer will give up 2/3 of a cup of coffee to get an extra donut.
        c. 3/2, which means the consumer will give up 1.5 donuts to get an extra cup of coffee.
        d. the price ratio, but we can't tell what that is without more information.

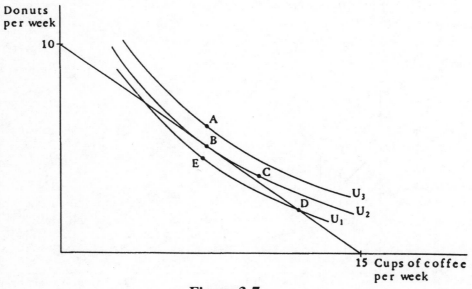

Figure 3-7

Questions 12 to 14 refer to Figure 3-8.

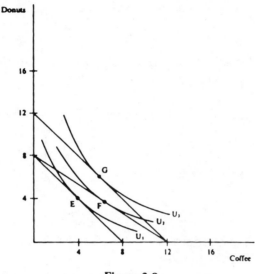

Figure 3-8

12.   The slope of indifference curve U_3 at point G is
        a. the same as the slope of U_2 at F.
        b. less than the slope of U_2 at F.
        c. the same as the slope at U_1 at E.
        d. greater than the slope of U_2 at F but less than the slope of U_1 at E.

13.   The consumer's marginal rate of substitution at F is
        a. 1/2.
        b. 2/3.
        c. 1.
        d. 2.

14.   Suppose the points E, F, and G are equilibria at successive points in time and that the consumer's income has not changed. We know that
        a. the price of donuts fell by 1/3 and then rose by 1/3.
        b. the price of donuts fell by 1/3 and then the price of coffee fell by 1/3.
        c. the price of coffee fell by 1/3 and then the price of donuts fell by 1/3.
        d. the price of donuts fell and then the price of coffee fell, but we need more information to determine how much they fell.

15. A consumer's marginal rate of substitution between coffee and donuts (MRS_{cd}) is 3. The consumer's tastes change upon discovering that coffee is bad for one's health. The consumer's new marginal rate of substitution will be
   a. greater than 3.
   b. less than 3.
   c. equal to 3 since the change does not affect the marginal rate of substitution.
   d. uncertain, since more information is needed.

16. If two goods are perfect substitutes, then the indifference curves are
   a. L-shaped.
   b. downward-sloping straight lines.
   c. downward-sloping straight lines with slope of -1.
   d. concave.

17. An inferior good
   a. is one that people prefer less rather than more.
   b. is usually a normal good over very low incomes.
   c. has an upward-sloping demand curve.
   d. all of the above.

18. Line CF in Figure 3-9 indicates that coffee is
   a. an inferior good.
   b. a normal good.
   c. a normal good at lower levels of income and an inferior good at higher levels of income.
   d. an inferior good at lower levels of income and a normal good at higher levels of income.

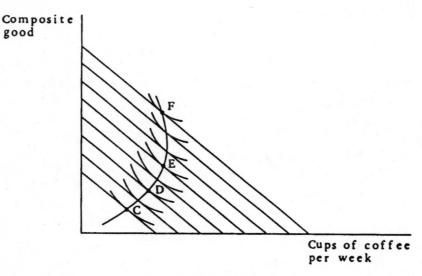

Figure 3-9

19.　A consumer is in equilibrium when he or she
　　a. receives the same utility from each good.
　　b. spends the same amount of money on each good.
　　c. equates the total utility received from each good.
　　d. equates the marginal utility per dollar spent on each good.

20.　A consumer is in equilibrium when
　　a. $MRS_{cd}/MU_c = MRS_{dc}/MU_d$.
　　b. $MRS_{cd} = P_c/P_d = MU_c/MU_d$.
　　c. $MRS_{cd}/MRS_{dc} = P_c/P_d$.
　　d. all of the above.

Discussion Questions and Problems

1.　Demonstrate that an individual's indifference curves cannot intersect without violating the assumptions concerning consumer preferences.

2.　Can a "good" ever become a "bad" to a consumer? Explain.

3.　"If you are indifferent between two market baskets, then you would allow someone else to decide which basket you receive, even if that other person is your worst enemy." Do you agree or disagree? Why?

4. Let income equal $15 a week, the price of a hamburger equal $1, and the price of a Coke equal 75 cents.
   a. Draw the budget line on Figure 3-10.
   b. Let the price of Coke increase to $1 and draw the new budget line.
   c. Return to the budget line in a. Now let the price of hamburger fall to 75 cents and draw the new budget line.
   d. Return to the budget line in part a. Let income fall to $7.50 a week and draw the new budget line.
   e. Return to the budget line in a. Let the prices double and income increase to $30 a week. Draw the new budget line.

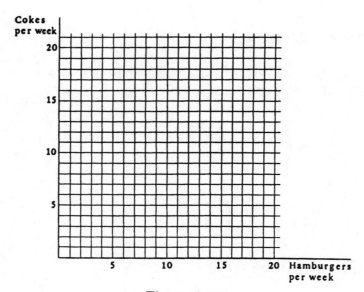

Figure 3-10

5.　Refer to Figure 3-11. Explain why B is the market basket chosen by the consumer.

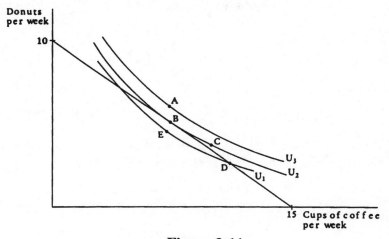

Figure 3-11

6.　Point E in Figure 3-12 represents the consumer's equilibrium basket of donuts and coffee. Suppose the consumer now learns that coffee will prolong life.
　　a. Draw an indifference curve that reflects this new information.
　　b. Identify the new equilibrium basket.
　　c. Does the consumer drink more coffee or less? Why?

　　d. Is the consumer better off, worse off, or as well off at the new equilibrium as the old? How can you be sure of your answer?

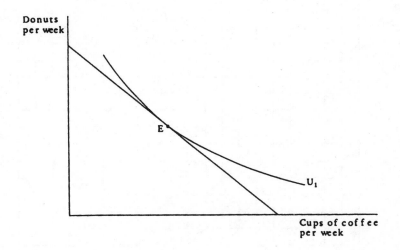

Figure 3-12

7.   What is the equilibrium like when the indifference curves are straight lines, the budget line is a straight line, and the slopes differ? What is the equilibrium like when the indifference curves are L-shaped? What happens in each case if relative prices change? Explain.

8.   In the first chapter, the authors claimed that relative prices matter in making economic choices. Use the tools in this chapter to support their claim.

9.   On Figure 3-13, draw indifference curves such that the consumer purchases 10 cups of coffee every week at every level of income.

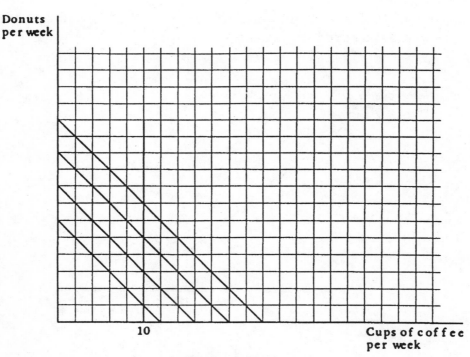

Figure 3-13

64

10. On Figure 3-14 draw a budget line for donuts such that the price of a donut is 50 cents for the first 10 donuts and 25 cents for any additional donuts. Assume income is $10 per week. Draw an indifference curve for Ann such that she consumes fewer than 10 donuts per week and label it A. Draw an indifference curve for Bill such that he consumes more than 10 donuts per week and label it B. Draw an indifference curve for Carol such that she might consume more than or less than 10 donuts per week and label it C. Does Carol's indifference curve violate our basic assumptions concerning human behavior? Why or why not?

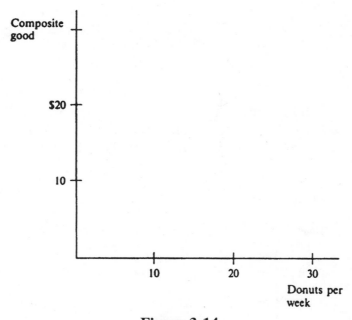

Figure 3-14

11. On Figure 3-14 draw a budget line for donuts such that the price of a donut is 50 cents for the first 10 donuts and $1 for any additional donuts. Assume income is $10 per week. Will Ann continue to consume less than 10 donuts per week? Will Bill still consume more than 10 donuts per week? How many donuts will Carol buy? Suppose Dan's indifference curve is such that he buys 10 donuts per week. What is Dan's MRS?

12.   Suppose there are only two goods X and Y, and X is an inferior good. Can Y also be an inferior good? What do we know about the income elasticity of demand for Y?

13.   Explain why True/False question #13 is false.

14.   On Figure 3-15 draw indifference curves for Robert with Robert's income on the vertical axis and Jack's income on the horizontal axis such that Jack's income is a "good" to Robert, but Robert gives money to Jack only when Jack has less income than Robert.

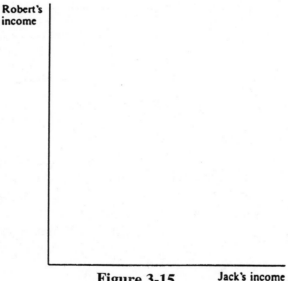

Figure 3-15   Jack's income

15. At an income of $60,000 Bill chooses not to buy a certain luxury car, but he does choose to buy one at an income of $120,000. If the price of the luxury automobile is $30,000, draw the relevant budget line and indifference curves in Figure 3-16. Explain your diagram.

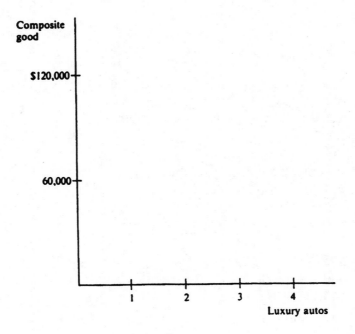

Figure 3-16

16. Explain why True/False question #15 is false.

17. Steve goes to Lake Tahoe for skiing. He can also party and gamble there. Skiing costs $5 an hour, partying $10 an hour, and gambling costs $7.50 an hour. The following is Steve's utility schedule.

Units	Skiing TU	Skiing MU	Skiing MU/P	Partying TU	Partying MU	Partying MU/P
1	125	—	—	150	—	—
2	225	—	—	290	—	—
3	295	—	—	390	—	—
4	345	—	—	480	—	—
5	385	—	—	560	—	—
6	400	—	—	600	—	—

Units	Gambling TU	Gambling MU	Gambling MU/P
1	150	—	—
2	285	—	—
3	405	—	—
4	480	—	—
5	540	—	—
6	540	—	—

a. Fill in the blanks in the schedule.

b. If Steve has $80 to spend, how will he allocate his time in order to maximize his utility?

c. Steve finds $32.50 in the snow. Now what will he do to maximize his utility?

d. If Steve has $80 and the price of skiing goes up to $ 10 an hour, what market basket will he buy? What if the price fell to $4 an hour?

68

The following questions relate to the material in the mathematical appendix.

18. Using the information in Discussion Question #1, what is the equation of the budget line in part a?

Questions 19 and 20 use the following information:

Dave has $20 a month to spend on Coke (C) and movies (M). The price of coke is $1 and the price of a movie is $4. Dave's utility function is $U = (C^{.2}) x (M^{.8})$.

19. What is the marginal utility of a Coke? What is the marginal utility of a movie?

20. How many Cokes and how many movies will Dave consume per month? What are the values of the marginal utility of Coke and the marginal utility of movies at Dave's equilibrium? What is the value of the marginal rate of substitution at the equilibrium rate of consumption?

ANSWERS

Review Questions

True/False

1. False, because we assume preferences are transitive
2. True
3. False
4. False
5. True
6. True
7. False
8. False
9. False, because the consumer must also be on the budget line
10. True
11. False
12. False
13. False
14. False
15. False

Multiple Choice/Short Answer

1. c
2. c
3. b
4. a
5. a
6. a. 8.33 books
   b. 16.67 tapes
   c. 2 tapes
   d. 1/2 book
   e. -1/2
   f. -1/2
   g. -2/3
   h. increased
   i. 5.56 books
7. c

8.   d
9.   a. B
     b. A and C
     c. E
     d. B
10. a. $9
     b. 90 cents
     c. -2/3
     d. -2/3
     e. 2/3
11. a
12. c
13. b
14. c
15. b
16. b. The units need not be the same.
17. b
18. c
19. d
20. b

Discussion Questions and Problems

1.   See Chapter 3, Section 3.1 and Figure 3.3 in the text.

2.   Yes. For a definite period of time it is possible for a consumer to not prefer consuming any more units of a good. For example, after consuming five pancakes, many people would consider a sixth pancake a "bad." However, they may desire additional pancakes a few days later.

3.   Agree. If you are truly indifferent, then you don't care which basket you receive. If that is really true, then there is no way the other person can harm you by choosing either basket.

4. See Figure 3-17
   a. Budget line is AB
   b. Budget line is CB
   c. Budget line is AD
   d. Budget line is EF
   e. Budget fine is AB A market basket on a higher indifference curve is not attainable because of the budget line. A basket on any other indifference curve on or within the budget line is less preferred than B. Market basket B is the only basket on U_2 that is attainable, so it is the most preferred basket.

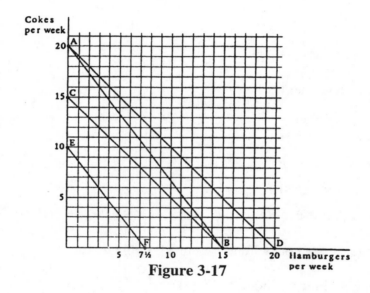

Figure 3-17

5. A market basket on a higher indifference curve is not attainable because of the budget line. A basket on any other indifference curve on or within the budget line is less preferred than B. Market basket B is the only basket on U_2 that is attainable, so it is the most preferred basket.

72

6. See figure 3-18.
   a. U_1' is the new indifference curve.
   b. E' is the new equilibrium.
   c. More coffee. The shift in the indifference curve means that $MRS_{cd} > P_c/P_d$ at point E. The marginal rate of substitution will fall only by moving down the indifference curve so the new equilibrium basket (E') will include more coffee than E.
   d. Better off. First, the welfare of the person at E is now higher because the new information can only make the consumer better off. Secondly, the shift in the indifference curve means that the curve intersects the budget line. This implies that the new tangency point will lie on a higher indifference curve.

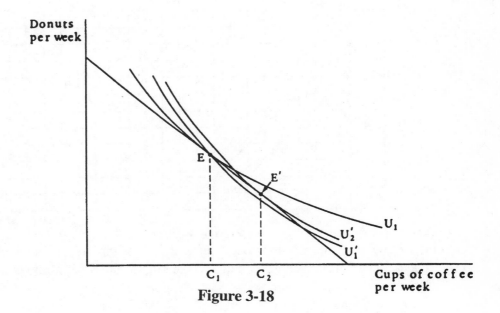

Figure 3-18

7.   Corner equilibrium. With L-shaped indifference curves, the equilibrium will always be at the point where the vertical portion and the horizontal portion of the indifference curves meet. For the linear indifference curves, a change in relative prices either will not change the equilibrium, or will move it to a corner solution on the other axis. For example, a person who considers Pepsi and Coca-Cola to be perfect substitutes will buy only Pepsi as long as the price of Pepsi is less than the price of Coca-Cola, but will buy only Coca-Cola if the price of Coca -Cola is less than the price of Pepsi. For the L-shaped indifference curves, changes in relative prices will not change the equilibrium.

73

8. Indifference curves are drawn without reference to price. The consumer only cares about the quantities of the goods he or she consumes. The consumer's budget line can be associated with an infinite number of prices and incomes so long as the relative prices are constant and the distance from the origin is fixed.

9. See Figure 3-19.

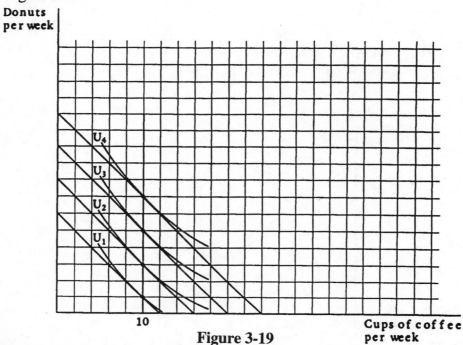

Figure 3-19

10. See Figure 3-20. Carol's indifference curve does not violate our assumptions concerning preferences. The two tangencies are due to the kink in the budget line.

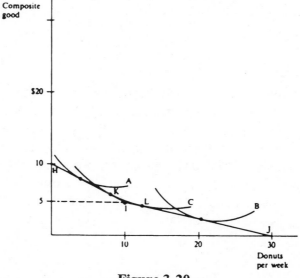

Figure 3-20

74

11.   Yes. Yes. Carol will consume fewer than 10 donuts per week. We can't tell what Dan's MRS is since the budget line is linked at 10 donuts per week i.e., it has no slope at 10 donuts per week.

12.   No. If X is an inferior good, then an increase in income results in less X purchased by the consumer and total expenditures on X must fall. Consequently, expenditures on Y must increase by the amount of the increase in income plus the amount expenditures on X fell by. (This must be the case if X and Y are the only goods.) Hence Y must be a normal good, and its income elasticity of demand must be greater than unity.

13.   In Figure 3-21, the original equilibrium is at E. The food stamps shift the budget line out to AGH. Given normal shaped indifference curves, the consumer will buy more of both food and all other goods, so some of the subsidy is used to buy nonfood items. It's possible the consumer would spend all the subsidy on food, which would occur if the new equilibrium was at J.)

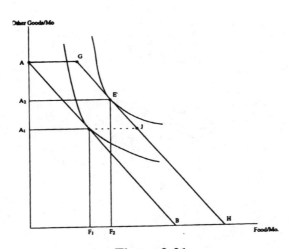

Figure 3-21

14. See Figure 3-22. The 45-degree line from the origin gives the points of equal incomes between Robert and Jack. The indifference curves must be tangent to budget lines with a slope of -1 to the left of the 45-degree line.

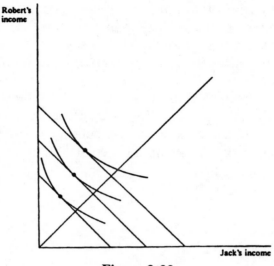

Figure 3-22

15. See Figure 3-23. At an income of $60,000, Bill's equilibrium basket is the corner solution involving zero luxury cars. At a higher income, Bill moves away from the corner solution and buys one unit of the luxury autos.

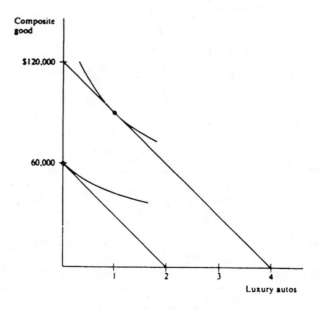

Figure 3-23

16. Diminishing marginal utility occurs when the additional utility received from consuming an additional unit of a good diminishes, holding consumption of all other goods constant. Diminishing marginal rate of substitution involves movement along an indifference curve, so that more of one good and less of another good is consumed. They are not the same because consumption of other goods is constant for the former, but consumption of other goods varies in the latter.

17. a.

Units	Skiing TU	Skiing MU	Skiing MU/P	Partying TU	Partying MU	Partying MU/P
1	125	125	25	150	150	15
2	225	100	20	290	140	14
3	295	70	14	390	100	10
4	345	50	10	480	90	9
5	385	40	8	560	80	8
6	400	15	3	600	40	4

Units	Gambling TU	Gambling MU	Gambling MU/P
1	150	150	20
2	285	135	18
3	405	120	16
4	480	75	10
5	540	60	8
6	540	0	0

b. 4 units of skiing, 3 units of partying, 4 units of gambling

c. 5 units of skiing, 5 units of partying, 5 units of gambling

d. 2 units of skiing, 3 units of partying, 4 units of gambling; 5 units of skiing, 3 units of partying, 4 units of gambling

18. The budget constraint is:

$$\$15 = \$0.75 \times C + \$1.00 \times H$$

This can be rearranged to $C = 20 - 1.33 \times H$. The vertical intercept of the budget line is 20 and the slope is -1.33.

19.   The marginal utility of Coke is found by taking the partial derivative with respect to Coke of the utility function:

$$U_c = .2(C^{-.8})(M^{.8}) = .2(M/C)^{.8}$$

The marginal utility of movies is found similarly:

$$U_m = .8(C^{.2})(M^{-.2}) = 0.8(C/M)^{.2}$$

20.   The relevant Lagrangian expression is:

$$L = (C^{.2})(M^{.8}) + \lambda(20 - \$1.00xC - \$4.00xM) \quad (1)$$

The first-order conditions are:

$$.2(C^{-.8})(M^{.8}) - \lambda = 0 \quad\quad\quad\quad\quad (2)$$
$$.8(C^{.2})(M^{-.2}) - \lambda 4 = 0 \quad\quad\quad\quad\quad (3)$$

$$20 - C - 4M = 0 \quad\quad\quad\quad\quad\quad (4)$$

Dividing (2) by (3) yields:

$$(1/4)(M/C) = 1/4 \text{ or } M = C \quad\quad\quad (5)$$

Substituting (5) into (4) yields:

$$20 - M - 4M = 0 \text{ or } M = 4 = C$$

Hence, the consumer purchases 4 Cokes and 4 movies.

To find the marginal utility of each good, substitute the equilibrium quantities of coke and movies:

$$U_c = .2(4/4)^{.8} = 0.2$$

$$U_m = .8(4/4)^{.2} = 0.8$$

c. The marginal rate of substitution equals the ratio of the marginal utilities:

$$MRS = MU_c/MU_m = 0.2/0.8 = 1/4$$

Note that this also equals the price ratio.

CHAPTER 4 *Individual and Market Demand*

_____

CHAPTER ANALYSIS

In this chapter, the theory of consumer choice is used to derive individual and market demand curves and to examine the effects of changes in income and prices on demand. Recall the difference between a change in demand and a change in the quantity demanded. A change in income or a change in the price of a related good will cause the demand curve to shift (change in demand), while a change in the price of the good itself causes a movement along the demand curve (change in quantity demanded). When the theory of consumer choice is used to analyze the effects of changes in income or in the price of related goods, it is analyzing a shift in demand. The theory of consumer choice is also used to derive demand curves and to analyze the responsiveness of consumers to changes in price movement along a demand curve.

4.1 The theory of consumer choice can be used to derive an individual's demand curve. Along a demand curve, only the price of the good itself is allowed to vary. Thus, the budget line is rotated so that the price of the good itself changes while the price of the other good (or all other goods) is held constant. Each budget line will be associated with an equilibrium market basket, so each price will be associated with a quantity demanded of the good. Review Figure 4.1 in the text to be sure that you understand how to derive a **price consumption curve** and a demand curve. Note that the horizontal axis of both graphs in Figure 4.1 is units of college education per year--the good we are interested in deriving a demand curve for. The vertical axes differ though. In the top figure, it measures other goods; while in the bottom figure it measures the price of a unit of college education.

4.2-4.4 A change in the price of a good has two effects on the consumption decision of the consumer: an **income effect** and a **substitution effect**. If the nominal price of one good falls the consumer can continue to purchase the same market basket as before and still have some money left over. Hence, the consumer is "richer"--his or her real income increased. (The opposite is true for a price increase.) The income effect has to do with the consumer's change in consumption due to the change in real income. The price decrease of one good also means that the relative price of the good has fallen (and that the relative price of the other good has increased). The substitution effect has to do with the consumer's change in behavior due to the change in relative prices.

The substitution effect measures the change in consumption due to the relative price change, holding real income constant. How would we know real income is constant? A consumer's real income is constant if the consumer stays on the same indifference curve associated with the original equilibrium. The substitution effect is unambiguous as long as indifference curves are convex--a consumer will substitute the relatively less expensive good for the relatively more expensive good, that is, increase consumption of the cheaper good. The income effect has to do with an increase or decrease in real income, implying the consumer ends up on a new indifference curve. The income effect depends on whether the good is normal or inferior. The income effect of a normal good reinforces the substitution effect, while the income effect of an inferior good opposes the substitution effect.

We can separate the substitution effect from the income effect by using indifference curve analysis. The substitution effect involves staying on the same indifference curve as the original market basket. Figure 4-1 shows the income and substitution effects for a price increase for a normal good. The original equilibrium is E (containing 20 cups of coffee per week) on budget line AB. The substitution effect holds real income constant, so we have to move along the original indifference curve, U. If the price of coffee increases, the slope of the budget line increases (line A'D'). Any tangency between a line with a steeper slope than AB and the indifference curve U must be to the left of point E. Thus less coffee and more of other goods is consumed because of the substitution effect.

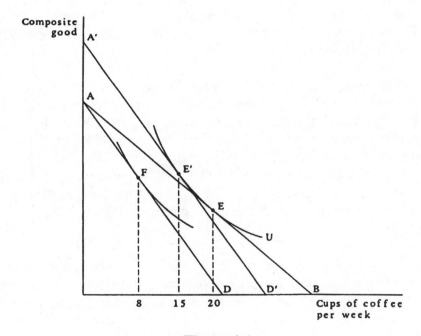

Figure 4-1

81

Because the absolute prices of all other goods have not changed, the new budget line has a vertical intercept at A. Thus, the new budget line is AD and the new market basket is F. The movement from E to E'(20 to 15) is due to the substitution effect, while the movement from E' to F (15 to 8) is due to the income effect. The good is a normal good since consumption fell when price increased. The textbook provides an illustration of using the substitution and income effects to analyze a proposal for both taxing gasoline (to raise the relative price of gasoline and reduce consumption of gasoline) and rebating the amount of tax to consumers so they are not poorer by the tax. Carefully review Figure 4.4 in the text to ensure you understand both the mechanics and the intuition of the analysis. Make sure you know why the representative consumer/taxpayer is worse off with the program.

The market demand curve is derived from the individual demand curves by adding the individual demand curves together horizontally. The market demand for a good at a specific price is the sum of the individual demands at that price.

4.5 Often a consumer would be willing to pay more for a good than they have to pay rather than do without the good. The difference between the total benefits received by a consumer from consuming some units of a good and the total cost of those units is known as **consumer surplus**. The height of the demand curve at a particular quantity measures the marginal benefit of consuming that unit of the good.

Suppose a part on Dave's demand curve for pizza is $8 and 3 pizzas per week. The $8 measures the value to Dave of eating the third pizza in a week. If he pays $8 for the third pizza there is no surplus for the third pizza. But, Dave's demand curve for pizza slopes down. He would have been willing to pay more than $8 for the second pizza and more yet for the first. Suppose that at a price of $12 Dave would buy one pizza a week, and a price of $10, two pizzas a week. Then Dave's consumer surplus is ($12 - $8) + ($10 - $8) + ($8 - $8) = $6. The total benefit of the three pizzas a week to Dave is $30 ($12 + 10 + 8). The total cost for Dave is $24. Again, we see that the consumer surplus equals $6. Graphically, consumer surplus is the area under the demand curve and above the price paid.

4.6 Since we obtain the individual's demand curve from the price-consumption curve, we can obtain the elasticity of demand from the price-consumption curve. When the price-consumption curve slopes down the consumer's total expenditures on the good increase as price falls, which means that the consumer's demand is elastic. When the price-consumption curve is horizontal, total expenditures are constant and demand is unitary elastic. When the price-consumption curve slopes up, total expenditures fall with price so demand is inelastic.

4.7 We have assumed that a consumer's demand for a good is independent of the demand for the good by other consumers. This does not have to be the case. A **network effect** exists when an individual consumer's demand for a good is influenced by the purchases made by other consumers. If the quantity demanded for a good is greater because other consumers are purchasing the same good, there is a **bandwagon effect**. Some goods are more valuable to a consumer if many others also consume the product. Examples include telephone service, e-mail, as well as goods that are "fashionable". The market demand curve is more elastic when there exists a bandwagon effect than when the quantity demanded of one consumer is independent of the consumption of other consumers. There are other goods, though, that have the opposite effect. A **snob effect** occurs when a consumer is less willing to consume a good the more widespread its usage. The consumer values the good more because it is more exclusive and not everyone is consuming it. The snob effect generates a more price inelastic market demand curve, other things equal.

4.8 Economists often try to test the theory of consumer choice by estimating demand curves. Three methods that are employed to test the theory are experimentation, surveys, and regression analysis. **Experimentation** is often carried on by firms trying to determine whether a new product can be produced and sold profitably, or whether a change in price would be profitable. Experimentation can give poor results if the "other things" that should be held constant when analyzing demand are not.

Surveys are used by firms as well as social science researchers. Much of the data used by economists is collected by the federal government by means of surveys. However, one must be careful, especially when asking people what they would do if faced with a certain situation, say a price for a product. Sometimes people behave differently when they actually confront the situation. Surveys tend to be more reliable when asking people about information (income, demographic information, etc), than when asking people about what they would do under certain specified situations.

The main method economists use to test the consumer theory presented in the text is **regression analysis**, or **econometrics**. Regression analysis is a statistical approach that uses existing data, and can be used to estimate a demand curve. In Chapter 2 we saw that the demand curve relates the price of the good with the quantity demanded, holding other things constant. The things held constant included income, prices of related goods, and the tastes of consumers. Under ideal conditions, we would want data on these variables in order to estimate the demand curve, but in practice, tastes tend to be unobservable and are not explicitly accounted for.

The authors use a demand relation for cable television to illustrate regression analysis. The model is reproduced:

$$Q_i = a + bP_i + cI_i + dP_{payi} + e_i$$

where Q_i measures the quantity demanded of basic cable for the ith consumer, P_i is the price the ith consumer pays, I_i is the households income, P_{payi} is the pay tier price, and e is an error term. The authors report the following results in the text and the appendix:

$$Q = \quad 9931 \qquad -230\,P \qquad -.01\,I \qquad -99.5\,P_{pay}$$
$$(638.97) \quad (44.58) \quad (.06) \qquad (31.14)$$
$$(15.54) \quad (-5.16) \quad (-.17) \qquad (-3.19)$$

The numbers in the top row are the estimated **coefficients**. The first term is the **intercept** and measures the quantity that would be chosen if the explanatory variables equaled zero. The coefficient on the price is -230, indicating that a $1 increase in price would cause quantity demanded to decrease by 230 subscribers. The negative coefficient on price indicates that the demand curve slopes down as theory predicts.

If we take values for the explanatory variables and plug them into the estimated equation, we can get a **predicted value** for the dependent variable (Q). For example, from Table 4.1 in the text, the values for the variables on the fifth system are $P=15$, $I=7950$ and $P_{pay}=10$. If we multiply 15 by -230, 7950 by -.01 and 10 by -99.5, we get -4524.5. We then add this to the intercept (9931) and calculate a predicted value of $Q = 5406.5$. The actual value for Q is 5100, so there is an **error** of 306.5. This can be done for each observation. Ordinary least squares calculates estimates so that the sum of the squared errors is at a minimum.

The second row in the equation above provides the **standard errors of the estimates** and the third row the **t-statistics**. The t-statistic is found by dividing the coefficient by the standard error. These are two ways of looking at whether a coefficient is important in a statistical sense. Even if the true value for one of the coefficients is zero, the estimated coefficient will not equal zero exactly. The relevant question is whether the estimated number is different enough from zero to conclude that the true value is not zero. Roughly, if the coefficient is more that twice the size of the standard error, we are confident that the coefficient is statistically different from zero. In the equation above, the coefficient on income is not statistically different from zero.

The Illustrations below provide two more examples of econometric estimates of demand.

ILLUSTRATIONS

Cigarette Prices and Consumption

Jeffrey Harris of the Massachusetts Institute for Technology developed a model of cigarette consumption using time-series data. He wanted to be able to estimate the effect of changes in the federal tax on cigarettes. The model is fairly simple, using only a few explanatory variables--the price of cigarettes, a time trend to measure changes in cigarette consumption over time that are unrelated to price, and the nicotine content in cigarettes. He obtained the following results (standard errors of the coefficients are in parentheses):

$$Q = 34.876 \quad - \quad 0.344\,P \quad - \quad 0.0162\,Yr \quad - \quad 0.129\,N$$
$$(0.046) \quad\quad (0.0008) \quad\quad\quad (0.031)$$

where Q measures average number of cigarettes smoked per adult per day, P is the real price of cigarettes, Yr is the time trend and N measures nicotine content of cigarettes. He used data from 1964 to 1993 to obtain his estimates. Again, a negative relationship between price and quantity demanded is found. Harris estimated the price elasticity of demand to be -0.47 for 1993. Since demand is inelastic, the government can increase tax revenues by raising the cigarette tax.

Since time-series data were used, Harris had to use the real price of cigarettes and not the nominal price. The time trend is needed because the number of people who smoke has been falling for the last thirty years because of health concerns.

(See Jeffrey E. Harris, "A Working Model for Predicting the Consumption and Revenue Impacts of Large Increases in the U.S. Federal Cigarette Excise Tax," National Bureau of Economic Research Working Paper No. 4803, July 1994.)

Price and Cigarette Consumption among Young Adults

Frank Chaloupka and Henry Wechsler estimate a demand equation for cigarettes among young adults. Their model is more involved than Harris' model, partially because they used a much larger cross-sectional data set. They use data from the 1993 Harvard College Alcohol Study, which also asked students about their smoking habits. The data set includes a sample of 16,277 college students, and included information about the students' smoking habits as well as socio-demographic information. The study used price and 40 other explanatory variables in estimating the demand relationship. The authors found cigarette prices had a negative effect on the quantity of cigarettes consumed, as theory predicts. They calculated several estimates of price elasticity, ranging from -.6 to -1.4. They also found that students who were married, who said religion was important to them, and who had college-educated parents consumed fewer cigarettes, on average than other students.

(See Frank J. Chaloupka and Henry Wechsler, "Price, Tobacco Control Policies and Smoking Among Young Adults," *Journal of Health Economics*, 6 (3) 1997.)

KEY CONCEPTS

price consumption curve
income effect
substitution effect
Giffen good
consumer surplus
total benefit
marginal benefit

network effects
bandwagon effect
snob effect
experimentation
surveys
regression analysis
econometrics
ordinary least-squares

REVIEW QUESTIONS

True/False

_____ 1. The consumer's level of well being is constant along a demand curve but varies with shifts in the demand curve.

_____ 2. At each point on a demand curve, the consumer's equilibrium condition is satisfied.

_____ 3. At each point on a demand curve, the height to the curve measures the *total* benefit of the good to the consumer.

_____ 4. The prices and the quantities of other goods are held constant along a demand curve.

_____ 5. The substitution effect of a normal good is in the same direction as the substitution effect of an inferior good.

_____ 6. The income effect of a normal good is in the same direction as the income effect of an inferior good.

_____ 7. The demand curve of a normal good must be downward sloping.

_____ 8. A Giffen good is an inferior good for which the income effect is larger than the substitution effect.

_____ 9. It is more likely that an individual consumer has an upward-sloping demand curve than for a market demand curve to be upward sloping.

_____ 10. An excise tax and rebate program has no effect on a consumer's well being when the rebate exactly equals the tax paid.

_____ 11. The price of a commodity is a good measure of the consumer surplus received from it.

_____ 12. For a downward sloping demand curve, the lower the price the greater the amount of consumer surplus.

_____ 13. An upward-sloping price-consumption curve indicates the good is inferior.

_____ 14. A consumer's demand for a good is never influenced by the purchases of other consumers.

_____ 15. The demand for a good that exhibits the snob effect is more elastic than the demand for a good that exhibits the bandwagon effect.

_____ 16. To estimate the price sensitivity of a Big Mac, McDonalds should lower its price at some restaurants while raising the price of a Quarter Pounder at the same time.

_____ 17. In estimating demand, regression analysis doesn't control for determinants of demand other than price.

_____ 18. The estimated coefficient in a regression measures the effect of the variable, holding other things constant.

Multiple Choice

1. The curve EF in Figure 4-2 is called a(n)
    a. price-consumption curve.
    b. income-consumption curve.
    c. demand curve.
    d. elasticity curve.

2. From the curve EF in Figure 4-2, we know that the demand for coffee is
    a. elastic at high prices and inelastic at low prices.
    b. inelastic at high prices and elastic at low prices.
    c. elastic everywhere.
    d. unit elastic everywhere.

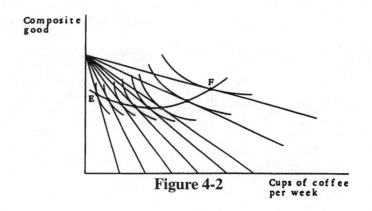

Figure 4-2

3. Which of the following can vary as we move down a demand curve?
    a. nominal income.
    b. tastes.
    c. prices of other goods.
    d. quantities purchased of other goods.

4. The height of a demand curve measures
    a. the total benefit received from consuming the good.
    b. the marginal benefit received from consuming that unit of the good.
    c. the real income of the consumer.
    d. the nominal income of the consumer.

5. A price decrease and an increase in income are similar in that
    a. both force the consumer to achieve a lower level of well being.
    b. both force the consumer to reach a lower indifference curve.
    c. both move the budget line outward.
    d. they are not similar at all.

6. The difference between a price decrease and an increase in income is that
    a. a price decrease does not affect the consumption of other goods while an increase in income does.
    b. an increase in income does not affect the slope of the budget line while a decrease in price does change the slope.
    c. a price decrease decreases real income while an increase in income increases real income.
    d. a price decrease leaves real income unchanged while an increase in income increases real income.

Questions 7 through 11 refer to Figure 4-3.

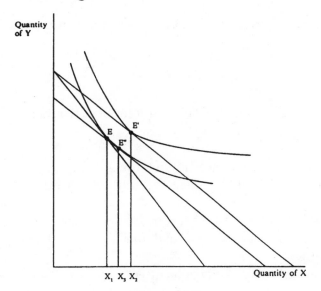

Figure 4-3

7. If E is the original equilibrium and E' is the new equilibrium, then
    a. the price of X increased.
    b. the price of X decreased.
    c. the price of X stayed the same and income increased.
    d. the price of X stayed the same and income decreased.

8. Which of the following is a true statement concerning the movement from E to E' ?
    a. Total expenditures on X have fallen.
    b. Total expenditures on X have risen.
    c. X is an inferior good.
    d. The price elasticity of X is greater than one.

9. The substitution effect is found by the distance
    a. X_1-X_3.
    b. X_3-X_2.
    c. X_1-X_2.
    d. E-E'.

10. The income effect is found by the distance
    a. X_1-X_3.
    b. X_3-X_2.
    c. X_1-X_2.
    d. E-E'.

11. If the original equilibrium was E' and the new equilibrium was E, then the substitution effect would be
    a. X_3-X_1.
    b. X_2-X_3.
    c. X_2-X_1.
    d. none of the above because the substitution effect would have to be measured on the indifference curve with E'.

12. For a demand curve to be upward sloping, the
    a. income effect must be larger than the substitution effect and the good must be a normal good.
    b. income and substitution effects must be the same size.
    c. good must be an inferior good and the income effect must be larger than the substitution effect.
    d. good must have a strong bandwagon effect.

13. Suppose a person had money taken away whenever the price of a good fell, and was given money every time price increased so that his or her real income was always constant. Then,
    a. the consumer's demand curve would be vertical.
    b. the consumer's demand curve would slope down.
    c. the consumer's demand curve would be unit elastic everywhere.
    d. none of the above. We need more information.

14. Which of the following is a true statement?
    a. All inferior goods are Giffen goods and all Giffen goods are inferior goods.
    b. All inferior goods are Giffen goods but not all Giffen goods are inferior goods.
    c. All Giffen goods are inferior goods but not all inferior goods are Giffen goods.
    d. None of the above is correct because there is no definite relation between inferior goods and Giffen goods.

15. A market demand curve can be derived by adding all the individual demand curves
    a. vertically.
    b. horizontally.
    c. in parallel.
    d. Any of the above as long as it is consistent.

16. In Figure 4-4, the consumer surplus is measured by
    a. OPCQ.
    b. CQB.
    c. APC.
    d. APC + OPCQ.

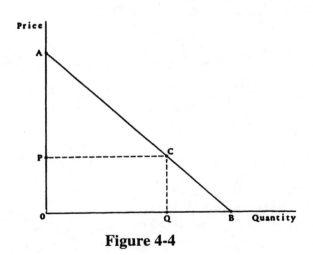

Figure 4-4

17. Consumer surplus is zero
    a. when the elasticity of demand is greater than one.
    b. when the elasticity of demand is less than one.
    c. on the last unit of the good purchased.
    d. on the first unit of the good purchased.

18. If the consumer's demand curve is linear, the price consumption curve will be
    a. linear and downward sloping.
    b. horizontal.
    c. U-shaped.
    d. ∩-shaped.

19. The difference between the snob effect and the bandwagon effect is that
    a. the snob effect is an example of a network effect but the bandwagon effect is not an example of a network effect.
    b. The bandwagon effect is an example of a network effect but the snob effect is not an example of a network effect.
    c. The market demand curve for a snob good is more inelastic than the market demand curve for a bandwagon good, other things constant.
    d. The snob effect generates an upward-sloping demand curve and the bandwagon effect generates a downward-sloping demand curve.

20. A possible problem in using a survey to collect information about demand is that
    a. a random sample is almost impossible to obtain.
    b. people often don't know what they really want.
    c. statisticians don't know how to interpret the results.
    d. people sometimes lie in surveys.

21. If an estimated demand equation is $Q = 25 - 0.005 P$. Quantity demanded will be ___ when $P = 0$ and ___ when $P = \$1000$.
    a. 25; 25
    b. 25; 20
    c. 20; 25
    d. 20; 15

22. Suppose a demand curve for coffee is estimated and that the estimated coefficient for a variable, X is -0.18. X is likely to be
    a. the price of cream because the coefficient is negative indicating a complement.
    b. the price of tea because the coefficient is negative indicating a substitute.
    c. income because coffee is a normal good.
    d. any of the above are possible.

Discussion Questions and Problems

1. It is important that you understand demand curves and the underlying indifference curves. To gain experience with the tools you have learned in this chapter, derive demand curves from indifference curves of different shapes and locations, for example, indifference curves that are very convex and others with less curvature. Derive a demand curve with a steep slope and another that is relatively flat.

2. How are the price-consumption curve and the demand curve related?

3. What information does a demand curve provide? (Be complete.)

4. Explain why a consumer's well being is not constant along a demand curve.

5. Explain why True/False question #4 is false.

6.	In Figure 4-5, draw budget lines and indifference curves such that the income-consumption curve is a straight line through the origin. What can we conclude about this person's demand curves for coffee and donuts?

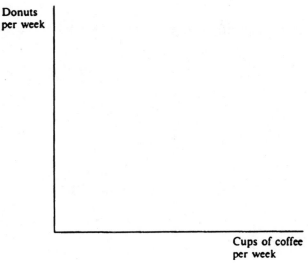

Figure 4-5

7.	At an income of $48 a week, Michelle buys 4 movies (P_m=$6) and 2 CDs ($P_{cd}$=$12). Suppose the price of movies increases to $8. What has happened to Michelle's nominal income? to her real income? Why is there an income effect when price changes?

8.	Explain why the substitution effect is the same whether a good is a normal good or an inferior good.

9. Suppose the government imposes a gasoline tax of 50 cents per gallon and gives everyone a $200 lump-sum rebate. We have the following information about three consumers:

	Gallons purchased/month (before tax)	Gallons purchased/month (after tax and rebate)
Bill	300	100
Sandra	600	400
Jim	800	700

a. How much tax does each pay?

b. Are they better or worse off after the tax and rebate?

10. What is a Giffen good? Why do we expect there to be very few Giffen goods?

11. The two panels in Figure 4-6 are identical and show identical increases in price. The substitution effect is provided in each case. Draw indifference curves in panel a for an inferior good and show the income effect. Do the same for a Giffen good in panel b.

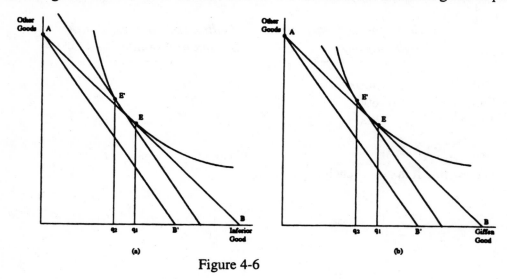

Figure 4-6

12. Explain why price is not a good measure of consumer surplus.

The schedule below is used in questions 13 and 14.

Price	Quantity Demanded
$5	1
4	2
3	3
2	4
1	5

13. The above schedule applies to an individual consumer. If the price is $2, what is the value of the consumer surplus? What is the maximum that the individual would spend to obtain 5 units of the good?

14. Suppose the consumer has a choice between two pricing schemes. In the first, price is $4 per unit. In the second, the person has to pay a flat fee of $4 for the privilege of buying as many units as desired at $2 a unit. Which would the consumer choose? Which generates the most consumer surplus?

15. Show that a price reduction generates greater increases in consumer surplus the more elastic the demand for the good.

16. What does the price-consumption curve look like for an inferior good?

17. In Figure 4-7 below, derive a demand curve for coffee when the price-consumption curve is horizontal. (Note that the budget lines indicate price falls by 50 percent each time.) What is the elasticity of demand for this demand curve?

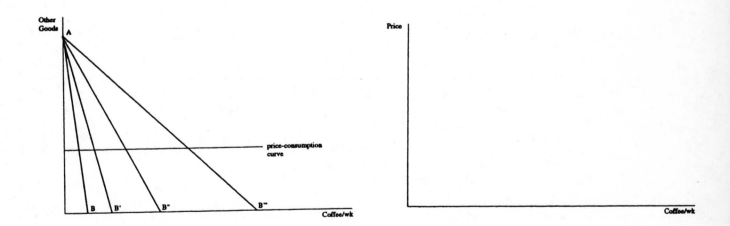

Figure 4-7

18.   Suppose the income elasticity of demand for a good is zero. What shape does the demand curve have? How do you know?

19.   Use Figure 4-8 to derive a demand curve for coffee that is vertical at 20 cups of coffee per week. What would the income-consumption curve look like? What is the price elasticity of demand? Could the demand curve be vertical at all prices?

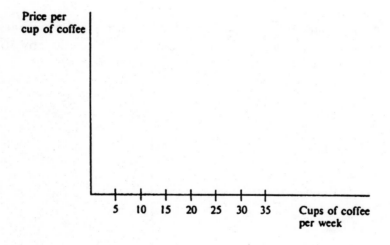

Figure 4-8

20. An individual's demand schedule for a good is below. Suppose there are 10 people in the market and each has this same demand schedule. Find the demand schedule for the market. In Figure 4-9, draw an individual's demand curve and the market demand curve. Calculate the arc elasticity of demand for the individual demand curve and the market curve when price increases from $5 to $6.

Price	Quantity	Price	Quantity
$10	0	5	5
9	1	4	6
8	2	3	7
7	3	2	8
6	4	1	9

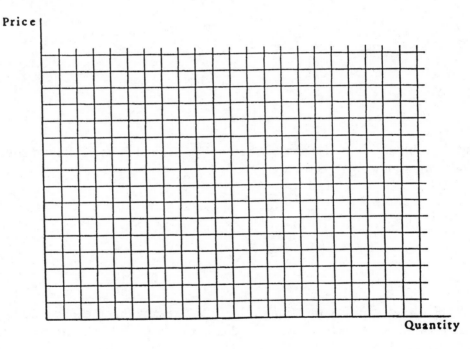

Figure 4-9

21. Suppose you want to market a new credit card. Would the good be an example of the bandwagon effect, the snob effect or neither. Explain.

22.   The econometric example used in the text estimated the demand for cable. The estimated coefficient on price was -330.94 when equation (1) was estimated, and -230 when equation (2) was estimated. Which estimate do you think is better? Why?

The following questions relate to the material in the mathematical appendix.

23.   Using the information from question 20 in chapter 3, find Dave's demand functions for Coke and movies. (Use general expressions for prices and income and then find the quantity demanded given the income and prices used.) What is the elasticity of demand for each? Are the goods normal goods or inferior goods.

24.   In the problem above, if income is $100, P_c is $1, and P_m is $5, how many cokes and how many movies will Dave consume?

25.   A Cobb-Douglas utility function is $U = X^a Y^{1-a}$. Show that the elasticity of demand for each good must be unity. What does this imply about the share of expenditures on each good?

ANSWERS

Review Questions

True/False

1.	False	10.	False
2.	True	11.	False
3.	False. It measures marginal benefits.	12.	True
4.	False	13.	False. It is price inelastic
5.	True	14.	False
6.	False	15.	False
7.	True	16.	False
8.	True	17.	False
9.	True	18.	True

Multiple Choice

1.	a
2.	a
3.	d
4.	b
5.	c
6.	b
7.	b
8.	a
9.	a
10.	b
11.	d
12.	c
13.	b
14.	c
15.	b
16.	c
17.	c
18.	c
19.	c
20.	d
21.	b
22.	a

Discussion Questions and Problems

1.   You should use the same budget lines in each so that only differences in indifference curves lead to differences in demand curves. If you have problems or questions, contact your instructor.

2.   The price-consumption curve traces out the equilibriums associated with alternative prices for one of the goods in an indifference curve mapping. Both the quantities of the good on the horizontal axis and the quantities of the good on the vertical axis are shown, and price is shown by the slope of the budget lines. The demand curve is found by using the price information from the budget line and the quantity demanded of the good on the horizontal axis for each price. The information of the price-consumption curve is used to derive the demand curve in price-quantity space.

3.   Demand curves show how many units will be demanded at various prices when incomes, prices of other goods, and tastes are held constant. "Demanded" means willing and able to pay. The price measures the relative price of the good against all other goods (composite good). Hence at any point on the demand curve, price equals the marginal rate of substitution, which measures the amount of the composite good the consumer will give up to gain an additional unit of the good. This, then, measures the marginal benefit of the unit to the consumer.

4.   Every point on the demand curve is an equilibrium represented by a tangency between an indifference curve and a budget line. The income effect of a price change implies that the consumer moves to a different indifference curve, which implies that the well being of the consumer has changed.

5.   The demand curve is derived from the price-consumption curve, which usually shows changes in the quantities of the goods on both axes when the relative price changes. Both the substitution effect and the income effect of a price change would suggest that the consumer would changes the quantities of both goods.

6.   See Figure 4-10. Since the income-consumption curve is a straight line through the origin, we know that the amounts purchased of both goods increase as income increases. Hence both goods are normal goods. Demand curves for normal goods are downward sloping so the demand curves for both coffee and donuts must be downward sloping.

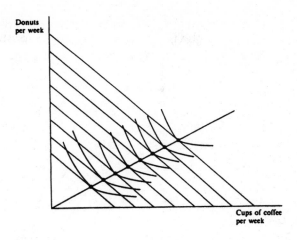

Figure 4-10

7. Michelle's nominal income doesn't change but her real income falls. This can be seen by the fact that she cannot buy 2 CDs and 4 movies any longer. Her options are more restricted after the price increase so her real income has fallen. Whenever the price of a good that a consumer buys changes, the real income of the consumer changes, and these changes affect the behavior of the consumer. This change in behavior due to the real income change is the income effect of a price change.

8. Whether the good is a normal good or an inferior good is determined by the position of one indifference curve relative to another indifference curve. The substitution effect is found by moving along the indifference curve the original equilibrium is on. Hence, the substitution effect is the same regardless of the direction of the income effect.

9. a. Bill pays $50; Sandra pays $200; and Jim pays $350.
   b. Bill is better off because the tax rebate is more than the tax he pays. Sandra is worse off (see Figure 4.4 in Browning and Zupan). Jim is worse off.

10. A Giffen good has an upward-sloping demand curve. A Giffen good is an inferior good with an income effect greater than its substitution effect. We expect Giffen goods to be very rare because the income effect is usually small. A change in the price of most goods does not affect the real income of most consumers very much. A good would have to consume a large portion of one's budget and be an inferior good to be a Giffen good.

11. See Figure 4-11. Note that the income effect in panel b must be greater than the income effect in panel a.

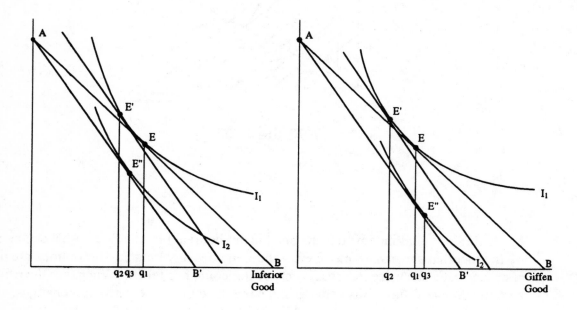

Figure 4-11

12. Price measures marginal value while consumer surplus relates to total value. As price falls, consumer surplus increases. Other things equal, lower prices will be associated with greater consumer surplus.

13. $6; $15.

14. The consumer would choose the second scheme. Consumer surplus is $2 under the second scheme and $1 under the first.

15. Figure 4-12 shows two demand curves that intersect at price P_1 (Point E). D_1, is more elastic than D_2 at price P_1. If price falls to P_2, consumer surplus increases more for the more elastic demand curve (EFH) than for the less elastic demand curve (EFG).

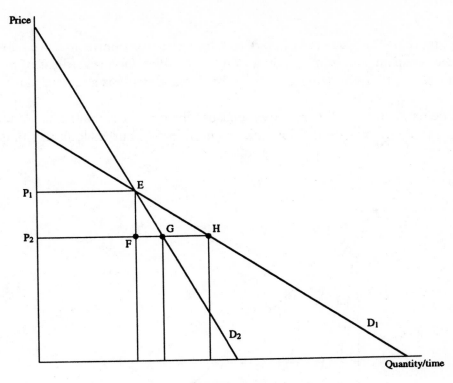

Figure 4-12

16. The price-consumption curve is upward sloping, indicating that demand is inelastic for an inferior good.

105

17. See Figure 4-13. Since the price-consumption curve is horizontal we know the consumer spends the same amount of money on the good regardless of price. Hence, the price elasticity of demand is one. The demand curve is a rectangular hyperbola.

18. The demand curve will slope down because the only effect is the substitution effect, which is always negative. (Note that the indifference curves look like those in Figure 3-19.)

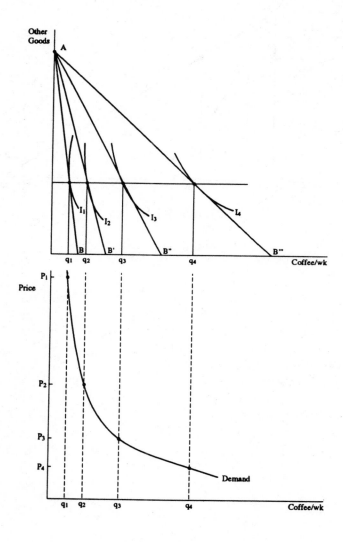

Figure 4-13

106

19.   The income-consumption curve is bending toward the vertical axis. (Note that this could not be true for very low incomes, since a zero income must be associated with zero units purchased and the income-consumption curve must go through the origin.) Price elasticity of demand is zero because the change in quantity demanded is zero for all price changes. The demand curve could not have zero elasticity everywhere, for when the price of a cup of coffee exceeded 1/20th of the individual's income, the consumer would have to consume fewer than 20 cups of coffee per week. See Figure 4-14.

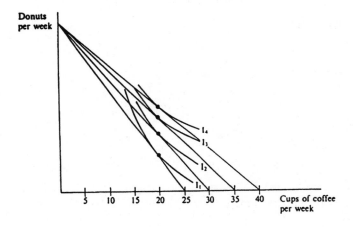

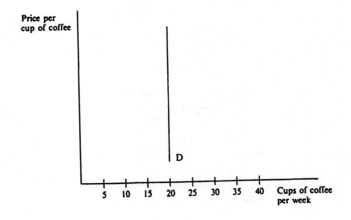

Figure 4-14

20.

Price	Quantity	Price	Quantity
$10	0	5	50
9	10	4	60
8	20	3	70
7	30	2	80
6	40	1	90

Individual price elasticity:

$$= [\Delta Q/(1/2)(Q_1 + Q_2)]/[\Delta P/(1/2)(P_1 + P_2)]$$

$$= [1/(1/2)(5 + 4)]/[1/(1/2)(5 + 6)]$$

$$= (1/4.5)/(I/5.5) = 11/9$$

Market price elasticity:

$$= [\Delta Q/(1/2)(50 + 40)]/[1/((I/2)/(5 + 6))]$$

$$= (10/45)/[1/(11/2)] = (2/9)/(2/11) = 11/9$$

The elasticities are the same. The demand curves are in Figure 4-15.

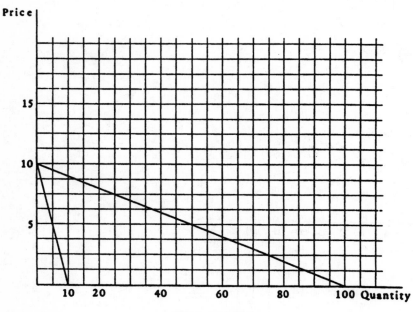

Figure 4-15

108

21. The credit card would likely have a bandwagon effect. As more people use it and it becomes accepted at more places, the demand for the card would increase.

22. The second estimate is probably better because the equation included other important determinants of demand--income and the price of a related good.

23. The first-order conditions from the Lagrangian were found in the answer to question 20 in chapter 3 and are:

$$(.2C^{-.8})(M^{.8}) - \lambda P_c = 0 \qquad (1)$$

$$(.8C^{.2})(M^{-.2}) - \lambda P_m = 0 \qquad (2)$$

$$I - P_c C - P_m M = 0 \qquad (3)$$

Multiplying both sides of (1) by C and both sides of (2) by M and rearranging terms yields:

$$C = [.2C^{.2}M^{.8}]/P_c \qquad (4)$$

$$M = [.8C^{.2}M^{-.8}]/P_m \qquad (5)$$

Substituting (4) and (5) into (3) and solving for lambda yields:

$$= C^{.2}M^{.8}/I \qquad (6)$$

Substituting the value for lambda into (4) and (5) yields:

$$C = .2I/P_c \qquad (7)$$

$$M = .8I/P_m \qquad (8)$$

Equations (7) and (8) are the demand functions for the two goods. Substituting the values for income and prices from before finds Dave consumes 4 Cokes and 4 movies. The elasticity of demand for each good is unity. (This is shown formally in the answer to number 18.) Both goods are normal goods since the income elasticity of demand is positive. We know this by taking the derivative of (7) and (8) with respect to income:

$$\partial C/\partial I = .2/P_c \text{ and } \partial M/\partial I = .8/P_m \qquad (9)$$

24. $C = .2(\$100)/\$1 = 20$

$M = .8(\$100)/\$5 = 16$

25. The Lagrangian for this function is:

$$L = X^a Y^{1-a} + \lambda(I - P_x X - P_y Y) \qquad (10)$$

The first-order conditions are:

$$aX^{a-1}Y^{1-a} - \lambda P_x = 0 \qquad (11)$$

$$(1-a)X^a Y^{-a} - \lambda P_y = 0 \qquad (12)$$

$$I - P_x X - P_y Y = 0 \qquad (13)$$

We can solve for the demand functions for X and Y (if you have problems, see equations (18) - (20) in the appendix in the text.):

$$X = aI/P_x \qquad (14)$$

$$Y = (1-a)I/P_y \qquad (15)$$

The elasticity of X is found by taking the derivative of (14) and multiplying it by P_x/X:

$$= [aI/P_x 2](P_x/X) = [aI/P_x](I/[aI/P_x] = 1$$

The same will be true for the price elasticity of Y. This suggests that the share of the consumer's income spent on each good is constant.

CHAPTER 5 *Using Consumer Choice Theory*

CHAPTER ANALYSIS

This chapter does not introduce any new tools; instead, it provides applications of the tools developed in Chapters 3 and 4. When you read the examples, pay close attention to the approach the authors take in analyzing the problems. In each example, indifference curves are constant throughout the analysis, while the budget line shifts in one way or another. Always be careful to distinguish between factors that affect the slope of the budget line and factors that affect the location of the budget line.

Housing Vouchers

The federal government provides assistance for housing to low-income families through the Section 8 program of the Housing and Urban Development Act of 1975. Low-income families live either in public housing or in apartments for which the landlord receives a subsidy from the government. The government also experimented with a housing voucher system, in which low-income families received a cash transfer for housing. Under the Section 8 program, the government provided an excise subsidy, while under the housing voucher system the government provided a cash transfer. As our theory predicts, it was found that many families receiving the cash transfer did not spend the entire cash transfer on housing, but spent a portion on other goods.

[See Robert Guenther, "Housing Vouchers Aren't Bane or Panacea, Tryouts Suggest," *Wall Street Journal*, June 26, 1982, p. 87.1

Diversification

As the textbook points out, many investors seek a diversified portfolio in order to reduce risk. In recent years, many investors have increased diversification by purchasing foreign stocks, bonds, mutual funds, or other assets. In this way, they reduce risk since firms in other countries are likely to have successes and failures at different times than American firms. Another factor to consider when diversifying a portfolio is one's non-financial assets. A worker at Boeing may want to hold financial assets in companies that are not in the same line of business as Boeing. Since the success or failure of Boeing is already important to the financial well being of an employee, it's good to diversify into other areas. The portfolio of a homeowner will differ from that of a renter. Mutual funds help smaller investors to diversify their investments. There are some mutual funds that permit the investor to invest in the entire New York Stock Exchange, reducing risk even more.

KEY CONCEPTS

excise subsidy

welfare cost

voucher program

endowment point

expected return

expected utility

lump-sum transfer

risk averse

risk neutral

risk loving

insurance

diversification

REVIEW QUESTIONS

1. The difference between an excise subsidy and an equal-sized cash grant is that
   a. the excise subsidy involves an income and substitution effect, while the cash grant involves an income effect only.
   b. the cash grant involves an income and substitution effect, while the excise subsidy involves an income effect only.
   c. the excise subsidy involves a substitution effect only, while the cash grant involves an income effect only.
   d. the cash grant involves an income and substitution effect, while the excise subsidy involves a substitution effect only.

2. In comparing an excise subsidy and a cash grant of the same amount, the recipient will
   a. always prefer the excise subsidy.
   b. always prefer the cash grant.
   c. be indifferent between them.
   d. sometimes prefer the subsidy and at other times prefer the cash grant.

3. In Figure 5-1, an excise subsidy on food lowers the price to consumers from P_1 to P_2 The welfare cost of the excise subsidy is
   a. P_1ADP_2.
   b. P_1ACP_2.
   c. ABCD
   d. ABC.

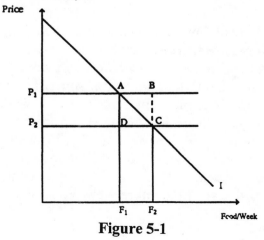

Figure 5-1

112

4.	The difference between an excise subsidy and a subsidy that involves a fixed quantity (like public schools) is
	a.	an excise subsidy shifts indifference curves, while a fixed-quantity subsidy shifts the budget line.
	b.	an excise subsidy can never make a consumer worse off, while a fixed-quantity subsidy sometimes causes a consumer to be worse off with the subsidy than without it.
	c.	an excise subsidy is cheaper for the government than a fixed-quantity subsidy.
	d.	an excise subsidy changes the slope of the budget line, while a fixed-quantity subsidy causes a parallel shift in the budget line.

5.	A fixed-quantity subsidy may result in some people consuming less education than they would without the subsidy because
	a.	education produced by the government is inferior to education produced privately.
	b.	some people can't be better off with the subsidy.
	c.	the government provides a fixed quantity and the consumer can't buy an extra amount of the good.
	d.	the quality of a good is better when the government subsidizes it.

6.	People who are better off with a fixed annual fee for trash disposal than with a per unit price for trash disposal will produce less trash under the fixed annual fee.	True	False

7.	Suppose an individual is considering two time periods and expects to earn $10,000 in each.
	a.	What is the maximum amount the individual can spend in the first year if the interest rate is 10 percent? In the second year?

	b.	What if the individual expects to earn $5000 in year 1 and $15,000 in year 2?

	c.	Redo part a. with an interest rate of 5 percent.

8.	If the interest rate increases,
	a. the price of current consumption increases relative to the price of future consumption.
	b. the price of current consumption decreases relative to the price of future consumption.
	c. the price of current consumption and the price of future consumption increase but there is no change in relative prices.
	d. None of the above.

9.	The total effect of a higher interest rate on current consumption is
	a. positive.
	b. negative.
	c. zero.
	d. Any of the above are possible.

10.	If the interest rate increases, then people will
	a. decrease their consumption in the first period.
	b. increase their consumption in the first period.
	c. decrease their consumption in the second period.
	d. increase their consumption in the second period.

11.	In Figure 5-2, the shape of the indifference curves indicate that
	a. risk is an inferior good.
	b. the investor is happiest when risk is zero.
	c. the investor will accept more risk only if he or she gets a higher return.
	d. the investor is risk-neutral.

12.	Suppose a stock will return 2% with probability .2, 6% with probability .4, 10% with probability .2, and 14% with probability .2. The expected return is
	a. 6%.
	b. 7.6%.
	c. 8%.
	d. 8.4%.

13.	The person with the total utility curve in Figure 5-3 is
	a. risk neutral.
	b. risk averse.
	c. risk lover.
	d. can't tell without more information.

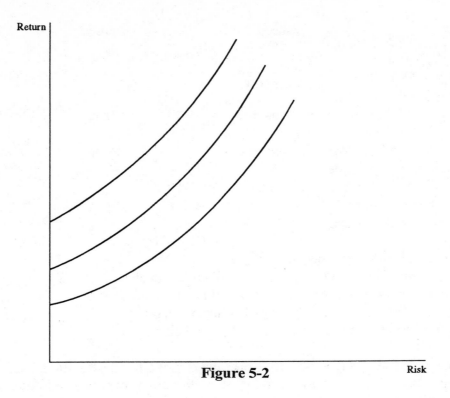

Return

Figure 5-2

Risk

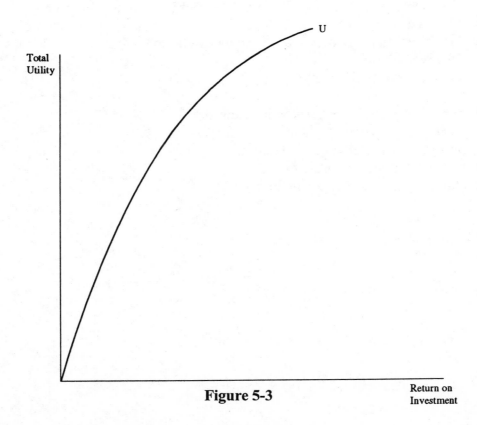

Total
Utility

U

Figure 5-3

Return on
Investment

14. If $U(E(R_i)) = E(U(R_i))$, the investor is
    a. risk neutral.
    b. risk averse.
    c. risk lover.
    d. can't tell without more information.

15. An example of risk-loving behavior is
    a. buying car insurance.
    b. purchasing a CD.
    c. getting a flu shot.
    d. playing a slot machine in Nevada.

16. When people buy insurance, they expect
    a. to pay more in premiums than they will collect in claims.
    b. to receive more in claims than they will pay in premiums.
    c. to pay in premiums what they will collect in claims.
    d. increase their expected return by reducing their risk.

17. An insurance company is willing to bear the risk of a fire destroying a house because
    a. they can predict whether the house will burn down in the future and can set premiums high enough to cover the risk.
    b. they invest the premiums in high-return stocks enabling them to pay for the house if it burns down.
    c. they insure many homes and can predict well the total number of homes that will be destroyed by fire.
    d. the owners are risk-lovers.

18. A diversified portfolio enables an investor to
    a. make a return without bearing any risk.
    b. maximize his or her expected return.
    c. reduce his or her exposure to risk.
    d. eliminate his or her exposure to risk.

DISCUSSION QUESTIONS AND PROBLEMS

1. Low-income households often receive a subsidy for housing. Using a graph, demonstrate that a low-income family prefers a lump-sum cash transfer to an excise subsidy on housing of equal value.

2. Demonstrate that a low-income family will consume less housing under a lump-sum cash transfer than with an excise subsidy of equal value.

3. Why does an excise subsidy on health care expand health care consumption more than a lump-sum subsidy on health care?

4. Show the welfare cost of an excise subsidy. What would it cost the government to give an equivalent lump-sum subsidy?

5. On Figure 5-4, show that a family may consume more education as a result of a fixed-quantity subsidy. Is it possible for someone to consume the same quantity of education without the subsidy as with the subsidy? Explain.

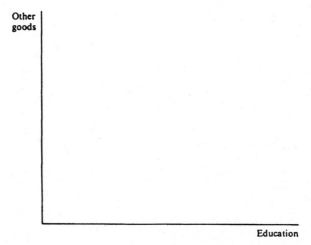

Figure 5-4

118

6. Some municipalities charge a flat fee for water. Water consumption tends to be higher in such municipalities than in municipalities that charge by the gallon. Show what would happen to an "average" consumer in a municipality that switched from charging a fixed annual fee to a per gallon charge.

7. Use Figure 5-5 to:

a. Draw the budget line for an individual who expects to earn $10,00 in both time periods, assuming an interest rate of 10 percent. Label it AA'.

b. Draw the budget line for someone who expects to earn $5000 in year 1 and $15,000 in year 2, assuming an interest rate of 10 percent. Label it BB'.

c. Redo a with an interest rate of 5 percent and label it CC'.

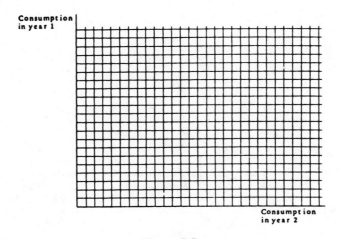

Figure 5-5

119

8. College students often receive offers for credit cards even though they currently are not working. Why would banks send cards to students and why would students use them?

9. Suppose there are two individuals, each with an income of $10,000 this year and next year. Frank consumes $10,833 the first year and $9000 the second, while Michelle consumes $9167 the first year and $11,000 the second.

   a. What is the interest rate? What does savings equal? Borrowing?

   b. In Figure 5-6, draw the budget line both individuals face and label it AB. Label Frank's equilibrium basket F and Michelle's M. Draw an indifference curve for each reflecting their respective equilibrium.

   c. Suppose the interest rate changes to 40 percent. Draw the new budget line and label it CD. Is Frank better off than before? Michelle? What happens to the consumption of each person in each period?

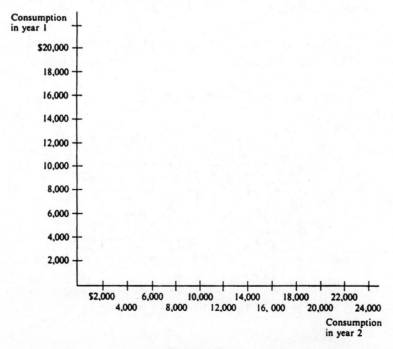

Figure 5-6

10. Suppose an individual's supply curve of savings is a vertical line. What can we conclude about the individual? In Figure 5-7, draw budget lines reflecting different interest rates and show the consumer's equilibrium on each.

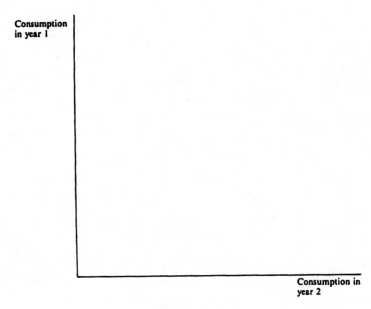

Figure 5-7

11. Why don't investors put all of their investment funds into assets with highest rates of return?

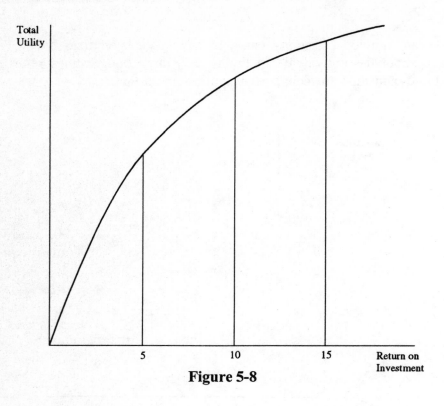

Figure 5-8

12.   Explain why the total utility curve in Figure 5-8 illustrates risk aversion.

13.   Why do people buy insurance? Young couples often don't have medical insurance. Why would they choose not to buy medical insurance?

14.   Why do many people buy mutual funds instead of stocks in individual companies?

ANSWERS

Review Questions

1. a
2. b
3. d
4. d
5. c
6. False
7. a. Maximum consumption in year 1 = $10,000 + $9090 = $19,090. Borrowing $9090 at 10 percent requires a payment in year 2 of $10,000. Maximum consumption in year 2 = $10,000x1.1 + $10,000 = $21,000.
   b. Maximum consumption in year 1 = $5000 + $13,636 = $18,636. Maximum consumption in year 2 = $5000x1.1 + $15,000 = $20,500.
   c. Maximum consumption in year I = $10,000 + $9524 = $19,524. Maximum consumption in year 2 = $10,000x1.05 + $10,000 = $20,500.
8. a
9. d
10. d
11. c
12. b
13. b
14. a
15. d
16. a
17. c
18. c

Discussion Questions and Problems

1. In Figure 5-9, the original budget line is AB and the family consumes q_1 units of housing a month. The excise subsidy reduces the price on housing, so the new budget line is AC. The new equilibrium is E'. A lump-sum transfer of equal value will increase the family's income, so we shift AB out to A'B', making sure it goes through E'. Since the slope of A'B' is greater than the slope of AC, the new equilibrium will be to the left of E' and on a higher indifference curve. Thus, the family is better off with a lump-sum transfer than an excise subsidy.

2. This can be seen by referring to Figure 5-9. The equilibrium under an excise subsidy is E' with q_2 units of housing purchased. Under a lump-sum transfer, the equilibrium is E" with q_3 units of housing purchased. Because of the convexity of indifference curves, $q_3 < q_2$ and the family will consume less housing under the voucher system than under the excise system.

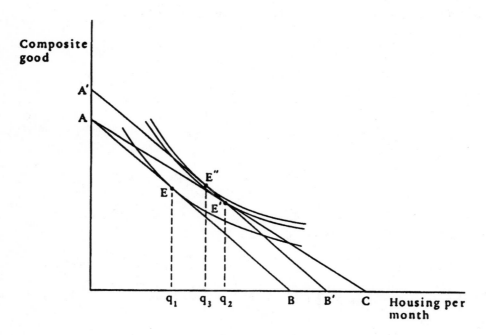

Figure 5-9

3. Both the excise subsidy and the lump-sum subsidy have an income effect on consumption, but the excise subsidy also encourages more consumption of health care because it lowers the relative price of health care. That is, there is also a substitution effect with the excise subsidy.

4. In Figure 5-10, the original equilibrium is E. An excise subsidy lowers price to P_2, and health care consumption increases to H_2. The extra consumer surplus for the consumer is P_1EGP_2, but the cost to the government is P_1FGP_2. That is, the cost is greater than the benefits by the area EFG. This triangle, EFG, measures the deadweight cost of the excise subsidy. The government could have gotten the consumer to increase consumption to H_2 by giving the consumer a lump-sum transfer of P_1EGP_2.

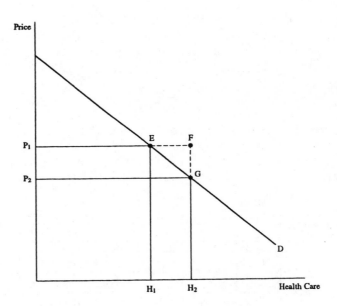

Figure 5-10

5. Refer to Figure 5-11. Initial equilibrium is at A. When the subsidy is added, the budget line shifts to MM'BN. The family maximizes utility by consuming E_2 units of education, which is more than was consumed before the subsidy. It is possible for a consumer to consume the same quantity of education before the subsidy as after if he or she consumed E_2 before the subsidy, that is, if the individual's indifference curve was tangent to MN at B.

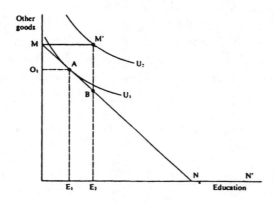

Figure 5-11

6. The analysis is identical to Figure 5.4 in the text.

7. See Figure 5-12.

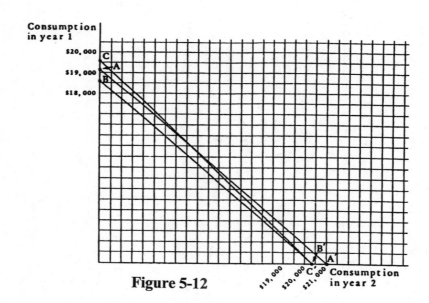

Figure 5-12

8. It is expected that college students will earn income once they graduate, and that their earnings will increase over time. Hence, the banks expect the borrowed money to be repaid over time. Similarly, the students can borrow against their expected future earnings in order to increase consumption while in school.

9. a. Frank borrowed $833 and must pay back $1000 in a year. Thus, $833(1+i) = $1000. Solving for i yields an interest rate of 20 percent. Savings equals $833 and so does borrowing.
    b. See Figure 5-13.
    c. Frank is worse off because he must move to a lower indifference curve. Michelle is better off. Frank will borrow less because the substitution effect and the income effect of the interest change both encourage Frank to consume less in the first period. Without more information we can not be sure whether Michelle will save more or save less than before.

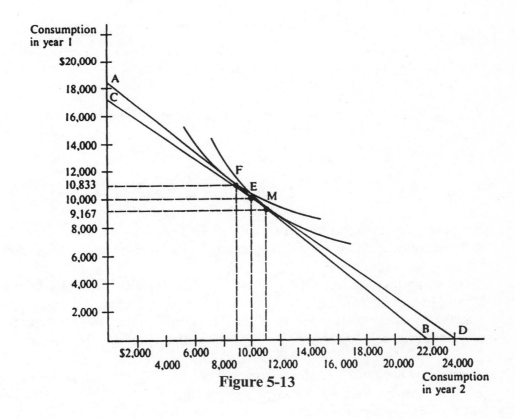

Figure 5-13

127

10.   The individual's income and substitution effects in year 1 exactly offset each other. In Figure 5-14 we see that consumption in year 1 stays the same while consumption in year 2 increases with higher interest rates.

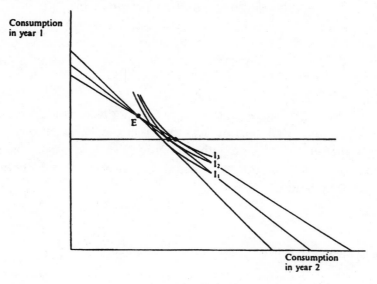

Figure 5-14

11.   Investors want a higher rate of return but don't want greater risk. They make tradeoffs between rates of return and risk, depending on their preferences with respect to risk.

12.   Suppose an investor has a risky investment that will yield 5 percent with probability of .5 and 15 percent with probability of .5. the expected return is 10 percent. In Figure 5-15, the investor receives more utility (U_2) from a return of 10 percent than with an expected return of 10 percent (U_4). Therefore, the investor is risk averse.

13.   People buy insurance in order to reduce their risk. They would rather face a known and certain payment than an unknown and possibly very large payment. Young couples often don't buy medical insurance because they believe the cost of insurance is too great for them. They believe the risk is low enough that they are unwilling to pay the premiums for the insurance.

14. There may be several reasons, including a desire to use someone else's expertise. However, one important reason is the opportunity to diversify since mutual funds are portfolios of many financial assets, including stocks of many firms.

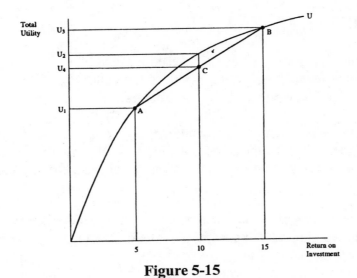

Figure 5-15

129

CHAPTER 6 *Exchange, Efficiency, and Prices*

CHAPTER ANALYSIS

In this chapter a model of pure exchange is described and used to analyze the nature and consequences of voluntary exchange, and to introduce the concept of efficiency. A new tool of analysis is introduced--the Edgeworth exchange box diagram.

6.1   Voluntary exchange is mutually beneficial; that is, people will not trade voluntarily unless they believe they will benefit from the trade. As long as an individual is not coerced into an exchange, that individual must expect to benefit from the exchange or the individual would not enter into it.

Mutually beneficial exchange between two parties can occur whenever their subjective valuations of the goods differ. The marginal rate of substitution measures an individual's subjective valuation of one good in terms of another good. Since the MRS depends on the quantities of the goods already held, the MRS changes slightly when people exchange one good for another. A good will flow from the person with the smaller MRS to the person with the larger MRS for the good. As exchange continues the MRSs of the individuals approach equality. When their MRSs are equal, exchange will cease.

Pure exchange can be studied using the **Edgeworth exchange box** diagram. Figure 6-1 illustrates how an Edgeworth exchange box is derived. Part a of the figure shows an indifference curve mapping of individual A, while b presents person B's indifference curve mapping. For both, it is assumed that 20 donuts and 30 cups of coffee per week are the maximum available. Part c is the same as b except that the origin, OB, has been rotated 180 degrees. Individual B is better off when moving in a southwesterly direction. By superimposing B's inverted indifference mapping (c) onto A's indifference mapping (a), we come up with an Edgeworth exchange box (d).

There are several important features of the Edgeworth box: First, the size of the box depends on the total quantities available of both goods. Second, there are two origins to keep straight. Third, individual A prefers moving toward B's origin while B prefers moving toward A's origin. Wherever the marginal rates of substitution for the two individuals differ, there is room for mutually beneficial exchange. However, when an indifference curve for A is tangent to an indifference curve for B, the MRS of A equals the MRS of B and there is not more possible gains from trade. The locus of all such points of tangency is called the **contract curve**. Finally, the equilibrium condition found by a tangency between the indifference curves of each person is not unique--there are many possible equilibria.

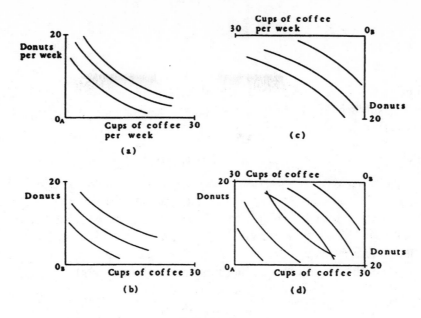

Figure 6-1

6.2-6.3 The Edgeworth box can also be used to demonstrate that voluntary change is **efficient (Pareto optimal)**. An efficient distribution is one in which the MRS of A is equal to the MRS of B. As we have seen, this occurs when an indifference curve for A is tangent to an indifference curve for B. Hence, any point on the contract curve is efficient. Review carefully Figure 6.3 in the text to ensure that you understand this. Note that points J, E, and K are all efficient, as are all other points on the contract curve. Efficiency is a weak concept, and cannot be used to determine whether point J is better than E or whether E is better than K. Clearly Mr. Edge prefers K to either E or J, but Ms. Worth prefers J to either E or K. Also, remember that the marginal rate of substitution for Edge equals the marginal rate of substitution for Worth at every point on the contract curve.

The two-person exchange model is often indeterminate. The model can be generalized to include many individuals. With many individuals in the market, each person is a **price-taker**. A price-taker cannot affect the prevailing market price. If we take an endowment point in the Edgeworth exchange box, there will be a line running through the point with a slope equal to the ratio of the prices of the two goods. Individuals will not bargain as they did in the two-person exchange model. Instead, they will accept the prices as beyond their control, move along the straight line to the contract curve. There is now a unique equilibrium for any endowment. Review Figure 6.4 in the text to make sure you understand this.

In general, an efficient distribution of goods requires that the marginal rates of substitution between any two goods are equal for all consumers: $MRS^1 = MRS^2 = ... = MRS^i$. When everyone faces the same prices for goods, each person will allocate his or her income such that the marginal rate of substitution equals the price ratio. Since everyone faces the same price ratio, all MRSs will be equal. The final equilibrium point in a competitive equilibrium is an efficient allocation of the goods among the consumers. Thus prices coordinate everyone's behavior in a way that results in an efficient distribution of goods.

6.4   Goods are scarce and available supplies must be allocated among the individuals who want them. In open markets, prices ration existing supplies by bringing the MRSs of all individuals into equality with the price ratio. When prices are not allowed to ration existing supplies, some non-price rationing mechanism will have to be used. Nonprice rationing generally are inefficient because MRSs of all individuals are not brought into equality. Recall that the height of the consumer's demand curve at a quantity measures the value of the last unit to the consumer. Figure 6.6 in the text illustrates that nonprice rationing tends to generate a result where individuals consume quantities such that the marginal value of the last unit consumed differs across consumers. That is, the MRSs of the individuals are not equal and the allocation of the supplies is not efficient.

ILLUSTRATIONS

The Economic Organization of a POW Camp

Exchange will almost always occur when people value goods differently. When R. A. Radford was a POW during World War II, he found that in POW camps markets developed for food, cigarettes, and other goods that the prisoners received in Red Cross parcels and from home. Articles were constantly traded among prisoners. Barter prevailed at first but was quickly replaced by a monetary system-with cigarettes used as money. The price of a good in cigarettes fluctuated with the supply of the good and the supply of cigarettes. Middlemen existed in the camps, and at times price controls were implemented to combat rising prices when parcels were late. The arrival of new prisoners generally caused prices to increase (an increase in the number of buyers for limited supply leads to an increase in prices), while receipt of extra rations depressed prices (an increase in supply leads to a decrease in prices).

[See R. A. Radford, "The Economic Organization of a POW Camp," *Economica* 12 (1945).]

Nonprice Rationing of Medical Care

A policy issue that perennially surfaces is the rising cost of medical care. President Clinton was first elected on a campaign of a health care plan that would help reduce medical costs. Many such plans involve greater government involvement and less reliance on market forces. If policy changes lead to some type of price controls, then other nonprice rationing methods will have to be used. Great Britain relies less on price and more on nonprice rationing to allocate medical care than is true of the United States or some other European nations. Henry Aaron and William Schwartz report that the rate at which new patients are accepted for dialysis treatment of kidney failure in Great Britain is about the same as the rate in France, Germany, and Italy for patients under 45 years of age. For patients between 45 and 54, the British rate is two-thirds of the rate in the other three European countries. The British rate is one-third of the other three countries for patients between 55 and 64, and less than one-tenth for patients over 64. That is, age is used, at least partially, to allocate medical care in Great Britain. Canada relies more on nonprice rationing methods also. It is common for Canadians to travel to the U.S. for treatments that they have difficulty obtaining in Canada.

[See Henry J. Aaron and William B. Schwartz, *The Painful Prescription: Rationing Hospital Care* (Washington, D.C.: The Brookings Institure, 1984)].

KEY CONCEPTS

Edgeworth exchange box
economic efficiency
Pareto optimality
contract curve
equity
price rationing
nonprice rationing

REVIEW QUESTIONS

True/False

_____ 1. Since voluntary exchange is mutually beneficial, people never are worse off after an exchange than before an exchange.

_____ 2. If one person gains from an exchange the other person must lose from the exchange.

_____ 3. For any point in an Edgeworth exchange box, it is impossible to make one person better off without making the other person worse off.

_____ 4. The vertical and horizontal dimensions of an Edgeworth exchange box indicate the total quantities of the two goods.

_____ 5. Exchange will tend to take place as long as both parties continue to benefit.

_____ 6. In an Edgeworth exchange box, whenever indifference curves of the two consumers are tangent, no further trade is possible.

_____ 7. A tangency of indifference curves implies that the two consumers' marginal rates of substitution are equal.

_____ 8. An efficient distribution of goods is characterized by equality between marginal rates of substitution.

_____ 9. All points on a contract curve are efficient.

_____ 10. There is one point on a contract curve that is better than the rest.

_____ 11. As long as all people are price-takers, the market equilibrium in the many-person exchange is efficient.

_____ 12. Prices serve a rationing function in determining how much of available supplies each person will get.

Multiple Choice/Short Answer

1. Two people will engage in exchange when they have different
    a. endowments of the good.
    b. incomes.
    c. marginal rates of substitution.
    d. tastes.

2. People engage in trade because
    a. they hope to gain by cheating other people.
    b. all people are traders by instinct.
    c. they expect to benefit from the trade.
    d. they are never satisfied.

3. The dimensions of an Edgeworth exchange box are determined by
    a. the amount of each good that one consumer has.
    b. the total amount of each good held by both parties.
    c. the limits set be each person's indifference curves.
    d. how much each person trades of each good.

Questions 4 to 12 refer to Figure 6-2.

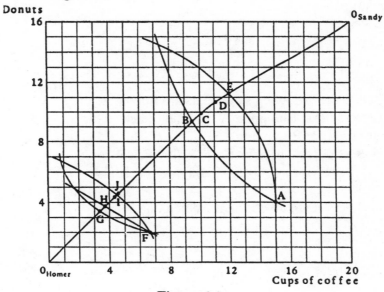

Figure 6-2

4.   For Sandy, the vertical axis is labeled _____ and the horizontal axis is labeled_____.
     a. donuts; cups of coffee
     b. cups of coffee; donuts
     c. donuts; donuts
     d. Can't tell without more information.

5.   If point A is the initial endowment point, how many donuts does Sandy have?
     a. 3
     b. 6
     c. 9
     d. 12

6.   At which point will Homer and Sandy end up if they trade?
     a. B
     b. C
     c. D
     d. Can't say for sure.

7.   The line connecting the two origins that contains points B, C, D, and E is called the ___
     _____.

8. Which of the points on the graph are Pareto optimal?
   a. B and E only
   b. C and D only
   c. A only
   d. B, C, D, and E

9. Indicate whether the following statements are true or false.
   a. Homer prefers point B to point A.   True   False
   b. Sandy prefers point B to point A.   True   False
   c. Homer prefers point E to point B.   True   False
   d. At point B, MRS Homer = MRS Sandy.   TrueFalse

10. Points B, C, D, and E are all efficient. Which one is best?
    a. B
    b. C
    c. D
    d. E
    e. None of the points are best.

11. Let the graph represent a many-person exchange situation.   Point F is the initial endowment point and the line through F is the price line. What point will be the final equilibrium?
    a. G
    b. H
    c. I
    d. J
    e. Can't tell from the information given.

12. In comparing points B and E, we know that
    a. the marginal rates of substitution are the same at B and E.
    b. Homer is better off at E than at B, while Sandy prefers B to E.
    c. both prefer B to E, since B is more equitable.
    d. B is Pareto optimal, but E is not.

13. Efficiency in the distribution of products among consumers occurs when
    a. the ratios of the quantities held are the same for all consumers
    b. P=MC.
    c. $P_x = MU_x$.
    d. consumers' marginal rates of substitution are equal.

14. An important function of price is to
   a. ration existing supplies among consumers.
   b. distribute goods fairly to the consumers who need them most.
   c. Both of the above.
   e. None of the above.

Discussion Questions and Problems

1. Explain why voluntary exchange is mutually beneficial.

2. Suppose there are two goods--coffee and donuts--and two people--Homer and Sandy.

   a. What determines whether they will trade?

   b. What determines which person trades coffee for donuts?

   c. What determines the final equilibrium? Is the final equilibrium unique?

3. Suppose POWs receive a Red Cross parcel weekly that contains three candy bars and four packets of tea. There is an American POW who would like to exchange tea for candy and a British POW who would like to exchange candy for tea. Use Figure 6-3 to answer the following.

    a. Draw an Edgeworth box that illustrates the above situation. (Make sure you label all axes and the endowment point.)

    b. Add indifference curves that are consistent with the information above.

    c. Show two possible outcomes for the exchange.

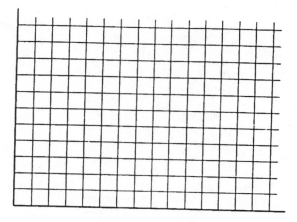

Figure 6-3

4. Figure 6-4 is an Edgeworth box depicting exchange possibilities for Homer and Sandy. Point A is the endowment point. The line connecting the origins is the contract curve.

    a. If the market price is 1 cup of coffee = 1 donut, what will be the equilibrium market baskets for each?

    b. If the market price is 1 cup of coffee = 2 donuts, what will be the equilibrium market basket?

    c. Can you make a summary statement of the relationship between prices, endowment, and the welfare of each person?

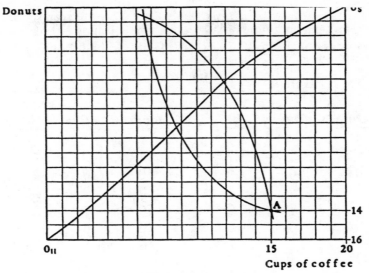

Figure 6-4

5. What is meant by the term *economic efficiency*? Explain how voluntary exchange leads to an efficient solution.

6. People compete for scarce goods. People cooperate with each other by means of voluntary exchange. These two statements appear to be contradictory. Can you reconcile them? If so, how?

7. How can there be more than one efficient distribution of goods? Which distribution of goods is "most efficient?"

8. Suppose Homer's endowment is 8 donuts and 11 cups of coffee and Sandy's endowment is 12 donuts and 9 cups of coffee. We also have the following information:

Homer			Sandy		
Donuts	Coffee	MRS_{cd}	Donuts	Coffee	MRS_{cd}
8	11	1.75	12	9	2.8
10	10	2.0	10	10	2.0
10	9	2.1	10	9	2.5
10	7	3.0	10	7	3.8
10	6	3.6	10	6	4.8
10	5	4.5	10	5	6.0

a. What will be the equilibrium distribution after exchange? What will be the relative price of a cup of coffee?

b. Suppose exchange has taken place, but before either Homer or Sandy consume any donuts or coffee, both stumble and each lose five cups of coffee. Will they trade again? Who places a higher value on coffee? What will happen to the price of coffee? Why?

c. Suppose that after the 10 cups of coffee had been lost, a third party enforces the original price of coffee 1C = 2D. Will there be trade between Sandy and Homer? Why or why not? Is this price control efficient? Explain.

9. It is said that prices serve a rationing function. Explain how prices carry out this function.

10. After the Arab oil embargo in the early 1970s the government set up a contingency plan that included rationing gasoline. Ration coupons were printed incase the plan was ever implemented. Some proposed that if the plan was implemented, consumers should be permitted to buy and sell coupons legally. Others disagreed and said it should be illegal to buy and sell coupons. Which plan would be the most likely to be efficient? Why?

11. Based on the mathematical appendix, explain why there are more than one efficient distributions of goods between two individuals.

ANSWERS

Review Questions

True/False

1. False. People sometimes make mistakes.
2. False
3. False. The statement is true for only points on the contract curve.
4. True
5. True
6. True
7. True
8. True
9. True
10. False
11. True
12. True

Multiple Choice/Short Answer

1. c. People with different endowments, incomes, or tastes will not trade if they have the same MRS. It is the relative importance of the goods that matter.
2. c.
3. b.
4. a.
5. d.
6. d. They will end up on the contract curve somewhere between B and E.
7. contract curve.
8. d.
9. a. False. He is indifferent between them.
    b. True.
    c. True.
    d. True.
10. e. Selecting between points on a contract curve involves value judgments.
11. b.
12. b.
13. d
14. a

Discussion Questions and Problems

1. Each party in a trade must *expect* to benefit since each can choose not to engage in trade. As long as people are not coerced, they will exchange goods with others only when they expect to benefit from the exchange. Of course, expectations are not always met.

2. a. If their MRSs differ, they will trade because they value an additional cup of coffee (an additional donut) differently. This allows both to be made better off by an exchange.
   b. The person who values coffee in terms of donuts the most will trade donuts for coffee. Note that the other person must value donuts in terms of coffee the most.
   c. When their MRSs for coffee and donuts are equal, trade will stop. The final equilibrium is not unique but will depend on their relative bargaining abilities.

3. a and b. See Figure 6-5.
   c. Points A, B, and any point on the contract curve between A and B.

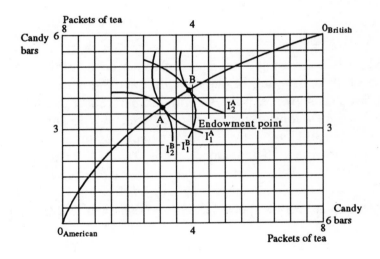

Figure 6-5

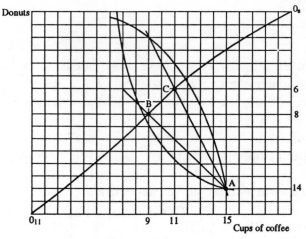

Figure 6-6

4. See Figure 6-6.
    a. The equilibrium is shown at point B, with Homer consuming 9 cups of coffee and 8 donuts and Sandy consuming 11 cups of coffee and 8 donuts.
    b. The equilibrium is shown at point C, with Homer consuming 11 cups of coffee and 10 donuts and Sandy consuming 9 cups of coffee and 6 donuts.
    c. The endowment is the amount of goods a person has initially. Prices determine the value of the endowment. The greater wealth permits the person to achieve a higher level of welfare. In the example, Homer's endowment consists mostly of coffee. When coffee is relatively expensive, he can reach a higher indifference curve than when coffee is relatively inexpensive. The opposite is true for Sandy.

5. Economic efficiency exists when it is impossible to make one person off without making another person worse off. Voluntary exchange leads to an efficient solution because people exchange goods as long as they can be made better off. Once their MRSs are equal, trade stops. But at this point, the MRSs of the people are equal so the solution is efficient.

6. This can be reconciled by reference to an Edgeworth box. When the two individuals are on the contract curve, the only way one person can be made better off is by making the other worse off. They are in conflict. But if we begin at a point off the contract curve, both can be made better off by voluntary exchange.

7.   There are many distributions where all individuals place the same *relative* importance on the goods, so there are many efficient distributions. There is not a most efficient distribution because that would involve making judgments concerning whose well-being is most important.

8.   a. Each person will consume 10 donuts and 10 cups of coffee. The price of a cup of coffee is two donuts: $MRS_{cd} = 2 = P_c/P_d$.
      b. Yes. Sandy values coffee relative to donuts more than Homer does. The price of coffee will increase because it is more scarce. The higher price rations the scarce good among Homer and Sandy.
      c. No. The price is $1C = 2D$ and is below both Homer's and Sandy's relative valuation of coffee. The price control is not efficient because $MRS^H_{cd} \neq MRS^S_{cd}$.

9.   Prices ration the existing supplies of a good by ensuring that the quantities of the good go to those who value them the most. The price measures how much of other goods must be given up to obtain an additional unit of the good. Those who are unwilling to give up the required amount of other goods will not obtain the good in question, while those who are willing will obtain the good.

10.   It is more likely that the plan that allowed legal sales of coupons would be efficient because voluntary exchange would ensure that marginal rates of substitution would be equalized.

11.   An efficient solution is found by maximizing one person's utility subject to a specified level of utility for the other person. The latter expression is equation (31) in the appendix. There is a different solution to maximizing Hank's utility for every possible value of k in (31).

CHAPTER 7 *Production*

CHAPTER ANALYSIS

The previous chapters concerned the demand side of product markets. This chapter begins the analysis of the supply side of the market. The relationships between the inputs used to produce commodities and the quantity of the commodities produced are the primary topics of this chapter.

7.1 A production function is a technical relationship between inputs and output, where output is the quantity of the commodity produced by the firm and inputs are resources used to produce the final product (output). For example, an automobile is the output of General Motors. The inputs used to produce the automobile include steel, aluminum, plastic, rubber, glass, paint, machine tools, engineers, technicians, laborers, and so on. A production function identifies the maximum quantity of a commodity that can be produced by each specific combination of inputs. In the United States, for instance, rice is produced by a process that requires large amounts of capital equipment such as tractors, while in Thailand rice is produced by more labor-intensive methods. The choice of which production method to use is determined by the price of the inputs, a topic that is examined further in Chapter 8.

7.2 Production responses can be studied in the short run and the long run. In the short run, at least one input is fixed at some level. New factories cannot be built overnight, for example, so capital is often fixed at the existing level in the short run. *There are no fixed inputs in the long run.*

It is important that you understand the relationships between total product, average product, and marginal product. Figures 7.1 and 7.2 in the text illustrate the total, average, and marginal product curves and their derivation. Note that when the marginal product curve lies above the average product curve, the average product curve is rising; when the marginal product curve lies below the average product curve, the average product curve is falling. These relationships hold for all marginal and average curves. Further, note that the total product curve increases as long as marginal product is positive.

The shapes of the product curves reflect the law of diminishing marginal returns, which states that as the amount of an input increases by equal increments, holding everything else constant, the resulting increments in output decrease beyond a certain point. That is, the marginal product of the variable input will eventually decline.

7.3 In the long run, all inputs can vary. Production can be analyzed by using isoquants, a tool similar to indifference curves. An isoquant contains all the combinations of inputs that will produce a particular level of output. Variable-proportions production functions generate convex isoquants. Movement along an isoquant can take place only in the long run, since all inputs are variable along the isoquant. The slope of an isoquant measures the marginal rate of technical substitution (MRTS), the amount of one input (such as capital K) that can be reduced without changing output when there is a unit increase in another input (such as labor L). Since isoquants slope down, the MRTS is negative, but the minus sign is dropped by convention. The marginal rate of technical substitution is also related to the marginal products of the inputs:

$$MRTS_{LK} = MP_L/MP_K$$

7.4 An important concept used in analyzing the long-run production process is that of returns to scale, that is, what happens to output when the use of all inputs changes proportionately. If output increases more than proportionately to the increase in inputs, there are increasing returns to scale; if output increases less than proportionately to the increase in inputs, there are decreasing returns to scale; and if output increases proportionately to the increase in inputs, there are constant returns to scale. Note that all inputs must increase by the same proportion.

7.5 Production functions can be estimated statistically. A specific functional form usually is assumed, and then data used to estimate the key relationships by regression analysis. A common production function used for the purpose of estimation is the Cobb-Douglas production function. For two inputs, it takes the form:

$$Q = aL^bK^ce$$

The function can be estimated by taking the natural logarithms of both sides of the equation. In practical terms, the most difficult part is measuring the capital stock. The values of b and c are crucial. Diminishing marginal returns for labor exist when $b < 1$, and diminishing marginal returns for capital exist when $c < 1$. If $b + c$ is equal to one, then constant returns to scale apply. If $b + c$ sum to less than one, then decreasing returns to scale apply, and if they sum to more than one, increasing returns to scale apply.

ILLUSTRATIONS

Marginal Average Relationship

The marginal-average relationship is an important concept that comes up repeatedly in economics. Whenever marginal product is greater than average product, it pulls average product up; when marginal product is less than average product it pulls average product down; and when marginal product equals average product, average product stays the same. The marginal-average relationship will show up in the next chapter as well. Average cost falls when marginal cost lies below average cost, rises when marginal cost lies above average cost, and is constant when marginal cost equals average cost. This relationship is true for the margin and average of anything.

We can use batting averages to illustrate this last statement. Ted Williams was the last baseball player to hit over .400 in a season. (A .400 batting average is when a player gets a hit 40 percent of the times he is at bat.) Suppose on a particular day, Williams' average was exactly .400. If he got up five times and had two hits, his average after the game would still be .400, because the marginal average (2 out of 5) exactly equaled his season average. If he had gotten three hits in five at bats, his new season average would be greater than .400 because his marginal was 60 percent. Finally, if he had gone 1 for 5, his new seasonal average would be less than .400 because his marginal was 20 percent.

Returns to Scale

The theoretical concept of returns to scale involves the effect on output of a proportionate change in all inputs used to produce the output. To illustrate the concept, let's use a simple example. You start up your own business of selling firewood. You get a chain saw and a pickup truck, go to the woods, cut down trees, and sell the firewood to consumers. Business is good, so you decide to double your scale. To do this, you get another pickup truck, another chain saw, and hire your twin to work with you. All inputs have exactly doubled. You might expect output to double, too, that is, constant returns to scale to prevail.

However, when firms expand they generally do not increase each and every input by the same proportion. In the example above, your twin might not work as quickly as you do, you might replace your pickup with a larger truck, or you might purchase a larger chain saw. That is, it is unlikely that you will exactly replicate the inputs you began with. This example also illustrates an important source of increasing returns to scale. One type of capital equipment may be appropriate when the scale of operations is small, yet inappropriate when the scale of operation is greater. Larger increases in output often accompany the transition from small-scale technique to large-scale technique.

KEY CONCEPTS

factors of production
production function
technologically efficient
fixed inputs
total product
average product
marginal product
law of diminishing marginal returns

short run
long run
variable inputs
isoquant
marginal rate of technical substitution
constant returns to scale
increasing returns to scale
decreasing returns to scale
Cobb-Douglas production function

REVIEW QUESTIONS

True/False

_____ 1. There is only one efficient technique to produce a certain quantity of output.

_____ 2. A production function identifies the physical constraints a firm faces.

_____ 3. The fixed input is held constant along an isoquant.

_____ 4. The short run is defined as a period less than 1 year.

_____ 5. A firm that is making plans to build a new factory is operating in the long run.

_____ 6. The marginal product of an input can be defined as the total output divided by the amount of the input used to produce that output.

_____ 7. The total product curve falls when the marginal product curve falls.

_____ 8. Diminishing marginal returns imply that workers hired first have more innate ability than those hired last.

_____ 9. The slope of an isoquant measures the marginal rate of technical substitution.

_____ 10. Isoquants differ from indifference curves in that the spacing between indifference curves does not measure changes in well being while the spacing between isoquants measures changes in output.

Multiple Choice/Short Answer

1. All the following are inputs in the production of computers except
    a. engineers.
    b. technological change.
    c. electricity.
    d. accountants.

2. A production function consists of production processes that are technologically _____ ____.

3. A fixed input is one for which
    a. it is impossible to vary the quantity used in the short run.
    b. it is impossible to vary the quantity used in the long run.
    c. it is too costly to vary the quantity used in the short run.
    d. the quantity used is fixed in the long run but varies in the short run.

4. If the average product of labor when 5 workers are employed is 10, and when 6 workers are employed is 12, then
    a. the marginal product curve lies above the average product curve between 5 and 6 workers.
    b. the marginal product curve lies below the average product curve between 5 and 6 workers.
    c. the total product curve is decreasing between 5 and 6 workers.
    d. marginal product is negative.

5. When the total product curve is increasing at an increasing rate,
    a. marginal product is positive but declining.
    b. average product is zero.
    c. the marginal product curve lies below the average product curve.
    d. marginal product is positive and increasing.

6. The law of diminishing marginal returns states that as the amount of an input increases in equal increments, the resulting increments in output
    a. will decrease but eventually increase.
    b. will eventually be negative.
    c. will eventually get smaller.
    d. will eventually be constant.

7.   Diminishing marginal returns is
     a. true only when moving along an isoquant.
     b. applicable to agriculture but not to manufacturing.
     c. applicable when making long-run plans.
     d. applicable whenever one or more inputs are held constant.

8.   On a given isoquant,
     a. the well being of the manager is held constant.
     b. output is held constant.
     c. capital is held constant.
     d. capital and labor increase proportionately.

9.   Technological change will effect
     a. a movement along an isoquant.
     b. a movement along a total product curve.
     c. a shift in the total product curve.
     d. greater economies of scale.

10. The slope of an isoquant measures
     a. the marginal rate of substitution.
     b. returns of scale.
     c. diminishing marginal returns.
     d. the ratio of the marginal products.

11. One possible factor that may give rise to increasing returns to scale is
     a. specialization of labor.
     b. increasing marginal productivity of labor.
     c. concave isoquants.
     d. the managerial function.

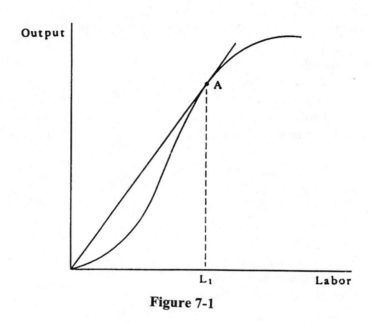

Figure 7-1

12. In Figure 7-1, the ray from the origin is tangent to the total product curve at point A. We know that when L_1 workers are employed,
    a. the average product of labor exceeds the marginal product of labor.
    b. the marginal product of labor exceeds the average product of labor.
    c. the average product of labor equals the marginal product of labor.
    d. We need more information to say anything about either average or marginal product of labor.

13. Suppose 5 laborers working on 10 acres of land are able to produce 4,000 bushels of corn, and 6 laborers working on 12 acres of land produce 5,000 bushels of corn. Production is characterized by
    a. increasing returns of scale.
    b. constant returns to scale.
    c. decreasing returns to scale.
    d. diminishing marginal returns.

14. Diminishing marginal returns is a _____-run concept while decreasing returns to scale is a _____-run concept.

15. A Cobb-Douglas production function exhibits constant returns to scale when
    a. b=1 and c=1.
    b. b+c = 1.
    c. b-c = 1.
    d. either b=1 or c=1.

16. Suppose a Cobb-Douglas production function has the following values: a=100; b=.6; c=.5. Then
    a. labor and capital exhibit diminishing marginal returns and the production function exhibits increasing returns to scale.
    b. labor and capital exhibit diminishing marginal returns and the production function exhibits decreasing returns to scale.
    c. labor does not exhibit diminishing marginal returns, capital exhibits diminishing marginal returns, and the production function exhibits decreasing returns to scale.
    d. we cannot say whether labor or capital exhibit diminishing marginal returns or not, but the production function exhibits constant returns to scale.

Discussion Questions and Problems

Questions 1 - 4 use the following data.

	Bushels of Corn per year					
Number of acres cultivated per year	Workers employed per year					
	1	2	3	4	5	6
1	50	150	275	375	450	500
2	150	370	550	700	825	900
3	240	500	740	940	1080	1160
4	300	660	920	1060	1190	1270
5	330	790	1050	1160	1250	1320
6	340	900	1050	1250	1300	1330

1. Using the above production function for corn, complete the following table:

Amount of land	Workers	Total output	Average product of labor	Marginal product of labor
3	0	0	-	-
3	1	___	___	___
3	2	___	___	___
3	3	___	___	___
3	4	___	___	___
3	5	___	___	___
3	6	___	___	___

2. In Figure 7-2(a), draw the total product curve for labor when the amount of land used is 3 acres. In Figure 7-2(b), draw the average product and marginal product curves. (Be sure you indicate the quantities on the axes.)

3. Suppose a farmer uses 1 worker and 1 acre of land. Over time, he expands production by increasing the use of both inputs proportionately. Does the farmer experience increasing, constant, or decreasing returns to scale as he expands?

154

4.	If the quantity of land is held constant at 3 acres, when do diminishing marginal returns for labor set in?

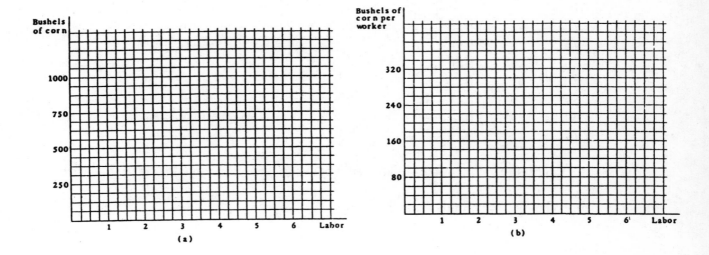

Figure 7-2

Questions 5 and 6 use the information in the following table.

Labor	Capital	Output
10	90	100
20	70	100
30	55	100
40	45	100
50	36	100
60	29	100
70	25	100

5. a. On Figure 7-3, draw the relationship between labor and capital given in the table.

   b. What do we call this figure?

   c. What is the $MRTS_{LK}$ when labor goes from 30 to 40 workers?

   d. What is the $MRTS_{LK}$ when labor goes from 60 to 70 workers?

   e. If the marginal product of the fiftieth laborer is 9, what is the marginal product of capital when the thirty-sixth unit of capital is employed?

6. Draw an isoquant for 50 units of output if constant returns to scale apply. Draw another isoquant for 120 units of output.

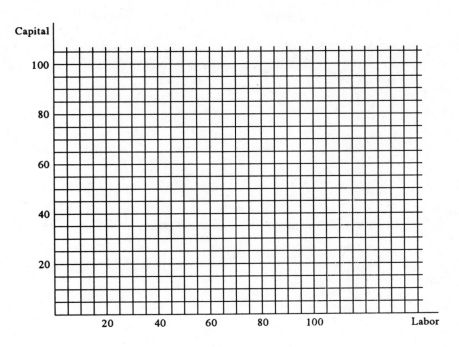

Figure 7-3

7. Suppose an isoquant is a straight line with a slope of -1. What does this imply concerning the marginal rate of technical substitution? What does it imply concerning the marginal products of the two inputs?

8. The marginal product of labor must fall over time because the labor force is increasing. Do you agree or disagree? Why?

9.   Some economists believe that constant returns to scale would prevail if all inputs could be exactly replicated. If this is true, explain why we observe increasing or decreasing returns to scale.

10. Distinguish between decreasing returns to scale and diminishing marginal returns.

11. Explain how marginal product and average product can be derived from the total product curve.

12. Suppose a firm uses 1,000 laborers, 600 units of capital, 3 acres of land, 25 tons of iron ore, and 30 tons of coal to produce 20 tons of steel. The firm expands and uses 1,500 laborers, 800 units of capital, 6 acres of land, 35 tons of iron ore, and 40 tons of coal to produce 30 tons of steel. Is this a case of constant returns to scale? Why or why not?

13. You are currently going to college. Consider yourself to be a "firm" utilizing inputs to produce an output. What is the output? What are the inputs you use to produce the output? Describe a situation when diminishing marginal returns applies.

14. Many firms use suggestion boxes or provide financial bonuses for employees who suggest a way of operating better. Suppose an employee suggests that the firm rearrange its floor plan to permit a better flow of materials and people. The firm does so and output increases by 3 percent without any increase in any of the inputs. Was the firm operating inefficiently before? How would the change be pictured using isoquants? (Assume the output before the change was 1,000 units a month.)

15. Can a production function that exhibits increasing returns to scale also display diminishing returns?

The following question relates to the material in the mathematical appendix.

16.   A production function for wheat is given by $W = AL^{.6}K^{.4}$.

      a. Derive the marginal products of labor and capital, and the marginal rate of technical substitution.

      b. If $A = 10$, $L = 100$ and $K = 75$, find W, MP_L, MP_K, and MRTS. Do the same for L 200 and K 150.

      c. If A increases to 20, what happens to W? What could cause such a change?

ANSWERS

Review Questions

True/False

1.	False.		6.	False.
2.	True.		7.	False.
3.	False.		8.	False.
4.	False.		9.	True.
5.	True.		10.	True.

Multiple Choice/Short Answer

1.	b		9.	c
2.	Efficient		10.	d
3.	c		11.	a
4.	a		12.	c
5.	d		13.	a
6.	c		14.	short; long
7.	d		15.	b
8.	b		16.	a

Discussion Questions and Problems

1.

Amount of land	Workers	Total output	Average product of labor	Marginal product of labor
3	0	0		
3	1	240	240	240
3	2	500	250	260
3	3	740	247	240
3	4	940	235	200
3	5	1080	216	140
3	6	1160	193	80

2. See Figure 7-4.

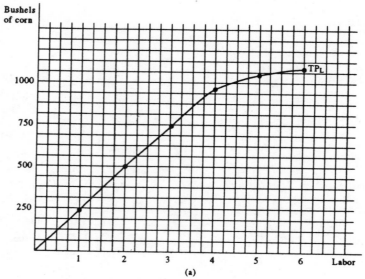

(a)

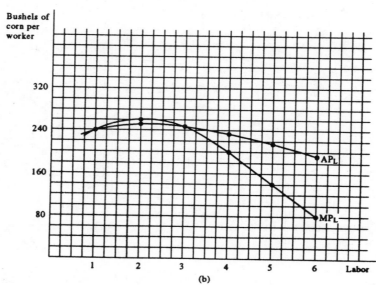

(b)

Figure 7-4

3. There are increasing returns to scale up through 4 units of each input and decreasing returns to scale after that.

4. Diminishing marginal returns set in when the third unit of fertilizer is used.

5. a. See Figure 7-5.
   b. Isoquant
   c. $(55-45)/(30-40)=-1$
   d. $(29-25)/(60-70)=(-)4/10=(-).4$
   e. $MRTS=(45-36)/(40-50)=(-)0.9$. $MRTS=MP_L/MP_K$, so $0.9=9/MP_K$. Thus $MP_K=9/0.9$ $=10$.

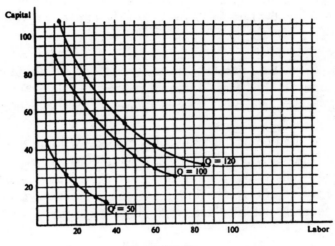

Figure 7-5

6. See Figure 7-5.

7. The MRTS is constant at all points on the isoquant. The ratio of the marginal products is constant too.

8. Disagree. Many other things can be happening too. Technical change may alter the production function, the capital stock may increase. education levels may change, etc.

9. When a firm expands, it generally does not exactly replicate all existing inputs. Instead, different types of capital may be employed that actually may alter the capital-labor ratio. That is, all inputs are not increasing proportionately. The movement to large-scale production will cause increasing returns to scale initially. When management becomes too spread out, decreasing returns to scale set in.

10. Decreasing returns to scale occur when a proportionate increase in all inputs results in a less than proportionate increase in output. It is a long-run concept. Diminishing marginal returns occur when adding equal increments of an input to a fixed amount of another input results in smaller additions to output. It is a short-run concept.

11. Average product is found by taking a line (ray) from the origin to a point on the total product curve. The slope of the line is the average product of labor associated with that point. Marginal product is found by the slope of a line tangent to the point on the total product curve. (Review Figure 7.2 on page 171 in the text if you have trouble.)

12. No. To determine whether scale economies exist or not, all inputs must be changed by the same percentage. In this case, output increased by 50 percent, laborers by 50 percent, capital by 33 percent, land by 100 percent, iron ore by 40 percent, and coal by 100 percent.

13. Output could be defined as the knowledge gained by going to college or by the diploma. Inputs include the faculty, classrooms, paper, books, the library, computers, land the college is on, as well as you. Diminishing marginal returns would apply whenever you try to increase your rate of output without increasing all inputs proportionately, e.g., attending class more frequently while holding studying time constant.

14. No. The firm was operating the best way it knew before the suggestion. The suggestion resulted in a change in technology. An isoquant labeled Q=1000 before the suggestion is now labeled Q--1030.

15. Yes. Increasing returns to scale occurs when all inputs are increased proportionately and output increases by a greater percentage. Diminishing returns occurs when at least one input is held constant.

16. a. $MP_L = \partial W/\partial L = .6AL^{-.4}K^{.4} = .6A\,(K/L)^{.4}$

   $MP_K = \partial W/\partial K = .4AL^{.6}K^{-.6} = .4A\,(K/L)^{-.6}$

   $MRTS = MP_L/MP_K = (.6A(K/L)^{.4})/(.4A(K/L)^{-.6}) = 1.5(K/L)$

b. $W = 10(100)^{.6}(75)^{.4} = 891.3$

$MP_L = .6(10)(75/100)^{.4} = 5.348$

$MP_K = .4(10)(75/100)^{-.6} = 4.754$

$MRTS = 1.5(75/100) = 1.125$

$W = 10(200)^{.6}(150)^{.4} = 1782.6$

$MP_L = .6(10)(150/200)^{.4} = 5.348$

$MP_K = .4(10)(150/200)^{-.6} = 4.754$

$MRTS = 1.5(150/200) \ 1.125$

c. $W = 20(200)^{.6}(150)^{.4} = 3565.2$

Technology must have changed since neither labor nor capital changed and output increased.

CHAPTER 8 *The Cost of Production*

CHAPTER ANALYSIS

8.1 Cost is an important concept in both economics and accounting, but the definition of cost differs in the two disciplines. To an accountant, the cost of a resource is the actual cash outlays expended on it; to an economist, the cost of a resource is the value of the resource in its next best alternative use. That is, to an economist all costs are opportunity costs, which include explicit and implicit costs. For a sole proprietorship an important implicit cost is the owner's time--what would the owner have earned working as an employee. For a corporation, the key implicit cost is the opportunity cost of its productive assets or its capital.

8.2-8.3 The distinction between the long run and the short run in analyzing production also applies to an analysis of costs. The various measures of cost are defined in Section 8.2 in Browning and Zupan. The firm's costs are determined by the production function and the prices of the inputs. Carefully review Figures 8.1 through 8.3 in the text to ensure that you understand the relationships between the various short-run costs. In particular, make sure you understand the relationship between the TVC curve and the total product (TP) curve--the shape of the TVC curve is determined by the shape of the TP curve. Further, the shape of the MC curve is determined by the shape of the marginal product (MP) curve. When MP is increasing, MC is decreasing, and when MP is decreasing, MC is increasing. Thus marginal costs eventually increase because of the law of diminishing returns. Similarly, the shape of the AVC curve is determined by the shape of the average product (AP) curve. The short-run cost curves are ultimately determined by the underlying production process and the ability of the firm to hire additional inputs at constant prices.

8.4 In the long run, all inputs can be varied, so the firm can find the optimal combination of inputs for a specific rate of output. As we saw in the last chapter, isoquants are analogous to indifference curves. Similarly, the isocost line is analogous to a consumer's budget line, with one important difference: the firm is not constrained to stay within a specific isocost line. The total costs of production can be chosen by the firm, whereas total income is not selected by the consumer. The firm wants to maximize profits, rather than output.

An **isocost line** identifies the combination of the two inputs that can be purchased at a given total cost. The slope of the isoquant curve equals the ratio of the input prices, just as the slope of the consumer's budget line equals the ratio of the prices of the goods. As long as the prices are constant, the isocost lines will be straight lines parallel to each other.

Figure 8-1 illustrates two ways to view the manner in which the firm determines the optimal combination of inputs. First, the firm can maximize output for a given total cost. If the firm decides it is willing to spend TC_2 dollars, it will seek to produce the most output possible given its cost constraint. In Figure 8-1, the firm must stay on or within the isocost line for TC_2. Hence the isoquant labeled Q_4 is not attainable. Isoquant Q_1, is attainable, but so are Q_2 and Q_3. Of these, Q_3 is the maximum output that can be produced for TC_2 dollars. Again, a tangency point determines the optimum. At point B, isoquant Q_3 is tangent to the isocost line for TC_2.

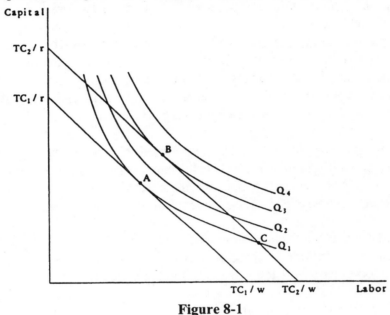

Figure 8-1

The second way to view the firm's optimization problem is in terms of **cost minimization**; that is, if the firm wants to produce Q_1 units of output, what is the least costly way of producing them? At point C, Q_1 units are produced at a cost of TC_2. However, this is not the least costly combination of inputs. The Q_1 units of output can be produced for TC_1 dollars at point A. This is the least costly method of producing Q_1 units of output. Note, too, that point A is the tangency between the isoquant and the isocost line.

The slope of the isoquant measures the marginal rate of technical substitution ($MRTS_{LK}$), and the slope of the isocost line is the ratio of the input prices (w/r). At a tangency point, their slopes are equal, or

$$MRTS_{LK} = w/r$$

Since $MRTS_{LK} = MP_L/MP_K$, it is true that $MP_L/MP_K = w/r$, or $MP_L/w = MP_K/r$. The optimum combination of inputs is one for which the marginal products per dollar's worth of all inputs are equal.

8.5 Up to this point, we have held input prices constant in order to identify the effects of output changes on costs. Of course, if the price of an input used to produce the firm's output changes, costs will change too. If the price of an input changes, the slope of the isocost line will change, and there will be a new optimal combination of inputs. The average and marginal cost curves will shift as well. A careful review of Figure 8-5 in the text will help you understand this relationship.

8.6-8.7 There are three long-run cost curves--total cost, average cost, and marginal cost. Every point on a long-run cost curve reflects a tangency between an isocost line and an isoquant and represents the least costly combination of inputs. The shape of the long-run cost curves are determined by the production process as well. As long as input prices are constant, increasing returns to scale in production imply that economies of scale exist, decreasing returns to scale imply diseconomies of scale, and constant returns to scale imply that the long-run average cost curve is horizontal. However, if the input mix changes as the firm changes scale, then economies of scale can exist, but would be unrelated to increasing returns to scale.

The structure of an industry is ultimately determined by the costs of production. When production is characterized by increasing returns to scale over larger ranges of output, the industry will tend to be made up of a few large firms. When decreasing returns to scale set in at relatively low levels of output, the industry tends to be made up of many small firms.

8.8 This section in the text provides an example of the use of the tools developed in this chapter to analyze an actual problem-pollution. Read the section carefully, if you *understand* the analysis you should have a good grasp of the tools presented in the chapter.

8.9 Many firms produce more than one product. Economies of scale apply to the production of a single product. But, it may be the case that production of one good enables the firm to produce another good at a lower cost than if production of the two goods were totally separate. Suppose an auto firm also produces trucks. Let TC(a) be the total costs of producing autos if the firm produced only autos, and TC(t) be the total costs of producing trucks if the firm produced only trucks. If TC(a,t) are the total costs of producing both trucks and autos, then **economies of scope** exist if TC(a,t) < TC(a) + TC(t).

8.10 Techniques used to estimate cost functions include **survivorship techniques** and regression analysis. A problem with regression analysis is that the data tend to be accounting data which often do not reflect the true opportunity costs of inputs.

ILLUSTRATIONS

Cost Curves and Market Structure

The key determinant of whether an industry is made up of many relatively small firms or a few relatively large firms is the long-run average cost curve. An industry can expand its output at lower cost by having one firm expand, if the firm's long-run average cost curve (LRAC) is still sloping downward. However, if the firm is at the minimum of its LRAC, then the industry can expand output at lower cost by having a new firm enter the industry. As long as increasing returns to scale are available, it is cheapest to have a single firm expand. When there are no longer increasing returns to scale, it is cheapest to have new firms produce the additional output.

Since increasing returns to scale are a technological phenomenon, industries characterized by increasing returns to scale in this country will also be characterized by increasing returns to scale in other countries. The automobile industry is made up of a few giant firms in the United States, but the same is true in Japan, Great Britain, France, and Germany. Empirical studies have found that industries that are highly concentrated (made up of a few large firms) in the United States tend to be highly concentrated in other industrial nations as well. [See Frederick Pryor, An International Comparison of Concentration Ratios," *Review of Economics and Statistics, 54* (May 1972), pp. 130-140.]

The Survivorship Principle

The survivorship principle is simple--firms that are too large or too small will lose business to firms that are the optimal size. George Stigler used this principle to measure economies of scale in the steel industry. He described the technique:

> Classify the firms in an industry by size, and calculate the share of industry output coming from each class over time. If the share of a given class falls, it is relatively inefficient, and in general is more inefficient the more rapidly the share falls.

[See George J. Stigler, "The Economies of Scale," Journal of Law and Economics, 1 (October 1958), pp. 54-71.]

KEY CONCEPTS

total fixed cost
total variable cost
total cost
marginal cost
average fixed cost
average variable cost
average total costs
isocost line

golden rule of cost minimization
expansion path
input substitution effect
economies of scale
diseconomies of scale
minimum efficient scale
economies of scope
diseconomies of scope
new entrant/survivor technique

REVIEW QUESTIONS

True/False

_____ 1. An implicit cost usually involves the use of resources owned by the owner of the firm.

_____ 2. Variable costs depend on how much output is produced.

_____ 3. The total variable cost curve is determined by the total product curve.

_____ 4. The law of diminishing marginal returns largely determines how variable and total costs vary with output.

_____ 5. At any given time, a firm faces a single isocost line.

_____ 6. A point of tangency between an isocost curve and an isoquant shows the maximum output attainable at a given cost as well as the minimum cost necessary to produce that output.

_____ 7. If the price of an input changes, there will be a new expansion path.

_____ 8. The shape of the long-run average cost curve is an important determinant of the market structure of the industry.

_____ 9. Every point on a long-run average cost curve is tangent to the minimum point of a short-run average cost curve.

_____ 10. If a firm experiences economies of scale, then it also experiences economies of scope.

Multiple Choice/Short Answer

1. A self-employed automobile mechanic uses his own tools, rents a building, buys replacement parts, and hires a teenager as a helper.
   a. List the inputs that generate explicit costs.
   b. List the inputs that generate implicit costs.

2. Working for someone else, the mechanic in question 1 could make $1500 a month and could rent tools for $20 a month. Rent on the building is $500 a month, replacement parts are $500 a month, and wages for the teenager are $400 a month. What are the total monthly costs?

3. An acre of land is used to raise wheat. If the farmer could make $2000 by growing corn on the acre, $1800 by growing oats, $1700 by growing soybeans, and $1500 by raising beef, what is the opportunity cost of the wheat?

4. Marginal cost is determined by
   a. the slope of the total fixed cost curve.
   b. the slope of the average variable cost curve.
   c. the slope of the total cost curve.
   d. the slope of the marginal product curve.

5. The law of diminishing marginal returns determines
   a. the shape of the short-run MC curve but not the shape of the AVC curve.
   b. the shape of the TVC curve but not the shape of the AVC curve.
   c. the shape of the MC and AVC curves.
   d. the shape of the TFC and AFC curves.

6. When the marginal product of a variable input decreases, marginal cost _____.

7. The slope of an isocost line measures
   a. the marginal rate of technical substitution.
   b. the marginal rate of substitution.
   c. the optimal combination of inputs.
   d. the ratio of the prices of the inputs.

Questions 8 to 10 refer to Figure 8-2.

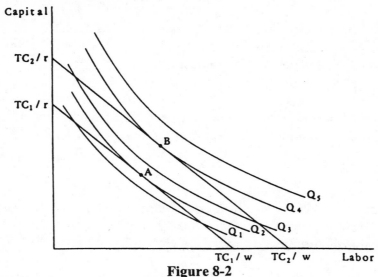

Figure 8-2

8. What is the maximum output that can be produced for a total cost of TC_1?

9. If the firm wants to produce Q_4 units of output in the least costly manner, how much will it have to spend?

10. Which of the following is true?
    a. $MRTS_{LK}$ at point A = $MRTS_{LK}$ at point B.
    b. $MRTS_{LK}$ at point A > $MRTS_{LK}$ at point B.
    c. $MRTS_{LK}$ at point A < $MRTS_{LK}$ at point B.
    d. All of the above are possible.

11. The optimal combination of inputs is one for which
    a. the marginal products of all inputs are equal.
    b. $MRTS_{LK}/MRTS_{KL} = w/r$.
    c. $MP_L/MP_K = w/r$.
    d. $MP_K/MP_L = w/r$.

12. A lower price of an input shifts the AC and MC curves of the firm
    a. upward.
    b. downward
    c. to the right.
    d. to the left.

172

13.   If the long-run average cost curve is U-shaped, then
      a. the production process is characterized by constant returns to scale.
      b. the production process is characterized by diminishing marginal returns.
      c. the production process is characterized by decreasing returns to scale.
      d. None of the above.

14.   Once a firm builds a plant, its options in the immediate future are determined by
      a. its long-run average cost curve.
      b. its short-run average cost curve.
      c. increasing returns to scale.
      d. constant returns to scale.

15.   Economies of scope exist when
      a. there are economies of scale on all the product lines of the firm.
      b. there are increasing returns to scale on all the product lines of the firm.
      c. firms produce a good that they use as an input when producing a second good.
      d. the total costs of producing two goods together are less than the sum of the costs of producing the goods separately.

16.   In the cubic total cost function $TC = a + bQ + cQ^2 + dQ^3 + e$, $a = 0$ means that
      a. marginal costs are zero.
      b. fixed costs are zero.
      c. economies of scale exist.
      d. economies of scope exist.

Discussion Questions and Problems

Questions 1 to 4 refer to the following table:

Acres of land	Tons of fertilizer	Bushels of wheat	Average product	Marginal product	TFC	TVC	TC	AVC	ATC	MC
1	1	40								
1	2	100	___	___	___	___	___	___	___	___
1	3	150	___	___	___	___	___	___	___	___
1	4	190	___	___	___	___	___	___	___	___
1	5	220	___	___	___	___	___	___	___	___
1	6	240	___	___	___	___	___	___	___	___
1	7	250	___	___	___	___	___	___	___	___
1	8	255	___	___	___	___	___	___	___	___

1. Let land rent for $500/acre and fertilizer cost $50 a ton. Fill in the blanks in the table.

2. There are four grids in Figure 8-3. Using the data from the table above, fill in the grids as follows: In part a draw the total product curve, and in part b draw the AP and MP curves. (Notice that some of the axes are labeled differently from those in Chapter 8.) In part c draw the TC, TVC, and TFC curves, and in part d draw the AVC, ATC, and MC curves

3. The price of fertilizer drops to $25 a ton. Fill in the table below and use these data to plot the new cost curves in Figures 8-3.

Acres of land	Tons of fertilizer	Bushels of wheat	Average product	Marginal product	TFC	TVC_2	TC_2	AVC_2	ATC_2	MC_2
1	1	40								
1	2	100	___	___	___	___	___	___	___	___
1	3	150	___	___	___	___	___	___	___	___
1	4	190	___	___	___	___	___	___	___	___
1	5	220	___	___	___	___	___	___	___	___
1	6	240	___	___	___	___	___	___	___	___
1	7	250	___	___	___	___	___	___	___	___
1	8	255	___	___	___	___	___	___	___	___

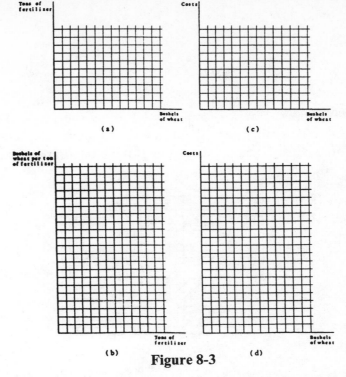

Figure 8-3

4. Use the tables in questions 1 and 3 and the graphs you produced in questions 2 and 3 as aids in answering the following questions.

   a. In what ways are the TP and TVC curves related?

   b. Why do diminishing marginal returns affect the MC and AVC curves?

   c. At what rate of output is the AVC curve at a minimum? The ATC curve? Why are they different rates of output?

   d. Is the minimum of the AVC curve at the same rate of output when the price of fertilizer equals $25 as it was when the price was $50? Why?

   e. Let the price of land double. What effect does this have on the MC curve? Why?

   f. Suppose a new type of fertilizer is developed that results in an additional 50 bushels of wheat per ton fertilizer applied. What is the effect on the AVC and MC curves?

5.　In Figure 8-4, draw a set of isoquants such that the production process tends to use relatively more labor than capital at low rates of output and relatively more capital than labor at higher rates of output. Add isocost lines and draw the expansion path.

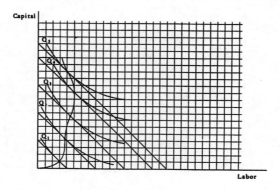

Figure 8-4

6.　Interpret a point of tangency between an isocost curve and an isoquant.

7.　"An expansion path that is a straight line through the origin implies constant returns to scale." Evaluate this statement.

8.　What is the shape of the long-run average cost curve if constant returns to scale prevail over the entire range of output? Why? What does the marginal cost curve look like? Why?

9.　Discuss how a long-run average cost curve is derived.

10. Discuss the relationship between long-run average costs and the market structure of an industry.

11. In what ways is an isocost line similar to a consumer's budget line? In what ways do they differ?

12. Suppose the price of labor is $50 a day and the price of capital is $ 100 per day. Draw the isocost curve in Figure 8-5 if the firm chooses to spend $10,000 a day. Add an isoquant tangent to the isocost curve at 120 units of labor. How many units of capital are employed? Let the price of capital fall to $80 a day. Draw the new isocost curve and add an isoquant to picture the new tangency point. Is the new tangency point also the firm's new equilibrium? Explain.

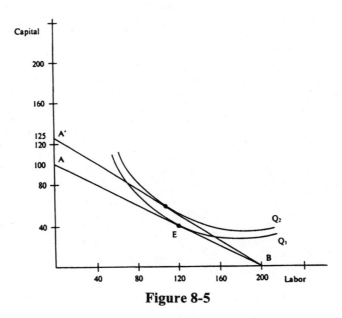

Figure 8-5

13. What happens to the marginal rate of technical substitution as we move along an isoquant? What happens to the marginal products of labor and capital?

14.   If the government requires that all automobiles meet certain emission standards, the cost for pollution control is higher than necessary. Do you agree or disagree? Why?

The following questions relate to the material in the mathematical appendix.

15.   Let $Q = L^{.5}K^{.5}$ be our production function, and let $w = \$5$ and $r = \$10$. What combination of labor and capital will a firm select if it wants to produce 1000 units at the least cost? What are the costs of producing 1000 units?

16.   Using the same prices and protection function as 15, find maximum output if the firm's spending constraint is $15,000. What is the output? How will the value of L, K, and Q change if r increases to $15?

ANSWERS

Review Questions

True/False

1. True
2. True
3. True
4. True
5. False
6. True
7. True
8. True
9. False. They are tangent but the tangency does not always involve the minimum point of the short-run average cost curve.
10. False

Multiple Choice/Short Answer

1. a. Renting a building, hiring a teenager, and buying parts
   b. The mechanic and the tools owned by the mechanic
2. $2920
3. $2000
4. c
5. c
6. increases
7. d
8. Q_2
9. TC_2
10. a
11. c
12. b
13. d
14. b
15. d
16. b

Discussion questions and problems

1.

Average product	Marginal product	TFC	TVC	TC	AVC	ATC	MC
40	40	$500	50	$550	$1.25	$13.75	$1.25
50	60	500	100	600	1.00	6.00	.83
50	50	500	150	650	1.00	4.33	1.00
47.5	40	500	200	700	1.05	3.68	1.25
44	30	500	250	750	1.14	3.41	1.67
40	20	500	300	800	1.25	3.33	2.50
36	10	500	350	850	1.40	3.40	5.00
12	1	500	400	900	1.57	3.53	10.00

2. See Figure 8-6.

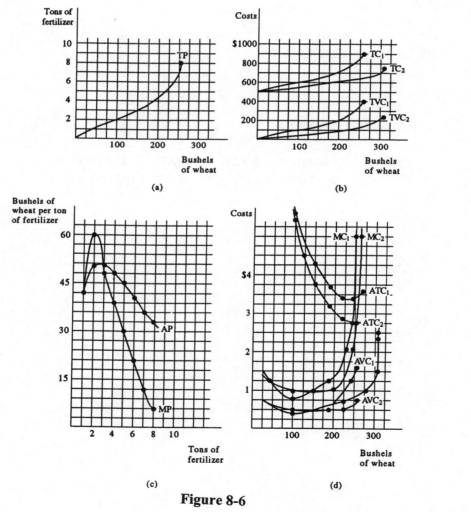

Figure 8-6

3.

Average product	Marginal product	TFC	TVC$_2$	TC$_2$	AVC$_2$	ATC$_2$	MC$_2$
40	40	$500	$ 25	$525	$.63	$13.13	$ .63
50	60	500	50	550	.50	5.50	.42
50	50	500	75	575	.50	3.83	.50
47.5	40	500	100	600	.53	3.16	.63
44	30	500	125	625	.51	2.84	.83
40	20	500	150	650	.63	2.71	1.25
36	10	500	175	675	.70	2.70	2.50
32	5	500	200	700	.78	2.75	5.00

For new cost curves, see Figures 8-6, parts c & d.

4.   a.   If the axes for the TP curve are labeled differently, the relationship between the TP and TVC curves is more apparent. With output on the horizontal axis of both graphs, we see that the TP and TVC curves have the same shape. The TVC curve is found by multiplying the number of units of the variable input used by the price of the variable input.

b.   Diminishing marginal returns determine the shape of the TP curve, which determines the shape of the TVC curve. Since the AVC and MC curves are derived from the TVC curve, the law of diminishing marginal returns ultimately determines the shape of the AVC and MC curves. This can be seen intuitively too. Diminishing marginal returns imply that output is increasing by smaller increments as the usage of the variable input increases. Since the price of the variable input is a constant, costs per unit of output must be rising.

c.   Between 100 and 150 bushels of wheat. Between 240 and 250 bushels of wheat. ATC includes fixed costs, and average fixed costs decline continuously. They pull ATC down over a large rate of output.

d.   Yes. Total variable costs were cut in half for every rate of output so the AVC curve shifts downward.

e.   None, because MC is affected by the variable input while land is the fixed input.

f.   The curves shift to the right.

5. See Figure 8-7.

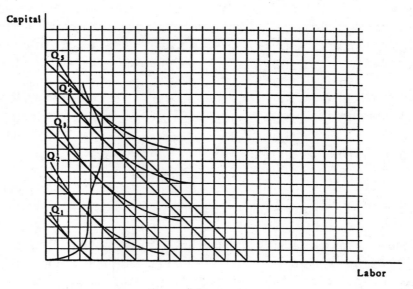

Figure 8-7

6. A tangency between an isocost curve and an isoquant implies that the slopes of each curve are equal. The slope of the isoquant is the marginal rate of technical substitution and the slope of the isocost curve equals the ratio of the input prices. Thus MRTS = w/r. Since MRTS = MP_L/MP_K we get $MP_L/w = MP_K/r$. To minimize costs, a firm should employ inputs such that the marginal product per dollars worth of all inputs is equal.

7. No. A straight-line expansion path merely means that the optimal amounts of the inputs increase proportionately to each other as output increases. It does not mean that they increase proportionately with output.

8. Horizontal line. A proportionate increase in inputs means costs increase proportionately, and since output is increasing proportionately too, average costs are constant. Marginal costs are also constant and equal to average costs, so the AC curve is the MC curve too.

9. The long-run average cost curve is the lowest average cost possible when all inputs are variable. Each point on the long-run average cost curve is associated with a different short-run scale of operation and is tangent to the short-run average cost curve associated with that scale of operation.

10. There is a tendency for firms to operate at the minimum point of their long-run average cost curves. Consequently, when the long-run average cost curve reaches its minimum at a rate of output that is large relative to the market demand, firms will be large and there will be only a few firms in the industry. When the minimum of long-run average cost is small relative to the market demand, many firms can exist in the industry.

11. The slope of the isocost line is the ratio of the input prices as the slope of the consumer's budget line is the ratio of the prices of the goods. However, a consumer has only one budget line that is relevant, while a firm has many because it can choose its level of spending.

12. See Figure 8-8. Forty units of capital are employed. The new tangency is not necessarily the firm's new equilibrium because the firm does not have to continue to operate at a daily cost of $10,000. It will find its profit-maximizing rate of output and then minimize its costs.

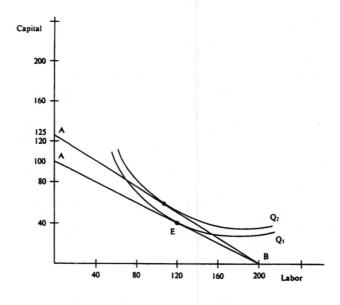

Figure 8-8

13. The MRTS decreases as we move down an isoquant. This means that the marginal product of the input that is being replaced is increasing while the marginal product of the input that is being added is decreasing.

183

14. Agree. The least costly method requires that the marginal cost of emission control be equal for all automobiles.

15. Set the Lagrangian equation:

$$Z = 5L + 10K + \lambda[1000 - L^{.5}K^{.5}] \qquad (1)$$

First order conditions are:

$$\partial Z/\partial L = 5 - \lambda 0.5L^{-.5}K^{.5} = 0 \qquad (2)$$

$$\partial Z/\partial K = 10 - \lambda 0.5L^{.5}K^{-.5} = 0$$

$$\partial Z/\partial \lambda = 1000 - L^{.5}K^{.5} \qquad (4)$$

Dividing (2) by (3) yields

$$1/2 = K/L \text{ or } K = 1/2 \, L \qquad (5)$$

Substituting (5) into (4) gives us the optimal quantity of labor:

$$1000 - L^{.5}(1/2L)^{.5} = 0 \qquad (6)$$

$$1000 = (1/2)^{.5}L \qquad (7)$$

so L = 1414.2 and K = 707.1. The costs of production are ($5)(1414.2) + ($10)(707.1) = $14,142.

16. Set the Lagrangian equation:

$$Z = L^{.5}K^{.5} + \lambda[\$15{,}000 - 5L - 10K]$$ (8)

The first order conditions are:

$$\partial Z/\partial L = 0.5L^{-.5}K^{.5} - \lambda 5 = 0$$ (9)

$$\partial Z/\partial K = 0.5L^{.5}K^{-.5} - \lambda 10 = 0$$ (10)

$$\partial Z/\partial \lambda = \$15{,}000 - 5L - 10K = 0$$ (11)

Dividing (9) by (10) yields:

$$K/L = 1/2 \text{ or } K = 1/2L$$ (12)

Substituting (12) into (11) gives as the optimal quantity of labor:

$$15{,}000 - 5L - 10(1/2L) = 0$$ (13)

or L = 1500 and K = 750. Output is:

$$Q = (1500)^{.5}(75)^{.5} = 1060.66 \text{ units.}$$

If r increases to $15, equation (10) becomes

$$\partial Z/\partial K = 0.5L^{.5}K^{-.5} - \lambda 15 = 0$$ (14)

and (12) becomes K = 1/3L. Equation (13) becomes:

$$\$15{,}000 - 5L - 15(1/3L) = 0$$

or 15,000 = 10L or L = 1500 and K = 500.

Output falls to:

$$Q = (1500)^{.5}(500)^{.5} = 866.$$

CHAPTER 9 *Profit Maximization in Perfectly Competitive Markets*

CHAPTER ANALYSIS

Chapters 7 and 8 presented material that is applicable to all firms--production functions and the costs of production. Although important, these two elements are not sufficient to explain the rate of output selected by a firm. The goals of the firm and the demand conditions facing the firm must be specified too. In Chapter 9 the **model of perfect competition** is presented. Microeconomists use the competitive model more than any other model to analyze the behavior of markets. Success in this and many other economics courses requires thorough understanding of the model of perfect competition and the ability to use it to analyze real world phenomena.

9.1-9.2 The assumptions of the competitive model are stringent and do not describe actual industries. Remember, though, that the realism of the assumptions of a model is not as important as the ability of the model to explain and predict economic behavior. There are four assumptions of the competitive model:
1. There are a large number of buyers and sellers such that all participants in the market are price takers. The justification for this assumption and its implications are discussed in Section 9.3.
2. There is unrestricted mobility of resources. This assumption, which is necessary to reach long-run equilibrium, is discussed more completely in Section 9.7.
3. It is assumed that the firms produce a homogeneous product so that consumers are interested only in price.
4. It is assumed that firms and consumers possess all relevant information necessary to make economic decisions.

We also assume that the firm seeks to maximize its profits. This assumption is often controversial, however it is used because it has proven to predict well.

9.3 A perfectly competitive firm faces a horizontal demand curve, which means that the firm can sell as much as it can produce at the market price. The competitive firm is a **price taker**-it must accept the price determined in the marketplace. Laborers looking for jobs are not able to set their wages. Rather, the market determines their wages. If an individual will not work for the market wage, someone else will. Similarly, wheat farmers cannot get more than the market price for their wheat since the amount they supply individually is so small relative to the entire market. The horizontal demand curve has an elasticity of infinity. Further, the demand curve is also the firm's average revenue curve and its marginal revenue curve.

9.4-9.5 The determination of the short-run profit-maximizing rate of output involves a two-stage process. First, the firm must decide whether to produce any units at all. If the firm shuts down, its losses will equal its fixed costs (TFC) since these must be paid even if no output is produced. A firm will operate as long as it can make a profit or as long as its losses are less than its TFC. A firm's profits or losses are found by subtracting total costs from total revenue:

$$\text{Profits (Losses)} = TR - TC = TR - TFC - TVC = (TR - TVC) - TFC$$

In the short run, the firm will operate when TR - TVC is greater than zero because total losses will be less than TFC. Another way of looking at the question of whether or not to produce is to examine average revenue and average cost. A firm will produce whenever average revenue (AR) exceeds AVC. Average revenue equals (PxQ)/Q = P, so the firm will produce when P > AVC. Thus, the minimum point on the AVC curve is called the **shutdown point** because the firm will not produce any output if it cannot cover its variable costs.

If P > AVC the next step is to determine the output level at which profits are maximized. The rule for profit maximization is that the firm should produce at the rate of output where MR = MC. Recall that profits equal TR - TC. If MR > MC, profits will increase because the addition to total revenue exceeds the addition to total costs, and the firm can increase profits by producing another unit. If MR < MC, the firm can increase profits by producing one less unit since the reduction to total costs exceeds the reduction to total revenue. Thus, whenever MR > MC the firm should expand output, and when MR < MC the firm should contract its rate of output. When MR = MC profits are at a maximum (or losses at a minimum).

Since the minimum point of the AVC curve is the shutdown point and the firm will produce at the rate of output where P = MC, the MC curve lying above the AVC curve can be thought of as the firm's supply curve. As we saw in the last chapter, the marginal cost curve slopes upward because of the law of diminishing marginal returns. Thus the firm will produce more units of output at higher prices and the firm's supply curve will slope upward.

We saw in Chapter 8 that a change in the price of the variable input shifts the marginal cost curve. Since the firm's marginal cost curve is also its supply curve, the firm will change its rate of output if the price of a variable input changes. Again, the firm will produce where P = MC as long as P > AVC.

9.6 The industry short-run supply curve is found by horizontally summing the supply curves of the firms in the industry. Review Figure 9.7 of the text to make sure you understand the derivation of the industry supply curve. Note, too, that the derivation assumes input prices are fixed because the marginal cost of the firm shifts when input prices change. Marginal cost curves slope upward owing to the law of diminishing marginal returns, so the industry supply curve also slopes upward. The competitive model is completed by adding the industry demand. The intersection of the industry demand curve and supply curve determines the market price and the market rate of output.

9.7-9.8 The same reasoning used to determine the short-run profit-maximizing rate of output is used to determine the long-run profit-maximizing rate of output. Of course, long-run cost curves are used rather than short-run cost curves since all inputs can be varied. If price is less than long-run average total costs, the firm will go out of business; otherwise the firm will produce at the rate of output where P = LMC. (Recall that P = MR in perfect competition.)

A short-run equilibrium is temporary and will change as entrepreneurs make decisions that change the rate of output of each firm and the number of firms in the industry. If short-run profits are being earned, new firms enter the industry because the expected return exceeds the opportunity costs of the entrepreneurs. If firms in the industry are making losses, firms will exit the industry because entrepreneurs are not covering their opportunity costs. These adjustments stop when firms earn zero profits-when revenues exactly cover the opportunity costs.

The **long-run supply curve** shows the amount supplied by the firms in the industry at any price after existing firms have responded fully to the price and all firms that want to enter or leave have done so. The shape of the long-run supply curve depends on how changes in industry output affect the prices of inputs. If entry or exit of firms does not change input prices, then the long-run supply curve of the industry is horizontal, or perfectly elastic. If industry expansion causes input prices to increase, the long-run supply curve of the industry slopes up.

Several points concerning the long-run supply curve are stressed in the text. Be sure that you understand these points.

9.9 It is not enough to know how the competitive model works—it is also important to be able to use it to analyze real-world phenomena. Of the four assumptions listed in Section 9.1, two are vital to the workings of the model. The first is that there are enough firms so they behave as price takers; this situation generates the horizontal demand curve. The second is unrestricted resource mobility, for this generates the long-run equilibrium condition-zero profits. When restrictions on the mobility of resources exist, the competitive adjustment process cannot work properly, and long-run profits can be made by firms in the industry.

ILLUSTRATIONS

Going Out of Business

A firm will shut down in the short run when price is below AVC, and it will go out of business in the long run when price is below LAC at every rate of output. Evidence of this behavior can be seen in virtually any town in the country. A building that once was a gas station is now an auto repair shop or a convenience store. A building that at one time housed a laundry now houses a pizza parlor; a tanning spa becomes a clothing store. In each case, a former business shut down because its price was too low to cover its variable costs, and eventually it went out of business. The durable assets are then transferred to another industry.

The Historical Development of Perfect Competition

The model of perfect competition described in the textbook evolved over time. Adam Smith discussed competition, but used the term more as popular discussion uses the term. That is, it denoted the idea of rivalry. George Stigler traced out the development of the concept of "perfect competition". He identified five conditions of competition that Smith noted: (1) the rivals must act independently; (2) the number of rivals must be enough to eliminate extraordinary gains; (3) the agents must have, "...tolerable knowledge of the market opportunities"; (4) there must be freedom to act on the knowledge, i.e., there must not be social barriers to entry or exit; and (5) enough time for resources to flow in the more profitable directions must elapse.

Stigler then traced out the manner in which economists altered and refined these points over time. Finally, in the early part of the last century, the assumptions used in the text were articulated. The result has been that the model of perfect competition is not a model of how firms behave or a model of competition as a process. There is no competitive behavior in the model of perfect competition. Instead, the model allows us to analyze how markets operate. As such, the model has proven to be very useful.

[For details see George J. Stigler, "Perfect Competition, Historically Contemplated," In *The Essence of Stigler,* ed. by Kurt R. Leube and Thomas Gale Moore (Stanford: Hoover Institution Press, 1986), pp. 265-88).]

KEY CONCEPTS

perfect competition	average profit per unit
free entry and exit	short-run firm supply curve
homogeneous product	shutdown point
survivor principle	short-run industry supply curve
price taker	zero economic profit
average revenue	long-run industry supply curve
marginal revenue	constant-cost industry
total revenue	increasing-cost industry
total profit	decreasing-cost industry

REVIEW QUESTIONS

True/False

_____ 1. In the model of perfect competition, consumers are assumed to view the products of the various firms in the industry as perfect substitutes.

_____ 2. If it can be shown that some firms do not seek to maximize profits, then the assumption of profit maximization is invalid.

_____ 3. A perfectly competitive firm is a price taker because the firm must take the market price as given.

_____ 4. The demand curve for a perfectly competitive firm is also its marginal revenue curve.

_____ 5. If MC > MR, the firm should produce at a larger rate of output.

_____ 6. If P < ATC, the firm will shut down to minimize its losses.

_____ 7. A perfectly competitive firm makes zero profits in long-run equilibrium.

_____ 8. When input prices are held constant, the short-run industry supply curve is derived by summing the firms' marginal cost curves horizontally.

_____ 9. The law of diminishing marginal returns is the basic determinant of the shape of the industry's short-run supply curve.

_____ 10. A perfectly competitive firm responds to a higher price by increasing its rate of output.

_____ 11. In the short run, an increase in market demand leads to a larger rate of output because new firms enter the industry.

_____ 12. A competitive industry's long-run supply curve is determined by how a change in industry output affects the prices of inputs.

_____ 13. The supply curves of inputs remain unchanged along an industry's long-run supply curve.

_____ 14. Economic profits are zero along a long-run supply curve.

_____ 15. The shape of the long-run supply curve depends on the supply curves of inputs.

Multiple Choice/Short Answer

1. If a firm is a price taker, then its demand curve is
   a. downward sloping.
   b. vertical.
   c. horizontal
   d. upward sloping.

2. Firms will consider themselves price takers when
   a. there is unrestricted mobility of resources.
   b. they collude with other firms.
   c. they produce a heterogeneous product.
   d. there are a large number of competing firms producing a homogeneous product.

3. For a competitive firm, the demand curve is also
   a. a total revenue curve.
   b. an average revenue curve.
   c. a marginal revenue curve.
   d. both b and c.

4. The price elasticity of demand for a perfectly competitive firm is
   a. less than 1.
   b. greater than I but less than infinite.
   c. infinite.
   d. uncertain without more information.

5. Profits are maximized where
   a. TR = TC.
   b. TR - TC = 0.
   c. the slope of the total revenue curve exceeds the slope of the total cost curve by the largest margin.
   d. total revenues exceed total cost by the largest amount possible.

6. Profits are maximized where
   a. MR = MC.
   b. P = ATC.
   c. price exceeds marginal cost by the largest amount.
   d. the slope of the marginal revenue curve equals the slope of the marginal cost curve.

Questions 7 to 11 refer to Figure 9-1.

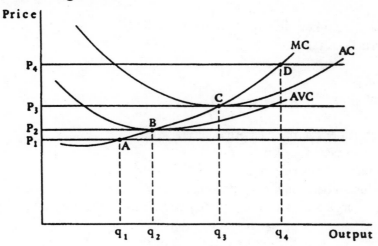

Figure 9-1

7.   If the price is P_1, what is the profit-maximizing rate of output?

8.   If the price is P_4, what is the profit-maximizing rate of output?

9.   If the price is P_3, what is the value of the firm's profits?

10.   What is the minimum rate of output the firm will produce (that is, what is the shutdown point)?

11.   What points are on the supply curve of the firm?
      a. A, B, C, and D.
      b. A, B, and C only.
      c. C and D only.
      d. B, C, and D only.

12.   If MR > MC, output should
      a. expand.
      b. contract.
      c. remain constant.
      d. expand or contract depending on whether P > AC.

13. A perfectly competitive firm will shut down in the short run when
   a. ATC > P > AVC.
   b. AVC > P > ATC.
   c. AVC > P.
   d. ATC > P.

14. The short-run industry supply curve slopes upward because
   a. the long-run supply curve slopes upward.
   b. of the existence of fixed costs in the short run.
   c. of the law of diminishing marginal returns.
   d. of decreasing returns to scale.

15. In the short run, an increase in demand will
   a. induce firms to charge a higher price and produce at the same rate of output.
   b. induce firms to produce at a larger rate of output as price increases.
   c. generate a low price as the quantity supplied increases.
   d. induce higher wages for workers in the industry.

16. In long-run equilibrium a perfectly competitive firm earns
   a. zero profits.
   b. modest profits.
   c. profits, but we can't say how large the profits will be.
   d. profits until new firms enter the industry.

17. For a competitive firm, as price increases
   a. output decreases.
   b. output stays the same, since the size of the plant is fixed in the short run.
   c. output increases.
   d. output will either increase or decrease depending on the shape of the firm's average cost curve.

18.   Refer to Figure 9-2. If industry demand increases from D_1 to D_2, then
    a. the firm's output will be q_1 in the short run and q_2 in the long run.
    b. industry output increases from Q_1 to Q_2 as new firms enter the industry.
    c. the firm can make a profit by changing a price below P_2 and take business away from the other firms.
    d. each firm increases output from q_1 to q_2 and earns economic profits in the short run.

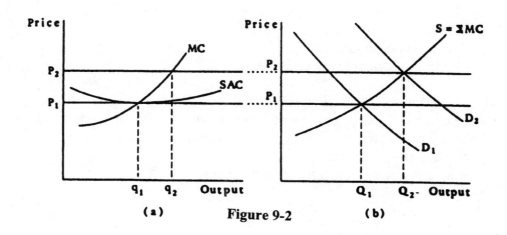

(a)   Figure 9-2   (b)

19.   If firms are making profits in the short run, then
    a. new firms will enter the industry until profits are zero.
    b. firms will make profits in the long run too.
    c. firms must not be price takers.
    d. cost curves are not defined properly.

20.   The key to the long-run adjustment in a competitive industry is
    a. the shape of the short-run supply curves.
    b. the market price elasticity of demand.
    c. profit seeking by firms.
    d. the price-taking behavior of firms.

21.   The shape of the industry long-run supply curve depends on
    a. the shape of the firms' short-run supply curves.
    b. the number of firms in the industry.
    c. whether new firms enter the industry.
    d. what happens to input prices as industry output expands.

22. Along an industry long-run supply curve
   a. input prices are held constant.
   b. the number of firms in the industry is constant.
   c. economic profits increase at higher rates of output.
   d. economic profits are zero.

23. What is the value of the long-run price elasticity of supply of a constant-cost industry?
   a. 0
   b. 1
   c. Between -1 and +1
   d. Infinity

24. If the price of the variable input decreases, what happens to the rate of output of the firm?
   a. Increases.
   b. Decreases.
   c. Remains constant.
   d. Can't tell without more information.

25. Which of the four assumptions of the competitive model is (are) necessary for the industry to reach the condition of long-run equilibrium? (There may be more than one answer.)
   a. Large number of firms
   b. Unrestricted resource mobility
   c. Homogeneous product
   d. All relevant information is known.

Discussion Questions and Problems

1. a. List the four assumptions of perfect competition and state what the function of each assumption is.

    b. Are there any industries in which these assumptions are fairly realistic?

    c. Can the perfect competition model be used in industries where the assumptions are not realistic?

2. Explain why a competitive firm's demand curve is also its marginal revenue curve and its average revenue curve.

3. Use the data in Discussion Question 1 of Chapter 8 and apply it to a competitive firm.

    a. If price is 90 cents, what rate of output will the firm produce? Why? Calculate the firm's profits.

    b. If price is $1.67 what rate of output will the firm produce? Why? Calculate the firm's profits.

    c. If price is $5.00, what rate of output will the firm produce? Why? Calculate the firm's profits.

    d. What is the shutdown point of the firm?

    e. Is there a relationship between price and output for the firm? If so, what is it?

4.   State the short-run profit-maximizing rule for a firm and explain why it ensures that profits are maximized.

5.   State the condition under which a competitive firm will go out of business and explain why it will do so.

6.   Use the data in Discussion Question 1 of Chapter 8 and let there be 100 firms in the industry. Find the points on the industry supply curve. If you graphed it, what would be its shape? Why?

7.   Explain the following statement taken from the text: ". . . we do not need to use the average cost curves to explain the determination of price and quantity in the short run. All the necessary information is contained in the industry supply and demand curves."

8.   Why will a firm continue to operate in the long run earning zero profits?

9.   What happens to the durable assets of a firm when it goes out of business ?

10.   Is it possible for fixed costs to increase in the short run? Explain.

11.   Use the data in Discussion Questions 1 and 3 of Chapter 8.

    a. If price is $2.50 and the price of fertilizer is $50 and land rents for $500, what is the profit-maximizing rate of output? How many units of fertilizer does the firm use? Calculate the firm's profits.

    b. Suppose the price of fertilizer falls to $25. What rate of output will the firm produce? How many units of fertilizer will it buy now? Calculate the firm's profits.

    c. Is the rate of output found in part b a short-run equilibrium? Explain.

12. Figure 9-3 illustrates two firms in a competitive industry with different cost curves. How can this be a long-run equilibrium?

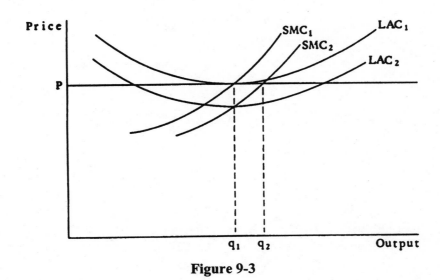

Figure 9-3

13. Explain how the shape of the long-run industry supply curve is determined?

14.   Using two graphs, one for the firm and one for the industry, explain thoroughly how a competitive industry moves from one long-run equilibrium position to another.

15.   Assume a new innovation is developed that reduces the costs of production for firms. What would be the effects on a competitive industry?

Questions 16 and 17 refer to Figure 9-4.

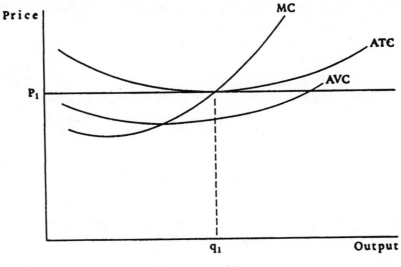

Figure 9-4

16. Suppose the price of the variable input increases.
    a. What happens to the cost curves? Why?

    b. What will happen to the quantity produced by the firm? Why?

    c. Will the firm still operate in the short run? Explain.

17. If the price of the fixed input increases:
    a. What happens to the cost curves? Explain.

    b. What will happen to the quantity produced? Why?

18. U.S. steelmakers face stiff competition from foreign producers. They propose higher tariffs on imported steel to save American jobs. What is the effect of higher tariffs on steel on the U.S. auto industry?

19. Suppose there is a market composed of 1000 individuals with identical demand schedules and 100 firms with identical cost schedules. An individual's monthly demand schedule is given below. The cost relations are:

$$TC = 36 + 3.8q + 0.01q^2 \qquad MC = 3.8 + 0.02q$$

Demand

(1) q	(2) P	(3) Q_D	(4) Q_D
1	$7.00	_____	_____
2	6.60	_____	_____
3	6.20	_____	_____
4	5.80	_____	_____
5	5.40	_____	_____
6	5.00	_____	_____
7	4.60	_____	_____
8	4.20	_____	_____
9	3.80	_____	_____

Supply

(5) q_f	(6) MC	(7) Q_s	(8) MC	(9) Q_s
90	_____	_____	_____	_____
80	_____	_____	_____	_____
70	_____	_____	_____	_____
60	_____	_____	_____	_____
50	_____	_____	_____	_____
40	_____	_____	_____	_____
30	_____	_____	_____	_____
20	_____	_____	_____	_____
10	_____	_____	_____	_____

a. Fill in columns, 3, 6, and 7.

b. Find the market equilibrium price and rate of output. Draw the market demand and supply curves in Figures 9-5(a).

c. Find the equilibrium price and rate of output for a firm. Draw the firm's demand and cost curves in Figure 9-5(b). What are the firm's profits?

d. Is this a short-run equilibrium or a long-run equilibrium? How do you know?

e. Suppose 600 more people enter the market. Fill in the new market demand schedule in column 4. What is the new short-run equilibrium price and rate of output for the market? For the firm? What are the profits for a firm? Add the relevant supply and demand curves to the graphs.

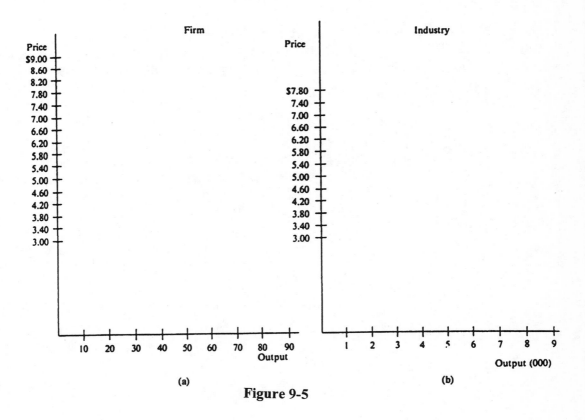

Figure 9-5

f. Suppose this is a constant-cost industry. What are the new long-run equilibrium prices and rates of output for the firm and the market? Where did the extra output come from?

g. Suppose, instead, that this is an increasing-cost industry, and the new cost relations for the firms are TC $= 36 + 4.4q + 0.01q^2$ and MC $= 4.4 + 0.02q$. Fill in columns 8 and 9. What are the new long-run equilibrium price and rates of output for the firm and the market? (Hint: Average cost is at a minimum at 60 units.)

h. What causes the differences in the long-run equilibriums in parts f and g?

i. Return to the original long-run equilibrium in part a. Suppose costs change such that TC $= 36 + 4.4q + 0.01q^2$ and MC $= 4.4 + 0.02q$. What are the new short-run equilibrium price and rates of output for a firm and the market? What are the profits for a firm?

j. Suppose this is a constant-cost industry. What are the new long-run equilibrium price and rates of output for the market and for a firm?

The following questions relate to the material in the mathematical appendix.

20.   The total cost function of a firm is:
$$TC = 10 + 2Q - 0.2Q^2 + 0.01Q^3$$

The price is $6.

a. What is the marginal cost function of the firm?

b. What are the total and average variable cost functions, and the average total cost function of the firm?

c. What are the fixed costs of the firm?

d. What is the profit-maximizing rate of output? What are the profits? How do you know the rate of output maximizes profits instead of minimizes profits?

e. What is the lowest price for which the firm will produce in the short run?

ANSWERS

Review Questions

True/False

1.	True	8.	True
2.	False	9.	True
3.	True	10.	True
4.	True	11.	False
5.	False	12.	True
6.	False. If P < AVC it will shut down.	13.	True
7.	True	14.	True
		15.	True

Multiple Choice/Short Answer

1. c
2. d
3. d
4. c
5. d
6. a
7. Zero
8. q_4
9. Zero
10. q_2
11. d
12. a
13. c
14. c
15. b
16. a
17. c
18. d
19. a
20. c
21. d
22. d
23. d
24. a
25. b

Discussion Questions and Problems

1. a. 1. Large number of buyers and sellers--ensures that no single buyer or seller can unilaterally affect price.
      2. Unrestricted mobility of resources--ensures the zero-profit condition of long-run equilibrium.
      3. Homogeneous product-allows us to define the industry easily and helps ensure price-taking behavior since the output of all firms is identical.
      4. Possession of all relevant information-ensures that one price prevails in the market and that individuals know which industries are profitable and which are not.
   b. The assumptions are fairly realistic for some elements of agriculture.
   c. Yes. The important point is how well the model explains and predicts and not the realism of its assumptions.

2. A demand curve relates price and quantity demanded. Total revenue equals (PxQ) while average revenue equals price. A demand curve is also an average revenue curve since it equals the price at every quantity. A competitive firm's demand curve is its marginal revenue curve because it is horizontal. Thus, the change in total revenues from selling one more unit will always equal price.

3. a. Zero. Price is below the minimum point of AVC. The firm is losing $500.
   b. 220 bushels of wheat. At this rate of output, P = MR = MC so profits are being maximized. The firm is losing $380.60 (TR = 220 x 1.67 = 367.40 and TC = $750). Note that the loss is less than the $500 loss when the firm shuts down.
   c. 250 bushels of wheat. P = MR = MC at this rate of output. The firm is making $400 in profits (TR = 250 x $5 = $1250 and TC = $850).
   d. The shutdown point is the minimum point of the AVC curve, which lies between 100 and 150 bushels of wheat
   e. When price is below AVC, output is zero and there is no relationship between price and output. When price is above the minimum point of the AVC curve, then output expands as price increases because of the shape of the MC curve.

4. The firm should produce where MR = MC. If MR > MC the firm can increase profits by producing one more unit because the addition to total revenue from producing the unit is greater than the addition to total costs. If MR < MC the firm can increase profits by producing one less unit because the reduction in total revenue from not producing the unit is less than the reduction in total costs. Since the firm can increase profits by increasing output whenever MR > MC and by reducing output whenever MR < MC, profits are at a maximum when MR = MC. Of course, this

applies only if P > AVC or the firm will shut down. Note, too, that for a competitive firm P = MR so the rule can be stated P = MC.

5.   A firm will go out of business in the long run if it can't cover all of its costs. These costs include the implicit costs of the inputs supplied by the owners of the firm. The return on these inputs is greater elsewhere so the owners will liquidate the firm and move these inputs to industries where the return is greater.

6.

Price	Output (bushels of wheat)
$ 1.00	15,000
1.25	19,000
1.67	22,200
2.50	24,000
5.00	25,000
10.00	25,500

The industry supply curve is upward sloping because the MC curves of the firms are upward sloping due to the law of diminishing marginal returns.

7.   The average cost curves will tell us whether the firm is making profits, but this is irrelevant to the determination of price and output in the short run. The supply curve of the industry is found by summing horizontally the supply curves of the firms. The firm's supply curve is its MC curve *above* AVC. Thus the firm will produce where its supply curve intersects its demand curve because at that point P = MC.

8.   Total costs include all opportunity costs, including the opportunity costs of the owners. Hence, if revenues cover all these costs, the owners couldn't do better anywhere else.

9.   The durable assets are used in other industries. This process may involve modifying the assets to some extent. If a particular input is so specialized that it cannot be used in other industries, it will be scrapped.

10.   Yes. Fixed costs are the costs that do not vary with output, but they can change. For example, the property tax on a plant can change.

11. a. 240 bushels of wheat. Firm uses 6 tons of fertilizer. It is losing $200. (TR = $2.50 x 240 = $600. TC = $800).

   b. 250 bushels of wheat. The firm uses 7 tons of fertilizer. It is losing $50. (TR = $2.50 x 250 = $625. TC = $675.)

   c. No. If the new price of fertilizer applies to all firms in the industry, the changes in output by all firms will cause a change in price and a new short-run equilibrium.

12. This can be a long-run equilibrium if Firm 2 (with LAC_2) has some inputs that are more efficient than those of Firm 1. Then Firm 2's costs curves do not reflect the opportunity cost of the more efficient inputs. When the opportunity costs of these inputs are calculated, the LAC_2 curve will shift upward to the LAC_1 curve.

13. The shape of the long-run industry supply curve is determined by the shape of the input supply curves. If the input supply curves are horizontal, then costs will not change as new firms enter the industry. The result is a constant-cost industry with a horizontal long-run supply curve. If the supply curves shape upward, it is an increasing-cost industry and the long-run supply curve is upward sloping. If the input supply curves slope downward, it is a decreasing cost industry and the long-run supply curve is downward sloping.

14. A competitive industry is in long-run equilibrium when all firms are making zero profits. In Figure 9-6 (b), this is point A. In Figure 9-6 (a), it is point a. If demand increases to D_2, price increases to P_2. In the short run, each firm moves along its MC curve until P = MC. This is point b in Figure 9-6 (a), with output q_2. Each firm in the industry is now making economic profits. As we move to the long run, new firms enter the industry. As they enter, industry output increases and price falls. If this is a constant-cost industry, new firms will enter until price falls all the way back to P_1. The new short-run supply curve intersects D_2 at point C. The price facing each firm is P_1 so all firms are now making zero profits (point a). The increase in industry output from Q_1 to Q_3 is supplied by new firms since all firms originally in the industry are producing q_1 units again.

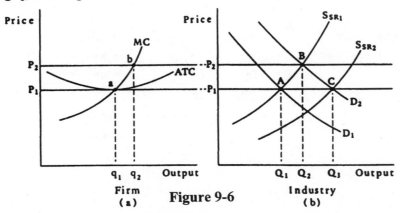

Figure 9-6

209

15.   The cost curves of firms shift downward, which means that the firms are now making profits. The profits will attract new entrants and encourage existing firms to expand output. The increased industry output causes price to fall until all firms are making zero profits once again.

16.   a. They shift upward because costs are higher at every level of output.

       b. The quantity produced by the firm will decrease. Since MC shifts upward and price remains constant, the new rate of output where $P = MC$ will be to the left of q_1.

       c. It may or may not depending on how much the curves shift upward. If price is above AVC, the firm will produce, but if the AVC curve shifts up so much that its minimum point is above P_1, the firm will shut down.

17.   a. The ATC curve shifts up but the AVC and MC curves do not shift because fixed costs do not affect variable costs.

       b. Quantity produced will not change since MC did not change. The firm will now make losses in the short run because the ATC curve shifted upward, though.

18.   Higher tariffs on steel raise the price of steel, which increases costs to U.S. automakers. The result is reduced output in the auto industry. If there is no change in tariffs on automobiles, imports of autos will increase.

19.

Demand

(1) q	(2) P	(3) Q_D	(4) Q_D
1	$7.00	1000	1600
2	6.60	2000	3200
3	6.20	3000	3200
4	5.80	4000	6400
5	5.40	5000	8000
6	5.00	6000	9600
7	4.60	7000	11200
8	4.20	8000	12800
9	3.80	9000	14400

Supply

(5)	(6)	(7)	(8)	(9)
q_f	MC	Q_s	MC	Q_s
90	5.60	9000	$6.20	9000
80	5.40	8000	6.00	8000
70	5.20	7000	5.80	7000
60	5.00	6000	5.60	6000
50	4.80	5000	5.40	5000
40	4.60	4000	5.20	4000
30	4.40	3000	5.00	3000
20	4.20	2000	4.80	2000
10	4.00	1000	4.60	1000

a.   See schedule above.

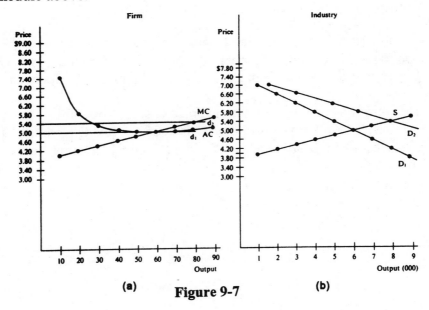

Figure 9-7

b. $Q_D = Q_s = 6000$ units at a price of $5.00. See Figure 9-7.

c. P = MC at $5.00. $q_f = 60$ units. See Figure 9-7. Profits TR - TC = pq_f - 36 - 3.8q - $0.01q^2$ = $5.00(60) - 36 - 3.8(60) - 0.01(60^2) = 300 - 36 - 228 - 36 = 0$.

d. This is a long-run equilibrium because each firm is making zero profits.

e. Market price is $5.40 where $Q'_D = Q_S = 8000$ units. The firm faces a price of $5.40, and each firm produces 80 units. Profits = $5.40(80) - 36 - 3.8(80) - 0.01(80^2) = 432 - 36 - 304 - 64 = 28. See Figure 9-7.

f. $P = 5.00; $Q_D = Q_S = 9600$ units; $q_f = 60$ units. Sixty new firms entered the market.

g. Since average costs are minimized at 60 units, long-run equilibrium exists at 60 units and $P = AC = MC$ at 60 units of output. Marginal costs for 60 units are $MC = 4.4 + 0.02(60) = 5.60. Therefore, equilibrium price must be $5.60. Quantity demanded at $5.60 is 7200 units. If each firm produces 60 units, there must be 120 firms.

h. The long-run supply curve is horizontal in part f but is upward sloping in part g because the increased demand for inputs in part g causes the prices of inputs to increase. Consequently, costs rise and the long-run supply curve is upward sloping.

i. We must find the quantity demanded, Q_D, in column 3 equal to the quantity supplied, Q_S in column 9, where $P = MC$. This occurs at a price of $5.40 where $Q_D = Q_S = 5000$ units. Each firm produces 50 units. Profits equal $11.

j. From part g we know minimum average cost is at 60 units. Therefore, $MC = 4.4 + 0.02(60) = 5.60. Equilibrium price is at $5.60, and $Q_D = 4500$ units. Each firm produces 60 units, so there are 75 firms. That is, 25 firms went out of business.

20.   a. Marginal costs are found by taking the derivative of the total cost function

$$MC = (dTC/dQ) = 2 - 0.4Q + 0.03Q^2$$

b. $TVC = 2Q - 0.2Q^2 + 0.01Q^3$
    $AVC = 2 - 0.2Q + 0.01Q^2$
    $ATC = (10/Q) + 2 - 0.2Q + 0.01Q^2$

c. $10

d. $\pi = TR-TC = \$6Q - 10 - 2Q + 0.2Q^2 - 0.01Q^3$
    $d\pi/dQ = 6 - 2 + 0.4Q - 0.03Q^2 = 0$
    $0.03Q^2 - 0.4Q - 4 = 0$

Therefore, Q = 20 and profits are $70.
The second derivative of the total cost function is $-.4 + 0.06Q$. When Q=20, this is positive so 20 units is a maximum. (Note: the other solution to the quadratic is negative so it cannot be a maximum.)

e. The shutdown point in the minimum point of AVC.

$$d(AVC)/dQ = -.2 + 0.02Q = 0$$

Therefore, the shutdown point is 10 units and price is $ 1.

213

CHAPTER 10 *Using the Competitive Model*

CHAPTER ANALYSIS

This chapter illustrates the various ways the competitive model can be applied. When you read the examples, pay close attention to the approach taken in the analysis. Note that the industry supply and demand curves are often the only tools used in the analysis. Be careful to distinguish between short-run and long-run effects.

ILLUSTRATIONS

Little Triangles Equal Big Bucks

In the text, the authors used graphs to show the gains from free trade and the losses to society of restrictions on trade. In several of the graphs, a triangle measured the gain or the loss. These triangles are small, so it may seem that the gains or losses may be small. However, these small triangles can equal large sums of money. Robert Crandall looked at the costs of the voluntary export restraints that prevailed in the auto industry in the early 1980s. By these "voluntary" quotas, Japanese imports were restricted. Crandall estimated the cost to American consumers was $4.3 billion in 1983, or approximately $160,000 per year for each job saved in the auto industry.

[See Robert W. Crandall, "Import Quotas and the Automobile Industry: The Costs of Protectionism," The Brookings Review, (Summer 1984), pp. 8-16.]

Common Agricultural Policy

The sugar example in the text shows the special treatment sugar producers receive from the government. Sugar is not alone, and neither is the U.S. government. Many agricultural products are protected or subsidized, and other industrial countries perform similar favors for their agricultural sectors. The European Union has had more difficulty coming to agreements on the agricultural sectors than in manufacturing or services. Members of the European Union differ with respect to how much they want to subsidize agriculture. The United States often has complained about the extent to which the European Union protects European farmers by keeping out U.S. agricultural products. It is estimated that the cost of the Common Agriculture Policy in 1990 was $36 billion. It is recognized that the Common Agriculture Policy will have to be changed before countries in Eastern Europe can be added to the European Union.

(For further discussion, see David W. P. Lewis, The Road to Europe: History, Institutions and Prospects of European Integration, 1945-1993, (New York: Peter Lang Publishing Inc., 1993).]

KEY CONCEPTS

consumer surplus
producer surplus
total surplus
efficiency in output
deadweight loss

excise taxes
welfare cost
excess burden
contestable markets
quotas

REVIEW QUESTIONS

1. Producers surplus is measured by
    a. profits.
    b. the area above the supply curve but below the price.
    c. the area below the demand curve but above price.
    d. the area below the supply curve.

2. It is possible that the owners of firms may not receive any producer surplus at all.
    True   False

3. Efficiency in output requires
    a. firms minimize costs.
    b. that firms make zero profits.
    c. output to be where marginal benefit equals marginal cost.
    d. both b and c.

4. In Figure 10-1, total surplus is maximized at output level
    a. 0.
    b. Q_1.
    c. Q_2.
    d. Q_3.

5. A price ceiling
    a. reduces total surplus because both producer surplus and consumer surplus fall.
    b. increases total surplus because both producer surplus and consumer surplus increase.
    c. reduces total surplus because the producer surplus falls by more than consumer surplus increases.
    d. has no net effect on total surplus because the reduction in producer surplus exactly equals the gain in consumer surplus.

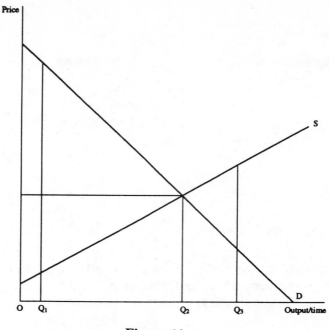

Price

S

D

O   Q₁   Q₂   Q₃   Output/time

Figure 10-1

6. As a result of an excise tax
    a. both the short-run and the long-run prices increase by the amount of the tax.
    b. the long-run price increases by more than the amount of the tax but the short-run price increases by less than the amount of the tax.
    c. the long-run price increases by less than the short-run price.
    d. the long-run price increases by more than the short-run price.

7. For a competitive industry, an excise tax
    a. generates short-run and long-run losses for firms.
    b. generates short-run losses for firms, and some firms exit the industry in the long-run.
    c. causes input owners of inputs in perfectly elastic supply to experience reduced prices for the inputs.
    d. both b and c.

216

8. Other things equal, the greater is the tax burden of an excise tax on consumers, the (more than one answer is correct)
   a. more inelastic the demand curve.
   b. more elastic the demand curve.
   c. more inelastic the supply curve.
   d. more elastic the supply curve.

9. For a competitive industry, the long-run burden of an excise tax depends upon
   a. the elasticities of demand and long-run supply.
   b. the elasticities of long-run and short-run supply but not the elasticity of demand.
   c. the elasticity of demand only.
   d. whether firms make long-run profits or not.

10. An excise tax generates a welfare loss when
    a. the tax is borne entirely by consumers.
    b. the demand curve is perfectly inelastic.
    c. the tax revenue is smaller than the loss in total surplus.
    d. the tax revenue is greater than the loss in total surplus.

11. While they were regulated by the CAB, airlines could not attract new customers by lowering price. Which of the following are tactics airlines did use to attract customers? (There may be more than one answer.)
    a. Offering discounts.
    b. Providing more flights.
    c. Providing movies on long flights.
    d. Providing food and complimentary drinks.
    e. Providing service to unprofitable cities.
    f. Providing attractive flight attendants.

12. If one airline successfully attracts new customers by using nonprice tactics, then
    a. other airlines will employ the tactics so that all airlines have more passengers.
    b. other airlines will lower price in response.
    c. other airlines will employ the tactics so that all airlines have higher costs and lower profits.
    d. None of the above.

13. Deregulation of the airline industry has resulted in
    a. higher fares.
    b. increases in accident rates.
    c. lower wages in the industry.
    d. all of the above.

14. Increased congestion at airports is due to
    a. increases in quantity demanded of airline service because of low fares.
    b. the failure of local governments to expand airport capacity.
    c. uniform landing and take-off fees regardless of the time of day.
    d. all of the above.

15. If a taxi medallion sells for $50,000, then
    a. the supply curve of taxi services must be upward sloping.
    b. there are more taxis than would exist in a free market.
    c. all owners of taxis are making $50,000 profits a year.
    d. the present value of the future stream of net increments to income equals $50,000.

16. If a taxi medallion sells for $50,000, then deregulation would
    a. force all owners of taxis to make zero profits.
    b. increase the value of a medallion.
    c. generate losses in wealth to existing owners equal to $50,000.
    d. generate losses in income of $50,000 a year to existing owners.

17. Suppose there is no trade between the United States and Taiwan, and that the domestic price of cabinets is less in Taiwan than in the United States. If free trade starts, then
    a. consumers of cabinets in both countries will benefit.
    b. producers of cabinets in both countries will benefit.
    c. consumers of cabinets in the United States will benefit and producers of cabinets in Taiwan will benefit.
    d. producers of cabinets in the United States will benefit and consumers of cabinets in Taiwan will benefit.

18. Using the information in 17 above, if the domestic demand for cabinets in Taiwan increased, then
    a. the price of cabinets in the United States will fall.
    b. the quantity supplied of cabinets by U.S. producers will fall.
    c. the quantity supplied of cabinets by U.S. producers will increase.
    d. the demand for cabinets in the U.S. will decrease.

19. The removal of a tariff on textiles would generate a net gain for the United States as a whole. This means that
    a. every U.S. citizen gains.
    b. citizens of the trading partners of the United States must be harmed.
    c. only the benefits to consumers are taken into consideration.
    d. the gains to textile consumers are larger than the loss to textile producers.

20. The dollars used to buy imports
    a. are used by foreigners to buy American exports.
    b. disappear from the American economy.
    c. cannot be used to buy American-made products so living standards in the U.S. fall.
    d. none of the above.

21. The quota on sugar imports harms (more than one answer may be correct)
    a. American consumers of sugar.
    b. American producers of sugar.
    c. foreign producers of sugar.
    d. foreign consumers of sugar.

22. The quota on sugar imports
    a. harms American consumers more than it benefits American producers so the United States is worse off on net.
    b. benefits American producers more than it harms American consumers so the United States is better off on net.
    c. harms American consumers by the same amount as it helps American producers so the United States is neither better off nor worse off on net.
    d. harms American consumers by more than it benefits American producers but benefits American taxpayers so that the United States is better off on net.

23. An increase in the tariff on steel would likely
    a. generate an increase in imports of products made out of steel.
    b. generate an increase in American auto production.
    c. encourage American steel firms to move to other countries.
    d. all of the above.

Discussion Questions and Problems

1. Explain how producer surplus is similar to consumer surplus.

2. What is efficiency in output?

3.   Explain how a competitive industry achieves efficiency in output.

4.   Explain why elasticities are relevant in determining the effects of an excise tax.

5.   Why aren't long-run profits affected by an excise tax?

6.   Using a graph, discuss the effects of removing rent controls in a city that has experienced rent controls for a long time. (Be sure you discuss short-run and long-run effects.)

7.   Explain how CAB regulation could generate prices above the free-market price, blockade entry into the market, and still have airlines making zero economic profits.

8.   Who has benefited and who has been hurt by airline deregulation?

9.   Many professions require a license to legally practice, e.g., doctors, dentists, lawyers. How would the market for physicians' services be similar to the market for taxi services? How would they differ?

10.   Several states have usury laws that set a maximum interest rate that can be charged on loans. What would be the effects of these laws?

11. Using a figure like Figure 10.11 in the text, show an equilibrium in which the U.S. exports wheat to the rest of the world. Relative to the situation where wheat is neither imported nor exported, show the changes in consumer and producer surplus in the U.S. when exporting takes place. What are the changes in consumer and producer surplus in the rest of the world?

12. Using the information in the Question 11, can we conclude that the U.S. gains as a result of the free trade in wheat? Does this mean that every person in the U.S. gained? Explain.

Questions 13 and 14 use Figure 10-2.

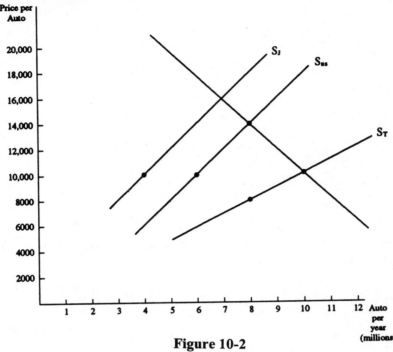

Figure 10-2

13. If the figure shows an equilibrium in the American auto market, how many cars are sold by domestic producers and how many are imports?

14. Suppose a quota of 2 million Japanese cars is imposed. Show the new equilibrium. What will be the new price? How many cars are sold by domestic producers and how many are imports? In the graph, show the changes in consumer and producer surplus.

ANSWERS

Review Questions

1. b
2. True
3. c
4. c
5. c
6. d
7. b
8. a, d
9. a
10. c
11. b, c, d, and f. (Airlines did service unprofitable cities, but this was initiated by the CAB and not by the airlines.)
12. c
13. c
14. d
15. d
16. c
17. c
18. c
19. d
20. a
21. a, c
22. a
23. a

Discussion Questions and Problems

1. Producer surplus is the gain to a producer from selling units of a good at a price above the minimum amount that would be necessary to compensate the seller. Graphically, it is the area above the supply curve and below the price. Consumer surplus is the area below the demand curve and above the price. In both cases, the agent is receiving more than they require in order to be in the market. The consumer would be willing to pay more than he or she has to pay, and the seller would be willing to sell for a lower price than he or she receives.

2. Efficiency of output occurs when the marginal benefit from an additional unit of a good equals the marginal cost of producing the extra unit

3. Efficiency in output occurs when price equals marginal cost. Price measures the extra benefit of an additional unit of the good, and marginal cost measures the extra costs to society of producing the extra unit. Competitive industries achieve efficiency in output because competitive firms produce where price equals marginal cost.

4. The more price increases as a result of an excise tax the more of the burden of the tax that consumers bear. Elasticities of supply and demand determine how much price increases after the tax is imposed. The more elastic demand is, the more quantity demanded changes with the tax, and the less price increases. Hence, the more elastic the demand, *ceteris paribus,* the less consumers bear the burden of the tax. The supply curve depends on the supply curves of inputs. The more elastic the supply curves of inputs, the more elastic the industry long-run supply curve, and the more price increases with the tax. Perfectly elastic input supply curves imply that input owners will not accept a reduction in the price of their input (they will move their inputs to other industries), so all the tax increase gets passed on to consumers. Consequently, the more elastic the supply curve the greater the burden of the tax that falls on consumers. (Review Figure 10.5 in the text if you have problems.)

5. Profits are always zero in the long run, so firm owners do not bear any of the tax in the long run. (However, if the owner of the firm also owns specialized inputs used in producing the good, then the owner as input owner bears part of the burden.)

6. In Figure 10-3, R_c is the legal maximum rent. There is a shortage of Q_d - Q_s. If controls are lifted, rents rise to R_{sr} since supply is relatively inelastic in the short run. In the long run, rental rates fall back to R_{lr}.

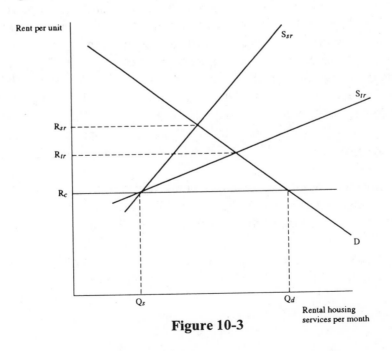

Figure 10-3

7.   The CAB set prices above the market's equilibrium price and allowed no new firms to enter the market. Firms still did not make economic profits because they engaged in nonprice competition, which raised their costs. In addition, some of the higher price went toward higher salaries for employees.

8.   Beneficiaries from deregulation include consumers who receive lower prices and owners of firms that entered after deregulation. Losers include owners of airlines that overexpanded after deregulation, employees of the major airlines, and consumers in some smaller cities who now pay higher fares.

9.   The American Medical Association restricts entry into the medical profession by restricting the number of students in medical schools. This results in higher salaries for physicians. Licenses cannot be sold as medallions can, so new graduates from medical school can earn economic profits. However, some of these profits are dissipated by extra costs incurred by students trying to get into medical school.

10.   Usury laws are a form of selective price control similar to rent control. If the equilibrium rate of interest is above the legal rate of interest, there will be a shortage of loanable funds. Banks might respond in several ways: requiring borrowers to leave a minimum amount in their checking accounts, raising the effective price of the loan; raise requirements for loan acceptance so that riskier borrowers cannot get a loan; or charging fixed fees to obtain loans. Borrowers who are not able to obtain funds in their own state may go to lending institutions in other states.

11.   Figure 10-4 illustrates. The equilibrium price in the U.S. without trade is P_1 and Q_1 units of wheat are sold. In the rest of the world, the equilibrium price and quantity are P_3 and Q_3. With trade, the U.S. increases production of wheat due to the higher price in the rest of the world. The trade equilibrium is at price P_2. In the U.S., consumers purchase Q_d units of wheat while suppliers produce Q_s units. The difference $(Q_s - Q_d)$ are exports of wheat to the rest of the world. In the right-hand figure, S_T is the sum of the supply curve for the rest of the world and the supply of exports of the U.S. Exports equal $Q_T - Q_R$, which also equals $Q_s - Q_d$. In the U.S., producer surplus increased by P_2AEP_1 while consumer surplus fell by P_2BEP_1. In the rest of the world, consumer surplus increased by P_3FHP_2 while producer surplus fell by P_3FGP_2.

12.   The U.S. gains as a whole because the increase in producer surplus is greater than the decrease in consumer surplus by the area BAE. Not every one in the U.S. gains by the trade since consumers face higher prices than they did before.

13.   10 million units are sold, of which 6 million are sold by American firms and 4 million by Japanese firms.

14. Figure 10-5 illustrates. Since the Japanese can only sell 2 million cars in the U.S., the new total supply curve is 2 million units greater than the American supply curve for all prices above $6000. The new equilibrium is at E', with a price of $12,000 for cars. Total sales of cars fall to 9 million, of which 7 million are made by American firms and 2 million by Japanese. Consumer surplus falls by AE'EB and producer surplus increases by AF'FB, so Americans are worse off on average.

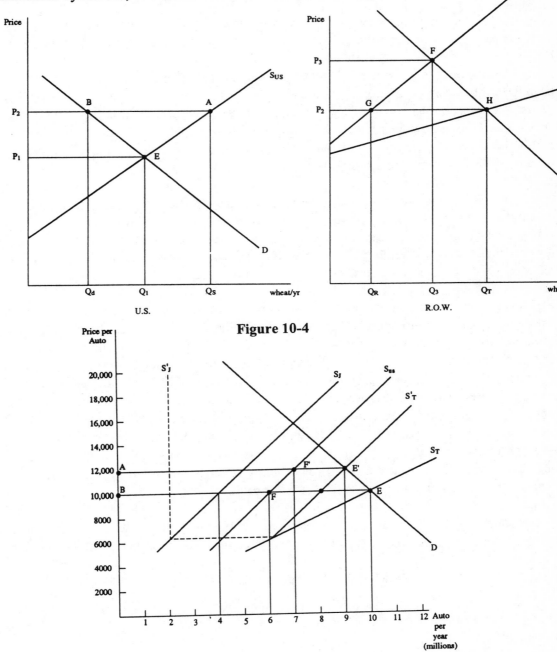

Figure 10-4

Figure 10-5

CHAPTER 11 *Monopoly*

CHAPTER ANALYSIS

Like the model of perfect competition, the monopoly model is not meant to describe the real world accurately. It is meant to be used as a tool to analyze certain types of economic behavior.

11.1 A **monopoly** is the sole producer of a good that has no close substitutes. Since it is the only producer of the good, a monopoly is the industry. The monopolist's demand curve is the industry demand curve, and since industry demand curves slope downward, the monopolist's demand curve also slopes downward. The shape of the demand curve is the key difference between a competitive firm and a monopoly--a competitive firm has a horizontal demand curve while a monopoly has a downward sloping demand curve.

In Chapter 9 we saw that marginal revenue equals price for a competitive firm and that the firm's demand curve is also its marginal revenue curve. For a monopoly, however, the marginal revenue curve is different from the demand curve, and price does not equal marginal revenue. The reason for the difference is that the monopoly demand curve slopes downward, indicating that the monopoly firm can sell more units only by lowering price.

11.2-11.3 The profit-maximizing rate of output of any firm, competitive or monopoly, occurs where marginal revenue equals marginal cost. Figure 11-1 illustrates the profit-maximizing rate of output for the monopolist. Since MR = MC at Q_1, Q_1 is the profit-maximizing rate of output. The price the monopolist charges is found by identifying the price on the demand curve for which Q_1 can be sold. At output rate Q_1 the firm can charge a price of P_1. Note that a monopoly will not necessarily be profitable. Figure 11-1 contains four average cost curves, and each is permissible since the marginal cost curve intersects each average cost curve at its minimum. If AC_2 applies, profits are equal to the area P_1ABC. However, if AC_3 applies, the firm earns zero profits, while if AC_4 applies, the monopolist operates at a loss. If AC_4 are long-run costs, the monopolist will go out of business. Note that the profit-maximizing (or loss-minimizing) rate of output is the same because the marginal cost curve is the same for each.

The monopoly price is related to the price elasticity of demand. It can be shown that the gap between price and marginal cost is inversely related to the elasticity of demand. That is:

$$(P - MC)/P = 1/\eta \text{ or } P = MC/(1-(1/\eta))$$

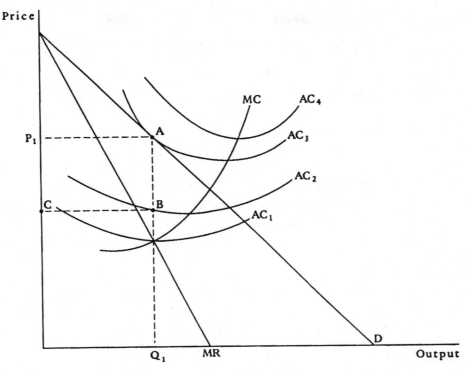

Figure 11-1

We also know that the monopolist will select a price-output combination that is on the elastic portion of its demand curve. This is because the monopolist produces where MR = MC. Since marginal costs are positive, marginal revenue must also be positive, and the demand curve is elastic when marginal revenue is positive.

An important characteristic to remember of firms that face downward-sloping demand curves, is that they do not have a supply curve. There is not a unique relationship between price and quantity in the case of monopoly as there is in perfect competition.

11.4 Pure monopoly is rare, but many firms may face downward-sloping demand curves. Any firm that faces a downward-sloping demand curve has some **monopoly power**. A measure of this monopoly power is the Lerner index:

Lerner index = (P - MC)/P

We have already seen that this ratio equals the inverse of the elasticity of demand. Hence, the more elastic the demand curve, the lower the Lerner index, which means the price markup is relatively low. In the extreme, a perfectly elastic demand curve would have a Lerner index equal to zero, indicating to monopoly power.

The extent of monopoly power is determined by the elasticity of the market demand curve and the elasticity of supply of other firms. The monopoly power of a firm will be greater if there are **barriers to entry** that keep out new firms. Recall that under perfect competition profits provide an incentive for new firms to enter an industry. In the case of monopoly, barriers to entry may prevent or retard the entry of new firms, enabling the monopolist to continue making profits in the long run.

The authors identify four categories of entry barriers:

1. **Absolute cost advantage**--the long-run average total cost of the incumbent firm is below that for rivals or potential entrants. This can be due to access to unique resources or more productive resources.
2. **Economies of scale**--a declining long-run average cost curve leads to "natural monopoly".
3. **Product differentiation**--consumers may be willing to pay more for one firm's product than another's because of real or perceived differences between them.
4. **Regulatory barriers**--the government grants **patents, copyrights, franchises** and **licenses** to firms that often prevent other firms form entering the industry.

11.5 Perfect competition and monopoly differ in several important ways. First, P = MC under perfect competition, while P > MC under monopoly. Second, monopoly produces at a lower rate of output, which generates a welfare cost to consumers. Third, the distribution of income between consumers and producers differs, since the economic profits made by the monopolist represent an increase in wealth for the owners of the monopoly while consumers lose purchasing power due to higher prices.

The deadweight loss of monopoly is shown in Figure 11.9 on page 314 in the textbook. The deadweight loss of monopoly is an example of static analysis. However, **dynamic analysis** of monopoly usually indicates that the social cost of monopoly may not be as great as the **static analysis** suggests. New products often are produced by monopolies, at least for awhile. If the alternative to the monopoly is no production of a good at all, society usually prefers the monopoly.

11.6 Public policy toward monopoly relies on two tools—**antitrust** and **price regulation**. The latter basically sets price ceilings on regulated firms. Since a monopoly increases price by restricting output, a price ceiling has the effect of eliminating the incentive to restrict output. In Figure 11-2, the unregulated monopolist would charge $15 and produce 600 units per month. If the government would set a price ceiling of $12, the monopoly would produce the perfectly competitive (efficient) rate of output. This result is due to the effect of the price ceiling. A price ceiling of $12 means that the firm can sell as many units as it wants (up to 1000 units) at a price of $10. To sell more than 1000 units, the firm would have to charge a price less than $12. The price ceiling essentially changes the monopolists downward sloping demand curve to a horizontal demand curve, at least out to 1000 units. Its demand curve becomes FBD and its marginal revenue curve becomes FBGMR. The monopolist maximizes profits by producing the rate of output where marginal cost equals marginal revenue, which is a rate of output of 1000 units and a price of $12--the competitive price-output combination.

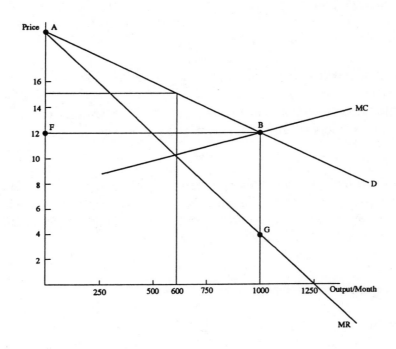

Figure 11-2

ILLUSTRATIONS

Barriers to Entry

The market for presidential candidates offers an example of barriers to entry. There are two dominant "firms" in presidential politics-the Democratic party and the Republican party. In 1980, Jimmy Carter was the Democratic candidate and Ronald Reagan the Republican. John Anderson entered the race as an independent candidate.

As representatives of their parties, Carter and Reagan were automatically on the ballots of all the states. As an independent, Anderson was not; in order to get his name on the ballot, he had to initiate petition drives in many states and court challenges in others. This activity required the use of funds that neither Carter nor Reagan had to spend. Further, Carter and Reagan received matching funds from the government, while Anderson had to obtain a minimum percentage of the vote in order to receive matching funds. Carter and Reagan were assured of equal time on TV and radio under the Fairness Doctrine, which did not apply to Anderson. Further, Anderson was not included in the nationally televised debates. It is more costly for an independent entrant to run for president than for representatives of the established parties because of various legal restrictions. Thus there are substantial barriers to entry in the market for president.

The 1992 and 1996 elections offered another third-party candidate--Ross Perot. Perot did better than any third-party candidate in the history of the country. He was included in the debates, and received considerable press coverage. He also had the financial resources to ensure he was on the ballots in all the states. Barriers to entry, though substantial, do not always mean that entry cannot take place at all.

The 2000 election illustrated barriers to entry again. There were two candidates other than the candidates of the major parties--Pat Buchanan represented Ross Perot's pary, the Reform Party, and Ralph Nader represented the Green Party. Neither candidate was included in the televised debates, which is a serious drawback for a third-party candidate.

The Aluminum Company of America

The Aluminum Company of America (ALCOA) was the sole domestic manufacturer of aluminum ingots from the late 1800s until World War II. Initially, the monopoly position of the firm was due to patents. When the patents expired in the early 1900s, ALCOA maintained its monopoly position by controlling the sources of the key input into the manufacturing process-bauxite. ALCOA signed long-term contracts with owners of bauxite supplies that guaranteed that they would sell only to ALCOA. These contracts were declared invalid by the courts in 1912. After 1912, ALCOA maintained its dominant position by quickly acting to meet any increases in demand with new capacity to produce aluminum. After World War II, ALCOA's position declined as new firms entered the market, aided by a government antitrust suit against ALCOA, the disposal of government-controlled aluminum plants during the war, and rapidly increasing demand for aluminum after the war.

KEY CONCEPTS

monopoly
monopoly power
price maker
barriers to entry
absolute cost advantages
economies of scale
natural monopoly

product differentiation
regularity barriers
Lerner index
deadweight loss
static analysis
dynamic analysis
antitrust laws

REVIEW QUESTIONS

True/False

____ 1. The sole producer of a good can charge whatever price it wants.

____ 2. When a demand curve slopes down, marginal revenue is always less than price.

____ 3. A monopoly produces where $P = MC$.

____ 4. The more elastic the demand is, the closer price is to marginal revenue.

____ 5. The supply curve of a monopoly is upward sloping.

____ 6. Monopolies always earn economic profits.

____ 7. Marginal revenue equals zero when the demand curve has an elasticity of one.

____ 8. For monopoly to exist, entry barriers must exist.

____ 9. The possibility of entry by new firms constrains the exercise of monopoly power.

____ 10. For the same market demand and cost conditions, price is higher and output is lower under monopoly than under perfect competition.

____ 11. The desire to make monopoly profits is a spur to innovation.

____ 12. As in perfect competition, a price ceiling in monopoly leads to reduced output.

Multiple Choice/Short Answer

1. A monopolist's marginal revenue curve lies below its demand curve because
   a. the average revenue curve is constant as quantity increases.
   b. the change in total revenue is constant as quantity increases.
   c. a monopoly does not have a supply curve.
   d. the demand curve slopes downward.

Questions 2 to 5 refer to Figure 11-3.

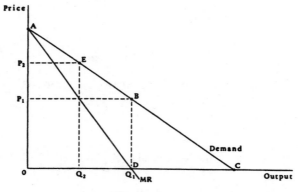

Figure 11-3

2. If MC = 0, what is the profit maximizing rate of output?

3. The demand curve is elastic
   a. over the range AB.
   b. over the range EB.
   c. at point E.
   d. over the range BC.

4. The demand curve is inelastic
   a. Over the range AB.
   b. at point B.
   c. over the range EC.
   d. over the range BC.

5. The demand curve is unit elastic
   a. over the range AB.
   b. at point E.
   c. at point B.
   d. over the range RC.

6. a. What is the price elasticity of demand when price is twice as large as marginal revenue?

   b. What is the price elasticity of demand when P = $20 and MC = $15?

7. If marginal revenue is greater than marginal cost, a monopolist will
   a. raise price.
   b. decrease output.
   c. increase output.
   d. shutdown.

Questions 8 to 11 refer to Figure 11-4.

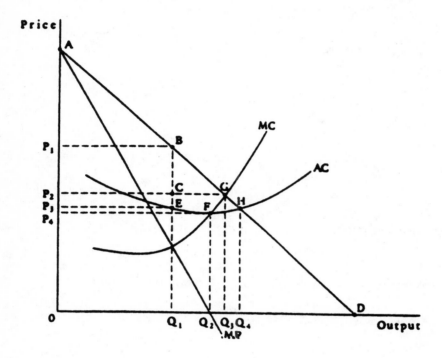

Figure 11-4

8. What price will a profit-maximizing monopolist charge?

9. The profits of the firm are measured by the area
   a. P_2GQ_3O.
   b. P_1BEP_3.
   c. P_1BCP_2.
   d. BCG.

10. The supply curve of the firm
    a. is the MC curve.
    b. is the MC curve that lies above point F.
    c. is the AC curve to the right of F.
    d. does not exist.

11.   The welfare cost of monopoly is measured by the area
        a. ABP_1.
        b. $ABCP_2$.
        c. BGC.
        d. P_1BGP_3.

12.   The Lerner index is
        a. $P > MC$.
        b. $(P - MC)/P$.
        c. $(MR - MC)/P$.
        d. $P(1 - 1(1/\eta))$.

13.   A natural monopoly is a monopoly owing to
        a. the control of a key input.
        b. a downward sloping long-run average cost curve.
        c. the government's granting the firm a monopoly.
        d. entry lags.

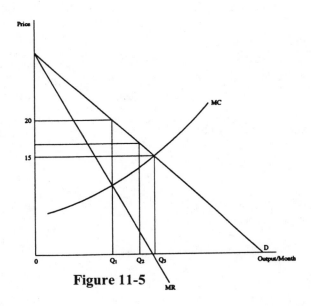

Figure 11-5

14.   Suppose the monopolist in Figure 11-5 knows that new firms will enter at any price
        above $17. What output will it produce?
        a. Q_1
        b. Q_2
        c. Q_3
        d. 0

15. The deadweight loss of monopoly is due to the fact that
    a. monopolists are greedy.
    b. monopolies earn economic profits.
    c. monopolies restrict output in order to raise price.
    d. a monopoly does not produce at the minimum point of its average cost curve.

16. Economic profits of a monopoly represent
    a. a transfer of income from consumers to producers.
    b. the inefficiency of monopoly.
    c. welfare cost of monopoly.
    d. all of the above.

17. A firm is observed making monopoly profits. Using dynamic analysis of monopoly, one would argue that
    a. the firm is inefficient and should be dealt with by antitrust or regulatory authorities.
    b. the firm's profits should be taxed away.
    c. the monopoly profits are not a concern as long as the firm is producing where P=MC.
    d. the profits are a reward for successfully developing a new product and the firm should not be dealt with by antitrust or regulatory authorities.

18. Dynamic analysis of monopoly
    a. reinforces static analysis in condemning the effects of monopoly.
    b. offers little difference from static analysis of monopoly.
    c. suggests that the welfare effects of monopoly are not as bad as static analysis suggests.
    d. indicates that monopolies always are beneficial on net to society.

Questions 19 and 20 refer to Figure 11-6.

19. If the government forces the monopolist to lower price from P_1 to P_2, the monopolist will change its rate of output from Q_4 to
    a. Q_1.
    b. Q_2.
    c. Q_5.
    d. Q_6.

20. If the price is set at P_3, output will be
    a. Q_3.
    b. Q_6.
    c. Q_7.
    d. Q_9.

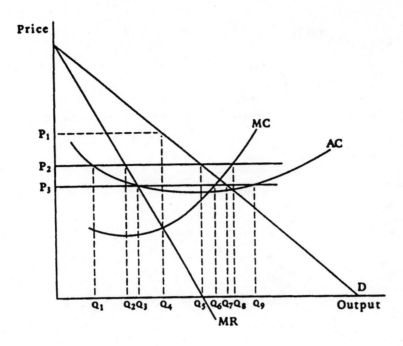

Figure 11-6

Discussion Questions and Problems

1. Explain why the marginal revenue curve lies below the demand curve.

2.   a. Fill in the following table:

Price	Quantity Sold	Total Revenue	Marginal Revenue	Price Elasticity
$22	0			
20	1			
18	2			
16	3			
14	4			
12	5			
11	5.5			
10	6			
8	7			
6	8			
4	9			
2	10			

b. If marginal costs were constant at $8, how much output would be produced by a perfectly competitive industry? How much by a monopolist?

c. If marginal costs were constant at $4, how much would be produced under perfect competition? Would the industry be on the elastic or inelastic portion of its demand curve? How much would be produced under monopoly? Is the monopoly on its elastic or inelastic portion of its demand curve?

3. Suppose that the firms in Discussion Problem 19 in Chapter 9 suddenly merged and became a monopoly, and the government prevents new firms from entering the industry. Further, assume that the monopolist's marginal cost curve is identical to the supply curve of the perfectly competitive industry.

a. Fill in the following table:

Price	Quantity Sold	Total Revenue	Marginal Revenue
$7.00	1000		
6.60	2000		
6.20	3000		
5.80	4000		
5.40	5000		
5.00	6000		
4.60	7000		
4.20	8000		
3.80	9000		

b. What output will the monopolist produce? What price will the monopolist charge? By how much does the monopolist restrict output?

c. Is the monopolist on the elastic portion of its demand curve? How do you know?

d. In Figure 11-7, draw the demand curve, marginal revenue curve, and marginal cost curve, and label the equilibrium.

e. Suppose demand goes up as in part e of Problem 19 in Chapter 9. Draw the new demand curve and the new marginal revenue curve. What will be the new short-run price and quantity?

f. What will happen in the long run?

g. Suppose that when the firms merged and became a monopoly, the government did not blockade entry. What would be the long-run effects?

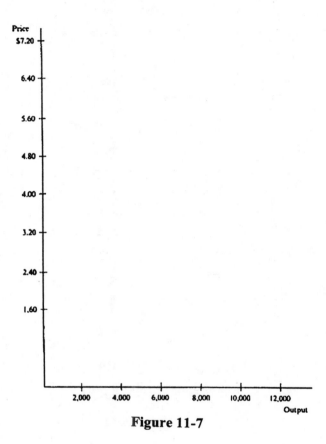

Figure 11-7

4.   a. Suppose marginal cost of gasoline is $1.00, and an isolated gasoline station in Nevada has a price elasticity of demand for gasoline of 2. What price will the station charge for gasoline?

   b. What is the Lerner index?

5.   Explain why a monopolist does not have a supply curve.

6. "Demand is infinitely elastic in perfect competition, so the more elastic the demand the more the firm is like a competitive firm. Therefore, if a firm has an elastic demand, it is not a monopoly." Do you agree or disagree and why?

7. A monopolist produces on the elastic portion of its demand curve, which suggests that the monopolist would rather lower price than raise price since total revenues increase when price is reduced. Why would we ever observe a monopolist raising price?

8. "The more narrowly a market is defined, the more likely a firm will be considered a monopoly." Do you agree or disagree, and why?

9. In the early 1900s, U.S. Steel owned the mines that produced the richest iron ore in the country. Was this a source of monopoly for U.S. Steel? Is U.S. Steel a monopoly today? Support your answer.

10. Will an unregulated monopolist always charge the price where marginal revenue equals marginal cost? Explain.

11. What is meant by monopoly power? How can firms that are not pure monopolies have monopoly power?

12. What is the source of the ill effects of monopoly? Explain.

13. Will perfect competition always result in more output and lower price than monopoly? Explain.

14. How does dynamic analysis of monopoly differ from static analysis? How is this related to antitrust policy?

The following questions relate to the material in the mathematical appendix.

15. Explain, mathematically, why $P = MR$ under perfect competition and $P > MR$ under monopoly.

16. The demand function for a monopolist is $P = 30 - .75Q$ and total costs are $TC = 20 + 9Q + .3Q^2$. What is the profit-maximizing rate of output? What are profits? What would be the price and output under perfect competition if the monopolist's marginal cost curve is the competitive industry's supply curve?

ANSWERS

Review Questions

True/False

1.	False	7.	True
2.	True	8.	True
3.	False	9.	True
4.	True	10.	True
5.	False. A monopoly does not have a supply curve.	11.	True
		12.	False
6.	False		

Multiple Choice/Short Answer

1. d
2. Q_1
3. a
4. d
5. c
6. a. 2
   b. 4
7. c
8. P_1
9. b
10. d
11. c
12. b
13. b
14. b
15. c
16. a
17. d
18. c
19. c
20. b

Discussion Questions and Problems

1. The demand curve slopes downward, which implies that the firm must lower price to sell additional units. This lower price applies to all units, however, and not just the additional units. The revenue earned on the output that could have been sold at a higher price falls as a result of the lower price. This reduction in revenue offsets, to a degree, the addition to total revenue from selling an additional unit. Since the addition to total revenue from selling an additional unit equals the price, and the lower price causes a fall in revenues from the output that could have been sold at a higher price, marginal revenue is less than price.

2. a.

Price	Quantity Sold	Total Revenue	Marginal Revenue	Price Elasticity
$22	0	0	0	
20	1	20	20	21
18	2	36	16	6.3
16	3	48	12	3.4
14	4	56	8	2.14
12	5	60	4	1.44
11	5.5	60.5	0.5	1.09
10	6	60	-0.5	.91
8	7	56	-4.0	0.69
6	8	48	-8.0	0.47
4	9	36	-12	0.29
2	10	20	-16	0.16

(Note: Elasticity of 1.09 at 5.5 units with MR = 0.5 is due to discrete movements in price and quantity and using the arc elasticity of demand formula.)

b. Perfect competition: P = MC = $8, so Q = 7 units; Monopoly: MR = MC = $8, so Q = 4 units and P = $14.

c. Perfect competition: P = MC = $4, so Q = 9 units. Inelastic. Monopoly: MR = MC = $4, so Q = 5 units and P = $12. Elastic.

3. a.

Price	Quantity Sold	Total Revenue	Marginal Revenue
$7.00	1000	$ 7,000	7.00
6.60	2000	13,200	6.20
6.20	3000	18,600	5.40
5.80	4000	23,200	4.60
5.40	5000	27,000	3.80
5.00	6000	30,000	3.00
4.60	7000	32,200	2.20
4.20	8000	33,600	1.40
3.80	9000	34,200	0.60

b. MR = MC at $4.60. Q   4000; P = $5.80. The monopoly has cut back monthly output by 2000 units.

c. Elastic. Marginal revenue is positive, so the monopolist must be on the elastic portion of the demand curve.

d. See Figure 11-8.

e. See Figure 11-8. The new output is between 5700 and 5800 units and price is between $5.90 and $6.00.

f. Nothing. The monopolist will continue to operate at this rate of output and price until cost conditions change or there is another demand change or it changes its scale of operation.

g. The industry would return to the competitive level as entry would occur until zero profits were made by all firms.

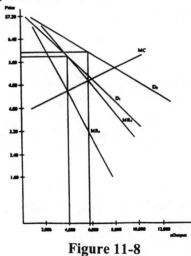

Figure 11-8

4.   a. $P = MC/(1 - (1/\eta)) = \$1.00/0.5 = \$2.00$
      b. Lerner index equals $(P - MC)/P = (\$2.00 - \$1.00)/\$1.00 = .5$. (Note that this is equal to $1/\eta$).

5.   A supply curve relates price and quantity supplied. Under monopoly, the profit-maximizing rate of output is found by the rule $MR = MC$. Then price is found from the demand curve. Since many demand curves can be associated with $MR = MC$ at a particular rate of output, many prices can be associated with the rate of output. That is, the price also depends on the demand curve.

6.   Disagree. If the demand curve is linear, the higher the price, the more elastic the demand. Hence an elastic demand may indicate that the monopoly is charging a high price. Further, we know a monopoly always produces on the elastic portion of its demand curve.

7.   The monopolist may raise price if its costs increase, if demand increases, or both. The firm wants to maximize profits and not maximize revenues.

8.   Agree. The determination of the market will be based on the availability of substitutes, which is also a key factor in determining whether the firm is a monopoly. A narrowing of the definition of the market means the number of goods that are accepted as close substitutes is reduced too, and this increases the likelihood that the firm will be considered a monopoly.

9.   Yes, because iron ore is a key input in the production of steel. U.S. Steel is not a monopoly today because it no longer controls a key input. New iron ore discoveries around the world and increased foreign competition have caused U.S. Steel to lose its monopoly.

10.   No. If the firm believes that new firms will enter at that price, but that a lower price would prevent entry and still allow the monopolist to earn some profits, it will charge a lower price.

11.   A firm has monopoly power when it faces a demand curve that slopes down. Many firms that are not pure monopolies face downward-sloping demand curves, often because of product differentiation. (Note that Chapter 13 discusses those cases in more detail.)

12.   The source of the monopoly's bad effects is the downward-sloping demand curve, which implies that marginal revenue lies below price. This results in the monopolist's restricting output to the rate for which $MR = MC$, which implies $P > MC$.

13. No. If there are substantial economies of scale, the costs of production for a monopolist may be lower than the costs if the industry was perfectly competitive. If so, it is possible for the monopoly to charge a lower price and produce more output.

14. Static analysis assumes that the existing goods and production processes are the only ones that matter, while dynamic analysis considers technological change and the introduction of new goods and services. Since society values new products, a firm that develops a new product still benefits society even if it charges a monopoly price. The alternative may be none of the good at all. Dynamic analysis suggests that antitrust policymakers should examine more than whether a firm currently is charging a monopoly price, but also look at how the firm obtained its position.

15. TR = PxQ but P = P(Q). Therefore, TR = P(Q)xQ and MR = P + (dP/dQ)/Q. Under perfect competition, a firm has no control over price so dP/dQ = 0 and MR = P. Under monopoly, dP/dQ < 0 so MR < P.

16.
$$\pi = TR - TC = 30Q - .75Q^2 - 20 - 9Q - .3Q^2 \tag{1}$$

To maximize profits, take derivative of (1) with respect to Q:

$$d\pi/dQ = 30 - 1.5Q - 9 - .6Q = 0 \tag{2}$$

Solving for Q yields the profit-maximizing rate of output of 10 units. Substituting 10 into (1) gives profits of $85.

Under perfect competition, P = MC:

$$30 - .75Q = 9 + .6Q \tag{3}$$

Solving for Q yields Q = 15.56 and P = 18.33.

CHAPTER 12 *Product Pricing with Monopoly Power*

CHAPTER ANALYSIS

Price discrimination is the practice of charging different prices for the same good. Perfectly competitive firms cannot price discriminate, so any real-world examples must involve firms with some degree of monopoly power.

12.1-12.3 There are three types or degrees of price discrimination. **First-degree price discrimination**, which is also called **perfect price discrimination**, is when the firm charges the maximum price consumers will pay for each unit sold. Figure 12-1 shows a demand curve in which one unit is demanded at a price of $10, two at a price of $9, and so on. If marginal costs are constant (and equal to average costs) at $3, the monopolist that charges a uniform price will sell four units at $7 each. Its profits are $16. Perfect price discrimination occurs when the monopolist charges the maximum price possible for each unit sold. That is, the consumer with the greatest demand for the good pays $10, the next consumer pays $9, the third $8, and so on. When this occurs, the marginal revenue and price are equal, just as they are in perfect competition. (However, price and marginal cost are not constant as is true in perfect competition). Under perfect price discrimination, marginal revenue equals marginal cost at eight units and the last unit is sold for a price of $3. The monopolist's total revenues are $10 + 9 + 8 + 7 + 6 + 5 + 4 + 3 = $52 and its total costs are $24. Hence, its profits are $28, which is $12 more than when a uniform price is charged.

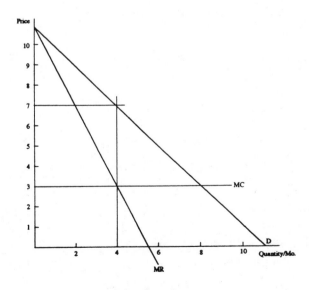

Figure 12-1

This example shows that price discrimination, especially first-degree price discrimination, increases the profits of the monopolist. Of course, most firms do not have the information necessary to engage in perfect price discrimination, and consumers have every incentive to not let firms know how much they actually value each unit of the good. Perfect price discrimination generates efficiency in output, just as perfect competition does. The difference is that the consumer surplus under perfect competition becomes profits for the monopolist under perfect price discrimination.

Second-degree price discrimination is the practice of charging a customer less per unit as the total number of units consumed increases. **Quantity discounts** are an example of second-degree price discrimination. **Third-degree price discrimination** occurs when a monopolist divides customers into two or more groups and charges different prices to each group. The monopolist maximizes profits by charging higher prices to groups with relatively inelastic demand for the good, and lower prices to the groups with relatively elastic demand for the good.

Three conditions must be met for firms to practice price discrimination. First, firms must have some degree of monopoly power. Second, the firms must be able to identify, at least roughly, the maximum amount a consumer will pay for a unit of the good. Third, the firms must be able to prevent resale of the product. Otherwise, those being charged a low price can sell the good to those being charged a higher price, and the firm would end up with few units sold at higher prices.

Third-degree price discrimination is the most common type of price discrimination. Suppose the monopolist can identify two groups of customers that have different elasticities of demand for the good. Further, the monopolist can keep the two groups separate and prevent resale. What price should it charge each group? A fact we already know is that the relationship between marginal cost and price depends on the elasticity of demand. If marginal cost is $5, and group A has an elasticity of demand of 5 while group B has an elasticity of demand of 1.5, then the monopolist will charge each group:

$$P_A = \$5/(1 - (1/5)) = \$6.25$$

$$P_B = \$5/(1 - (1/1.5)) = \$15$$

The group with the more elastic demand pays a lower price than the group with the less elastic demand.

To find the prices graphically, the horizontal summation of the marginal revenue curves of the two groups must be found. The firm then equates marginal cost with the summed marginal revenue curve. This value for marginal cost is then used to find the optimal output in each submarket. In Figure 12-2, $\Sigma MR = MC = \$5$ (Point F). In submarket A, $MC=MR=\$5$ at Point G, implying an output rate of about 52,000 units, and a price of $6.25. In submarket B, $MC=MR=\$5$ at point H, generating an output rate of 10,000 and a price of 15.

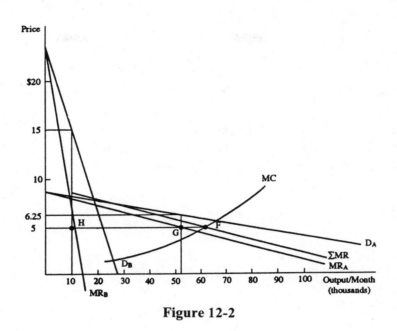

Figure 12-2

12.4 A common form of second-degree price discrimination is the two-part tariff. Under this pricing scheme, there is a fixed fee per time period and a uniform per-unit price. If Figure 12-1 applied to a person instead of a group of people, the monopolist could charge the person a flat fee of $28 and a per unit fee of $3 and replicate the perfect price discrimination result. Again, the monopolist is generally not going to be able to capture all of the consumer surplus for itself, especially when different customers have different demands for the good. Make sure you are familiar with Figures 12.6 and 12.7 in the textbook. Note that the price per unit will be lower under a two-part tariff than under uniform monopoly pricing.

12.5 Another common type of price discrimination is **intertemporal price discrimination**. Under this pricing scheme, the monopolist lets the customers self-select into those who pay a higher price from those who pay a lower price. Someone who wants to see a new movie right away, pays a relatively high price, while those who are willing to wait can pay a lower price at a discount movie theater or on either cable or home videos. The group with the less elastic demand pay more than those with the more elastic demand.

Peak-load pricing is not a type of price discrimination because the different prices are due to differences in costs. Since electricity usage varies during the year and during the day, the costs of providing the electricity also vary. The marginal cost of electricity becomes very high during the peak demand periods, which usually are very hot days in the summer. By charging a price equal to marginal cost during both the peak periods and the off-peak periods, the electric utility encourages conservation of electricity during the peak periods and the use of electricity during the off-peak period.

ILLUSTRATIONS

Telephone Pricing and Price Discrimination

Local phone companies often price discriminate. They charge businesses more for basic phone service than they charge households. This is because the demand for phone service among businesses is much less elastic than the demand for phone service by households. (Why?)

The California Electricity Market in 2001

The Spring and Summer 2001 brought severe shortages in electricity in California. While one reason for the shortages is that demand grew rapidly and there has not been sufficient numbers of new power plants built, another problem is that the incentives to conserve at the right times are not in place. Electricity generation illustrates several concepts developed in this and earlier chapters. The peak demand problem is one that exists in electricity markets. Many products are characterized by variable demand. For example, the demand for toys is much greater in the months preceding Christmas than in the rest of the year. The peak demand problem is not severe in this case because the toys can be made at a steady rate and stored until the peak demand period. This solution is not feasible with electricity. If there is a peak demand period, either the capacity must be in place to handle the demand or there will be brownouts or blackouts. The peak demand period for electricity is during the work week at day time on hot days in the summer. Many electric utilities encourage consumers to postpone nonessential electric usage to evening to reduce demand during the peak demand period. For example, vacuum and run the dishwasher in the evening rather than during the middle of the day when businesses are operating and people are using their air conditioners. If the utilities would charge a higher rate for electricity during the peak demand times, consumers would be encouraged to reduce consumption during the peak times and shift their consumption to off-peak times. The probability of a brown out would decrease as a result. However, to engage in peak-load pricing, the utilities would have to have meters installed at homes and businesses that could keep track of usage by time of day. Most utilities in the U.S. have not done so, although such meters are common in France and some other countries. Peak-load pricing is not price discrimination because the costs differ by time of day for supplying the services, whereas the differential for basic service is price discrimination.

KEY CONCEPTS

price discrimination
first-degree price discrimination, or perfect price discrimination
second-degree price discrimination
third-degree price discrimination
resale
two-part tariff
entry fee
intertemporal price discrimination
peak-load pricing

REVIEW QUESTIONS

True/False

_____ 1. Price discrimination can increase both the total surplus generated by a market and the monopolist's profits

_____ 2. First-degree price discrimination transfers all consumer surplus from consumers to the monopolist.

_____ 3. Perfect price discrimination is inefficient because monopolist's make large profits.

_____ 4. Senior-citizen discounts are a type of second-degree price discrimination.

_____ 5. Price discrimination is more likely with services than with manufactured goods.

_____ 6. Any firm with monopoly power can price discriminate.

_____ 7. The group with the more elastic demand pays a higher price when a monopolist price discriminates.

_____ 8. Under a two-part tariff, the price per unit is lower than under uniform monopoly pricing.

_____ 9. A monopoly can make profits even when setting price equal to marginal cost under a two-part tariff scheme.

_____ 10. Peak-load pricing is a form of third-degree price discrimination.

Multiple Choice/Short Answer

1. Perfect price discrimination is another term for
    a. first-degree price discrimination.
    b. second-degree price discrimination.
    c. third-degree price discrimination.
    d. none of the above. It is a distinct type of price discrimination.

2. Under first-degree price discrimination, consumer surplus is
    a. the same as under perfect competition.
    b. more than under third-degree price discrimination.
    c. equal to the producer surplus.
    d. zero.

3. If different customers are paying different prices, the firm is trying to increase profits by engaging in
    a. first-degree price discrimination.
    b. second-degree price discrimination.
    c. third-degree price discrimination.
    d. two-part tariffs.

4. Quantity discounts are a type of
    a. first-degree price discrimination.
    b. second-degree price discrimination.
    c. third-degree price discrimination.
    d. peak-load pricing.

5. Grocery stores that charge customers with coupons lower prices are engaging in
    a. first-degree price discrimination.
    b. second-degree price discrimination.
    c. third-degree price discrimination.
    d. two-part tariffs.

6. Which of the following is not a condition for price discrimination?
    a. Monopoly power
    b. The ability to distinguish different customers with different costs
    c. The ability to distinguish types of customers by their elasticities of demand
    d. The ability to keep the groups of customers separate

7. When a firm price-discriminates, it maximizes its profits by
   a. setting the price in each market equal to the marginal cost of servicing that market.
   b. charging the higher price to the market with the most customers.
   c. charging a higher price to the customers with a relatively high elasticity of demand and a lower price to those with a relatively inelastic demand.
   d. charging a higher price to the customers with a relatively low elasticity of demand and a lower price to those with a relatively elastic demand.

8. A monopolist is charging one group of customers $10 per unit and another group of customers $6 per unit. If the monopolist instead charged a uniform price for all, the price would be
   a. greater than $10.
   b. between $6 and $10.
   c. less than $6.
   d. can't tell without more information.

9. Under third-degree price discrimination, the
   a. number of customers is the same in both groups.
   b. ratio of price to marginal revenue is the same in both submarkets.
   c. elasticity of demand is the same in both submarkets.
   d. marginal revenue is the same in both submarkets.

10. Disneyland used to charge a fee to enter the park and a fee for each ride. This pricing tactic is called a(n) _____ .

Questions 11-13 utilize Figure 12-3.

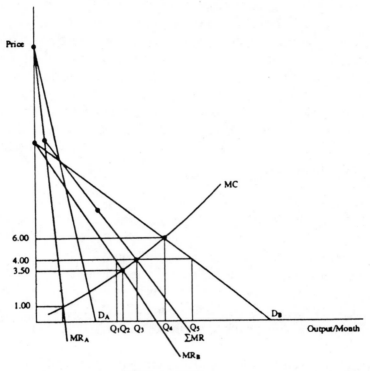

Figure 12-3

11. The relevant marginal cost in submarket A if the monopolist is price discriminating is
    a. $1.00
    b. $3.50.
    c. $4.00
    d. $6.00.

12. The output to submarket B if the monopolist price discriminates is
    a. Q_1.
    b. Q_2.
    c. Q_3.
    d. Q_4.

13. The total output produced by the price-discriminating monopolist is
    a. Q_2.
    b. Q_3.
    c. Q_4.
    d. Q_5.

Questions 14-16 utilize Figure 12-4.

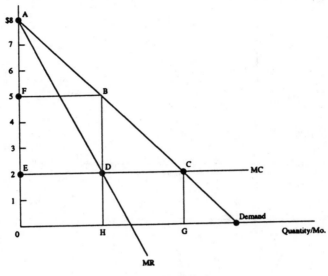

Figure 12-4

14. If all customers have the same demand, the optimal two part tariff is
    a. monthly fee of ABF and per unit price of $5.
    b. monthly fee of FBDE and per unit price of $2.
    c. monthly fee of BDC and per unit price between $2 and $5.
    d. monthly fee of ACE and per unit price of $2.

15. Suppose there are two customers--one with the demand curve marked "Demand" and the other with the demand curve marked "MR". If the monopolist set the two-part tariff as in the previous question, what would happen?
    a. The monopolist's profits would increase.
    b. The person with the demand curve "Demand" would drop out, reducing the profits of the monopolist.
    c. The person with the demand curve "MR" would drop out, reducing the profits of the monopolist.
    d. Everything would be the same as in question 14.

16. If there are two customers as in the previous problem, the monopolist can increase profits by
    a. raising the per unit price a little while still setting a fixed fee of ACE.
    b. charging a fixed fee less than ADE and a per unit price a little larger than $2.
    c. charging a fixed fee of ADE and a per unit price of $2.
    d. charging a uniform price of $5.

Questions 17 to 20 refer to Figure 12-5.

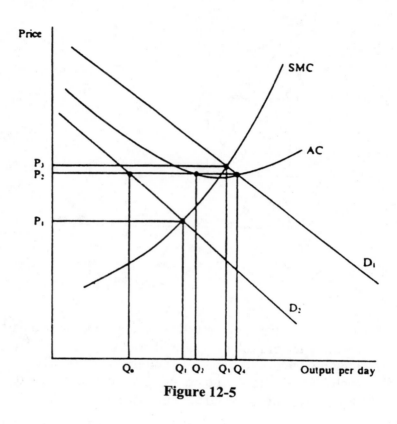

Figure 12-5

17. The peak-demand curve is demand curve _____.

18. If the firm was required to charge price P_2 all the time, the firm would have to build a plant large enough to produce
   a. Q_1 units per day.
   b. Q_2 units per day.
   c. Q_3 units per day.
   d. Q_4 units per day.

19. If the firm could use peak-load pricing, it would have to build a plant large enough to produce
   a. Q_1 units per day.
   b. Q_2 units per day.
   c. Q_3 units per day.
   d. Q_4 units per day.

20.   At a uniform price of P_2, quantity demanded for off-peak times would be_____,
       while quantity demanded during off-peak times if peak-load pricing were used would be

       _____.
       a. Q_0; Q_1.
       b. Q_0; Q_3.
       c. Q_1; Q_2
       d. Q_1; Q_1.

Discussion Questions and Problems

1.   Explain why the demand curve becomes the marginal revenue curve under first-degree
      price discrimination.

2.   Indicate whether the items below are examples of price discrimination and briefly state
      your reasons.

      a. A movie theater charges a lower price to children than adults.

      b. Airlines charge lower prices for children than for adults.

      c. A telephone company charges lower prices for long-distance calls made in the
          evening.

      d. The Postal Service charges the same price for all first class mail.

      e. The American Economic Association charges higher dues to full professors than to
          assistant professors.

3.   Since first-degree price discrimination offers a firm the largest profits possible, why don't firms engage in the pricing practice more often?

4.   Do discounts for senior citizens on city buses meet the conditions for price discrimination? Would senior citizen discounts on meat at the local grocery store meet the conditions for price discrimination? Explain your answer.

5.   Figure 12-6 provides the demand and marginal revenue curves for two groups of customers. Assume the conditions for price discrimination are met. Find the profit-maximizing rates of output and prices for the two groups. Explain how you found them.

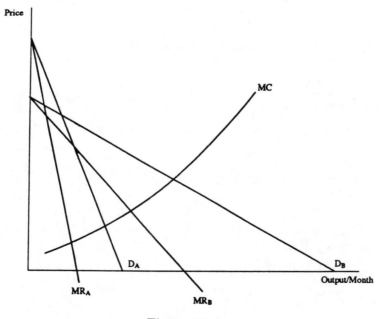

Figure 12-6

6. Suppose the marginal cost of a visit to the doctor is $30, and that wealthy patients have an elasticity of demand of 1.25, while poor patients have an elasticity of demand of 5. What prices would a profit-maximizing physician charge?

7. Figure 12-7 reproduces most of what is in Figure 12-2. Find the price and output if the monopolist charged a uniform price to all customers. Who benefits and who is harmed when the monopolist price discriminates?

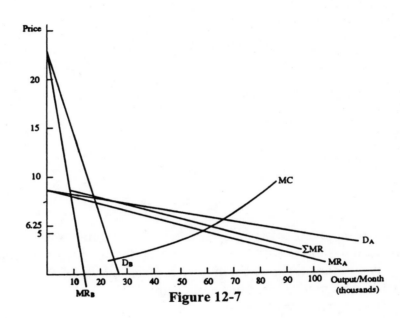

Figure 12-7

8.   If all consumers have the same demand curve for a product and the producer utilizes a two-part tariff, how much consumer surplus will consumers receive? Explain. What happens if consumers have different demand curves?

9.   What is intertemporal price discrimination and how does it work? How is the resale problem solved?

10. The peak-load problem often accompanies public utilities that are regulated because they are natural monopolies. There appears to be a contradiction, since natural monopoly is associated with declining average cost curves while the peak-load problem is associated with rising marginal costs during the peak demand period. Can you reconcile this apparent contradiction?

11. The demand for many products is not stable over time (that is, there are peak-demand periods), but prices do not increase significantly during the peak-demand period. How do manufacturing firms handle this problem of variable demand? Why can't electric companies or phone companies do the same?

The following question relates to the material in the mathematical appendix.

12. A monopolist faces two markets for its product and can keep the markets separate. The demand curve for market A is $P_A = 80 - 5Q_A$ and for B is $P_B = 170 - 20Q_B$. Total costs are $TC = 20 + 10(Q_A + Q_B)$.

a. Find the profit-maximizing output and price for each market.

b. What are the values for MR_A and MR_B?

c. What is the elasticity of demand in market A? Market B?

ANSWERS

Review Questions

True/False

1. True
2. True
3. False
4. False
5. True
6. False. Monopoly power is only one necessary condition.
7. False
8. True
9. True
10. False. it isn't price discrimination at all.

Multiple Choice/Short Answer

1. a
2. d
3. a
4. b
5. c
6. b
7. d
8. b
9. d
10. two-part tariff
11. c
12. a
13. b
14. d
15. c
16. b
17. D_1
18. d
19. c
20. a

Discussion Questions and Problems

1. First-degree price discrimination is when each unit is sold at the maximum price possible. The extra revenue obtained from each unit is the price, so P=MR.

2. a. Price discrimination. Prices differ while costs do not.
   b. Price discrimination. Prices differ while costs do not.
   c. Not price discrimination. Costs differ.
   d. Price discrimination. Price is the same but costs differ depending on distance.
   e. Price discrimination. Prices differ while costs do not.

3. Firms would like to, but are not able to for several reasons. They may not be able to prevent resale, or may not have the necessary monopoly power. More importantly, they do not have the information about specific customers that would enable them to know the maximum price for each unit each customer would be willing to pay.

4. The conditions for price discrimination are (1) seller must possess monopoly power, (2) seller must be able to separate the markets, and (3) the elasticity of demand must differ between the two groups. Price discounts for senior citizens on city buses meet these conditions while price discounts on meats do not. The bus lines can prevent senior citizens from selling the bus rides but grocers cannot prevent resale of meat.

5. Figure 12-8 shows how the prices in the two submarkets are found. The two marginal revenue curves are horizontally summed (ΣMR). The firm sets ΣMR = MC (point E), which determines the total output Q_{A+B}. The total output is divided between the two submarkets by finding the rate of output in each where marginal revenue in each market equals C. Q_A units are sold in market A at a price of P_A, and Q_B units are sold in market B at a price of P_B.

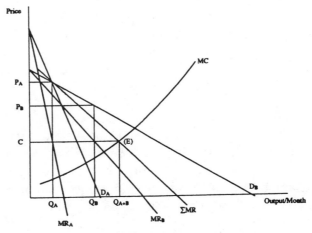

Figure 12-8

267

6. Wealthy patients: P = $30/(1-(1/1.25)) = $30/.2 = $150.
    Poor patients: P = $30/(1-(1/5) = $30/.8 = $37.50.

7. See Figure 12-9. We need the total market demand curve, which is the horizontal
    summation of D_A and D_B (ΣD). $\Sigma MR = MC$ at point F, which generates a price of about
    $6.90. Type A customers are better off with price discrimination because they receive a
    lower price while Type B customers are worse off with price discrimination. They pay
    $15 under price discrimination instead of $6.90 under uniform pricing.

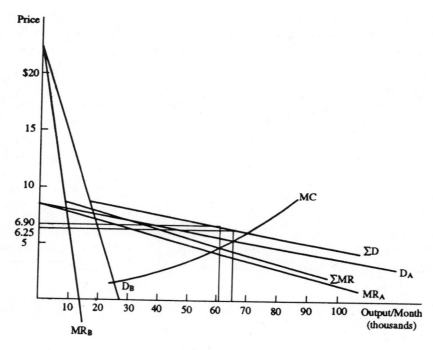

Figure 12-9

8. Zero since the two-part tariff allows the firm to capture the entire consumer surplus.
    The seller charges an entry fee equal to the dollar value of consumer surplus, and a per
    unit price equal to the marginal cost of production. A firm will not be able to capture
    the entire consumer surplus of all consumers if consumers' demands differ. Per unit
    price will be above marginal cost and the entry fee will be reduced somewhat.

268

9.   Intertemporal price discrimination is price discrimination over time. If customers differ in terms of how quickly they want to consume a good, then this can be an effective form of price discrimination. People who want the good right away pay a relatively high price, while those who are more patient pay a lower price at some time in the future. Resale is not a problem since the lower priced units appear only after a considerable period of time.

10.   The declining average cost curve is a long-run cost curve used by the firm for planning and determining how large to build its plant. The peak-load problem occurs for a given sized plant, so it involves short-run marginal costs.

11.   Manufacturing firms can produce at a steady rate and use inventories to handle unstable demand. Storage is not feasible technically for many electric companies or phone companies.

12.   a. $\pi = TR_A + TR_B - TC$ (1)

              $= 80Q_A - 5\,Q_A{}^2 + 170Q_B - 20Q_B{}^2 - 20 - 10(Q_A+Q_B)$ (2)

              $\partial\pi/\partial Q_A = 80 - 10Q_A - 10 = 0;\ Q_A = 7$ (3a)

              $\partial\pi/\partial Q_B = 170 - 40Q_B - 10 = 0;\ Q_B = 4$ (3b)

              $P_A = 80 - 5Q_A = 80 - 5 \times 7 = 45$ (4a)

              $P_B = 170 - 20Q_B = 170 - 20 \times 4 = 90$ (4b)

    b. $MR_A = 80 - 10Q_A = 80 - 70 = 10$ (5a)

              $MR_B = 170 - 40Q_B = 170 - 160 = 10$ (5b)

    c. $MR = P(1-1/\eta)$ (6)

              $\eta = P/(P-MR)$ (7)

        Therefore

        $\eta_A = 45/(45-10) = 45/35 = 9/7 = 1.286$

        $\eta_B = 90/(90-10) = 90/80 = 9/8 = 1.125$

CHAPTER 13 *Monopolistic Competition and Oligopoly*

CHAPTER ANALYSIS

Most real-world industries are neither perfectly competitive nor monopolistic; rather, most fall somewhere in between. In this chapter the two intermediate market structures of monopolistic competition and oligopoly are developed and explained.

13.1 The key difference between perfect competition and **monopolistic competition** is **product differentiation**. Perfect competition assumes that all firms in the industry produce a homogeneous product. Monopolistic competition assumes that the product of each firm differs slightly from the products of the other firms in the industry. This causes the demand curve facing the firm to slope downward. However, there is free entry into the industry and there are many firms in the industry, so the monopoly power of any single firm is slight. Examples of monopolistically competitive industries include gasoline stations, restaurants, and drugstores.

The short-run equilibrium position is illustrated in Figure 13.1 in the text. Review this figure and the accompanying text carefully to be sure you understand how the short-run equilibrium is determined. Note that the short-run equilibrium looks like the monopoly result. The long-run equilibrium condition is the same for monopolistic competition as for perfect competition-zero profits. This result follows from the assumption of free entry to and exit from the industry. However, since the firm's demand curve slopes downward, price exceeds marginal cost in monopolistic competition as it does under monopoly.

There are three major differences between the long-run equilibriums of perfect competition and monopolistic competition. First, each firm under monopolistic competition is not producing at the minimum point of its long-run average cost curve. This must be true because the LAC curve is tangent to the demand curve. Since the demand curve slopes downward, this tangency is to the left of the minimum point of its LAC curve; that is, **excess capacity** exists and there is inefficiency in production. Second, P > MC under monopolistic competition and there is inefficiency in output. Figure 13.2 in the text illustrates these two points. Third, the firm will engage in **nonprice competition** since goods are not homogeneous. However, many economists today question whether the "realism" of monopolistic competition enables us to understand market forces any better than relying on the models of perfect competition and monopoly.

13.2-13.3 Many important industries in the United States (such as steel and autos) are composed of a few very large firms. Such an industry is called an **oligopoly**. The key characteristic of oligopoly is **mutual interdependence**; each firm knows that its actions will affect its rivals and that the rivals are likely to respond in some way. Therefore, the firm must take into consideration the possible responses of rivals to any change in output or price it makes. Since the possible reactions are numerous, it is virtually impossible to present a single model of oligopoly.

The **Cournot model** assumes that the firms do not recognize their mutual interdependence. Each firm makes decisions by assuming the other firms will continue to produce their current rate of output. While the assumption is unrealistic, the prediction of the model--that the price and market output are closer to the perfectly competitive equilibrium as more firms are in the industry--is attractive to many economists. The **Stackelberg model** alters the Cournot model by assuming that one of the firms learns the behavior of the others and exploits this knowledge by taking the role of the leader. Economic warfare breaks out if more than one firm tries to be leader. The **dominant-firm model** tends to be used when one firm in the industry is much larger than the other firms. The dominant firm assumes the other firms will be price-takers once it sets the price. The dominant firm can calculate the supply responses of the competitive fringe to all possible prices, and the select the price-output combination that maximizes its profits. Note that each of these models suffers from an important problem—each assume that new firms will not enter the industry even though economic profits are made by the firms in the industry.

13.4 There is a strategy firms in an oligopolistic industry can follow that will allow greater profits than any of the models discussed above. The firms can cooperate with each other and **collude**. The goal of the collusion is to replicate the monopoly price-output equilibrium, which would maximize joint profits. When collusion involves a formal agreement they have formed a **cartel**.

Cartels and less formal collusive agreements suffer from at least three problems. First, while it is profitable to form a cartel, it is even more profitable to cheat by secretly selling more output than agreed to in the cartel agreement. Second, members of the cartel are likely to disagree over the optimal price-output combination. This is especially likely if the costs differ of the members. Third, the profits of the cartel encourage new firms to enter the industry, which makes the cartel difficult to maintain. Informal agreements suffer from an additional problem--it is difficult to detect cheating.

ILLUSTRATIONS

Cartels in Denmark

While cartels are illegal in the United States, they are, or have been, legal in many European countries. In Denmark, for example, cartels are legal and must register with the government. In studying Danish cartels, Bjarke Fog found that formation of cartels was difficult because the firms in the industry disagreed over what price to charge and how to divide sales among themselves. Hence many industries that attempted to organize a cartel failed to do so. Fog also found that existing cartels had problems, again caused by differences in views about the optimal price. In addition, it was difficult to get members to change existing plans in response to different demand or supply conditions. Fog found one cartel, for example, that had not raised its price in more than 10 years even though costs had risen steadily and profit margins had fallen. Forming and maintaining a cartel in the real world is a difficult undertaking even when the cartel is legal.

[See Bjarke Fog, "How Are Cartel Prices Determined?" *Journal of Industrial Economics 5* (November 1956): 16-23.]

Oligopoly and Collusion

Most economists believe that oligopolists will attempt to collude in order to maximize joint profits. Collusion is more likely to succeed in some situations than in others, however. Since it is profitable to cheat on collusive agreements (see Section 13.4 in the text), cartels must find a way to monitor and police their collusive agreements. The number of homogeneity of sellers is important, but so are conditions on the buyer's side of the market. George Stigler identified three factors on the buyer's side of the market that make it easier to detect if anyone is cheating on the cartel. When these buyer's conditions are met in an industry, it is easier for the firms in the industry to collude. The factors that facilitate collusion are (1) large numbers of relatively small buyers because it is difficult to offer price cuts to a lot of buyers without rivals knowing about it; (2) reporting of price by the buyers; and (3) frequent repeat buying on the part of customers. When these conditions exist, it is easier for the cartel to discover that one firm is attempting to cheat on the agreement by secretly cutting price.

[See George Stigler, "A Theory of Oligopoly," *The Organization of Industry* (Homewood, IL: Irwin, 1968).]

KEY CONCEPTS

monopolistic competition
differentiated products
excess capacity
oligopoly
Cournot model
reaction curve
Stackelberg model
residual demand curve
dominant firm model
cartel

REVIEW QUESTIONS

True/False

____ 1. Product differentiation means that consumers do not view the product of one firm as exactly identical to the product of another firm.

____ 2. The demand curve for a monopolistically competitive firm slopes downward but is fairly elastic.

____ 3. Under monopolistic competition, price exceeds marginal cost in the short run, but equals marginal cost in the long run.

____ 4. Like perfect competition, the long-run equilibrium condition for monopolistic competition is zero profits.

____ 5. If advertising leads to higher consumer prices, it is undesirable.

____ 6. The Cournot model assumes that rivals seek to coordinate their behavior.

____ 7. The Cournot model predicts that the more firms in the industry the closer the price gets to the competitive price.

____ 8. The Stackelberg model assumes the firms collude and seek to maximize joint profits.

____ 9. In the dominant-firm model, the industry produces too many units for the price set by the dominant firm if the dominant firm ignores the actions of the smaller firms.

____ 10. The residual demand curve in the dominant firm model is perfectly elastic.

____ 11. A cartel wants to replicate the price-quantity combination that would exist if the industry was a monopoly.

____ 12. Cartels that successfully raise price and profits face the problem of entry by new firms.

Multiple Choice/Short Answer

1. Which of the following assumptions of perfect competition does not apply to monopolistic competition?
    a. Many buyers and sellers
    b. Free entry and exit
    c. Homogeneous product
    d. Both b and c

2. Will the demand curve for a firm under monopolistic competition be horizontal or downward sloping?

3. Long-run equilibrium in monopolistic competition is characterized by which of the following? (There may be more than one answer.)
    a. Excess capacity
    b. Monopoly profits as a result of collusion
    c. Zero profits
    d. More profits than under perfect competition but less than under monopoly
    e. $P=MC$

4. The key characteristic of oligopoly is
    a. product differentiation.
    b. excess capacity.
    c. mutual interdependence.
    d. all of the above.

5. The major difficulty in analyzing oligopoly is
    a. that the product of oligopolistic industries is heterogeneous.
    b. taking account of how a firm believes its rivals will respond to any changes in output it makes.
    c. knowing whether or not collusion for the firms is profitable.
    d. accounting for different sizes of firms is an oligopolistic industry.

6. The Cournot model assumes that each firm
    a. believes that the other firms will continue to charge the price they are currently charging.
    b. works with the other firms to maximize joint profits.
    c. knows exactly how other firms will respond to anything it does.
    d. believes the other firms will hold output constant regardless of what it does.

7. Under the Cournot model, industry output
   a. is the same as the monopoly rate of output.
   b. lies between the competitive rate of output and the monopoly rate of output.
   c. it is the same as the competitive rate of output.
   d. is indeterminate.

8. Reaction curves for Artesia and Utopia are given in Figure 13-1. If Artesia is producing 80 units of output, Utopia's profit-maximizing rate of output is
   a. zero
   b. 20
   c. 40
   d. 100.

9. In Figure 13-1, the equilibrium output is
   a. 60 units for each firm.
   b. 60 units for Artesia and 120 units for Utopia.
   c. 40 units for each
   d. indeterminate without more information.

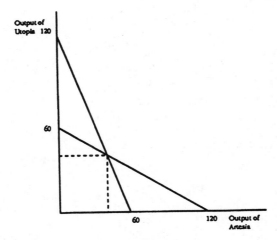

Figure 13-1

10.	The dominant firm model is illustrated in Figure 13-2. What are the output rates of the smaller firms and the dominant firm, respectively?
a. Q_1, Q_2
b. Q_2, Q_3
c. Q_1, Q_4
d. Q_1, Q_3

11.	In Figure 13-2, if new firms joined the industry and were part of the fringe firms in the industry, the dominant firm's output
a. would fall and price would fall.
b. would fall and price would rise.
c. would increase and price would fall.
d. and price would remain the same.

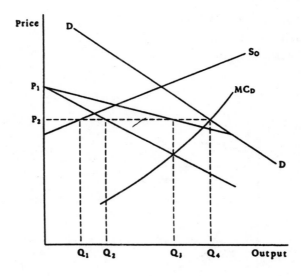

Figure 13-2

12.	The elasticity of demand for the dominant firm is greater,
a. the greater the dominant firm's market share.
b. the greater the elasticity of supply of the competitive fringe.
c. the lower the elasticity of the market demand curve.
d. the lower the price.

13. If output in an industry under perfect competition is 5000, and is 3000 under monopoly, then a cartel's ideal rate of output is
   a. 5000 units.
   b. 3000 units.
   c. between 3000 and 5000 units.
   d. indeterminate without more information.

14. Suppose a cartel exists in an industry, but one firm refuses to join. Which of the following firms could make the greatest profits? (Assume all firms have identical cost curves).
   a. The firm outside the cartel.
   b. A loyal member of the cartel.
   c. Any of the firms before the cartel was formed.
   d. Can't tell without more information.

15. Which of the following can explain OPEC's early success?
   a. The price elasticity of demand for oil is low in the short run.
   b. The price elasticity of supply for oil is low in the short run.
   c. Many oil-importing nations adopted policies that strengthened OPEC's position.
   d. All of the above contributed to OPEC's early success.

Discussion Questions and Problems

1. The major difference between monopolistic competition and perfect competition is that firms produce differentiated products in the former and homogeneous products in the latter. How does product differentiation generate the differences between the two models?

2.   In Figure 13-3 show a short-run equilibrium position for a firm under monopolistic competition such that the firm makes some short-run profits. Explain why it is a temporary equilibrium.

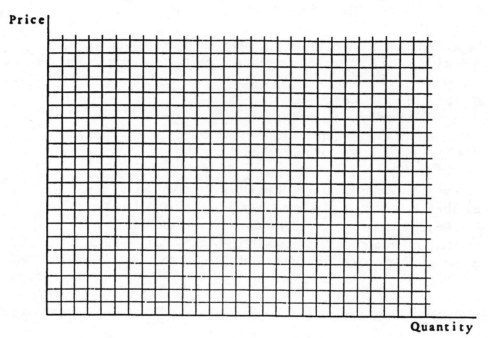

Figure 13-3

3.   What are the similarities and differences between perfect competition and monopolistic competition? Monopoly and monopolistic competition?

4.   What is excess capacity and how is it related to the model of monopolistic competition?

5.   Why is True/False Question #5 false? Suppose all advertising were banned. Would consumers be better or worse off? Why?

6.   Evaluate the following statement: "Oligopoly is the only market structure where firms engage in rivalrous behavior."

7.   Figure 13-4 gives the market demand curve and the marginal revenue curve if the industry was a monopoly. What are the rates of output for perfect competition and for monopoly? Suppose there were two identical firms (Firm A and Firm B) in the industry with constant marginal costs equal to MC. Derive the reaction curves for each. What is the Cournot equilibrium?

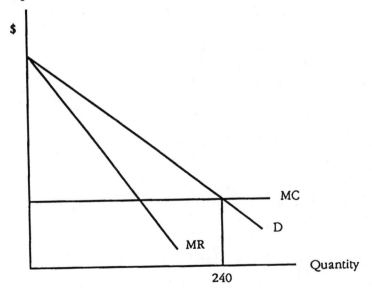

Figure 13-4

279

8. The Cournot model can be generalized to n equal-sized firms. The industry output equals $(n/(n + 1)) Q_c$, where Q_c is the competitive rate of output. What will the industry output rate be if there are two firms? Three? One hundred? One thousand? What relationship between the number of firms in an industry and oligopoly output does this suggest?

9. Explain how the dominant firm derives its demand curve.

10. In the dominant firm model, what happens if the supply curve of the smaller firms becomes more elastic?

11. Suppose the demand curve for a market has an elasticity of demand of 0.8, the market share of the dominant firm is 80%, and the elasticity of supply of the competitive fringe is 4. What is the elasticity of demand for the dominant firm? If the firm increases price by 10 percent, what will happen?

12. Suppose the dominant firm in an oligopolistic industry believed it was actually a monopoly. What would be the effects? How can the firm find the equilibrium price?

13. Explain how cartel theory and oligopoly are related. Does this imply that most firms in oligopolies are colluding? Why or why not?

14. Suppose that entry into all industries is essentially free in the long run. Does this imply that monopoly is not an important problem in the United States? Explain.

ANSWERS

Review Questions

True/False

1.	True	7.	True
2.	True	8.	False
3.	False	9.	True
4.	True	10.	False
5.	False	11.	True
6.	False	12.	True

Multiple Choice/Short Answer

1.	c	8.	b
2.	Downward sloping	9.	c
3.	a, c	10.	d
4.	c	11.	a
5.	b	12.	b
6.	d	13.	b
7.	b	14.	a
		15.	d

Discussion Questions and Problems

1. With differentiated products, consumers do not view the product of one firm as exactly identical to the product of another firm. Hence the firm can increase its sales by lowering price-its demand curve slopes downward. All the differences between the two models are due to the demand curve sloping down under monopolistic competition.

2. In Figure 13-5, P* and Q* are the short-run equilibrium price and quantity, respectively. This is an equilibrium because the firm has no incentive to change its rate of output (MR = MC). The firm is making profits since P > SAC. It is a temporary equilibrium because profits will induce new firms to enter the industry.

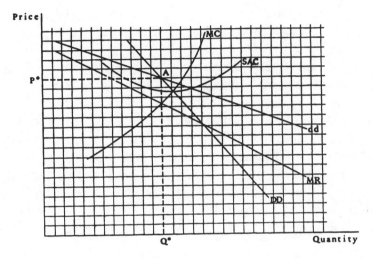

Figure 13-5

3. Perfect competition and monopolistic competition are alike except that goods are homogeneous under perfect competition and heterogeneous under monopolistic competition. Both monopoly and monopolistic competition have downward-sloping demand curves, but there is free entry in monopolistic competition, so firms cannot make long-run profits. However, price is greater than marginal cost under monopolistic competition.

4. Excess capacity means that firms produce at too low a rate of output, that is, to the left of the minimum point of their average cost curves. Excess capacity is an implication of monopolistic competition because the long-run equilibrium is characterized by zero profits and the firm faces a downward sloping demand curve. A downward sloping demand curve can be tangent to the average cost curve only to the left of the minimum point of the average cost curve.

5. Advertising may convey information that consumers value enough that they would be willing to pay a higher price for the product. Consumers would generally be worse off if all advertising was banned. Advertising informs people about what products are

available, where they can be bought, prices, warranties, etc. Without advertising, consumers would find shopping much more difficult.

6. The statement is correct. Under perfect competition, firms have no effect on other firms, so they do not engage in rivalrous behavior. By definition, a monopoly has no rivals. Under monopolistic competition, firms behave as if they have no effect on rivals because each firm is small relative to the market. Only in oligopoly do firms take into consideration how their actions will affect their rivals.

7. Perfect competition—240; monopoly—120 (half of perfect competition's rate of output with linear demand and marginal cost).

    Firm A will assume Firm B's output will not change. Firm A will produce at a rate of output equal to one-half the difference between the competitive rate of output (240) and B's rate of output. So, if B produces zero, A will produce 120 ([240-0]/2); if B produces 120, A will produce 60 ([240-120]/2); if B produces 100, A will produce 70 ([240-100]/2); and so forth. Since A and B are identical, B's reaction function is identical to A's reaction function. Figure 13-6 shows the two reaction curves. The Cournot equilibrium is at E, where the two reaction curves intersect. Each firm produces 80 units of output.

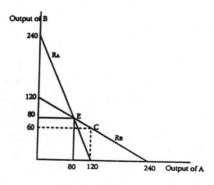

Figure 13-6

284

8. Two firms: $(2/3)Q_c$; three firms: $(3/4)Q_c$; one hundred firms: $(100/101)Q_c$; one thousand firms: $(1000/1001)Q_c$. These numbers suggest that the more firms in the industry, the more like a competitive industry it is.

9. For each price, the dominant firm calculates how much the competitive fringe will produce, and subtracts this quantity from the market demand curve to find the quantity demanded at the price on its demand curve. Figure 13-7 illustrates. At price P_1, the competitive fringe will produce enough output to satisfy the entire market quantity demanded, so the quantity demanded for the dominant firm is zero. At price P_2, the competitive fringe produces zero units, so the demand curve for the market is the demand curve for the dominant firm. Hence, the demand curve for the dominant firm is GAD_m.

10. In Figure 13-7, a more elastic supply curve means that S_f intersects the market demand curve to the right of F. This means that point G moves down the vertical axis, and the portion of the demand curve for the dominant firm, GA, becomes more elastic.

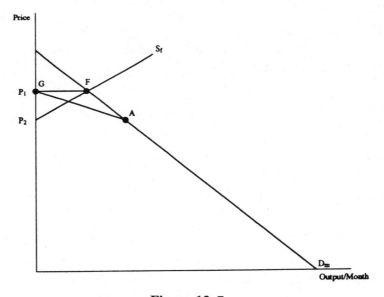

Figure 13-7

285

11. $\eta_D = \eta_M (1/\eta_S) + \varepsilon_{SF} (1/\eta_S) - 1$

         $= 0.8(1/.8) + 4(0.6) - 1$

         $= 0.8(1.25) + 4(1.25) - 1$
         $= 1 + 5 - 1 = 5$

12.   The firm would take the industry demand curve as its demand curve and equate marginal cost and marginal revenue to find the profit maximizing rate of output. However, the rest of the firms would take the price set by the dominant firm as their competitive price and produce additional output. As a result, more output is produced than planned by the dominant firm, and price falls.

13.   Cartel theory suggests that collusion is easier when there are just a few firms in the industry, and oligopoly is concerned with industries made up of a few firms. This does not imply that all firms in oligopolies are colluding because there are forces that make collusion difficult--for example, new entrants, number of buyers, product heterogeneity and cost differences.

14.   No. Firms can make substantial monopoly profits in the short run and generate substantial resource misallocations. It also depends on how long the adjustment from the short run to the long run takes.

CHAPTER 14 *Game Theory and the Economics of Information*

CHAPTER ANALYSIS

This chapter continues the analysis of markets by introducing game theory, which is a mathematical technique used to study choice involving strategic interaction, and the economics of information. The latter is relevant since real-world markets are not characterized by perfect information.

14.1-14.2 **Game theory** is a mathematical tool that can be used to analyze **strategic decision making**. It has been used to analyze the cold war, labor negotiations, advertising decisions, and oligopoly. There are three elements to a game theory model. **Players** are the decision makers, **strategies** are the potential choices that can be made by the players, and **payoffs** are the outcomes of those strategies. The strategies can be fairly simple, such as always do one thing, or can be much more complicated. In economics, most payoffs are designed as profits or losses from pursuing a particular strategy.

Many new terms are introduced in this chapter. Therefore a list of terms with a definition and a few comments is provided.

Payoff Matrix: a matrix representing how each combination of choices affects the profits of each firm.

Dominant strategy: when one choice is best no matter what the other player does.

Nash equilibrium: a set of strategies such that each player's choice is the best one given the strategy chosen by all the other players. Nash equilibrium is the most common analyzed by game theorists. A Cournot equilibrium is also a Nash equilibrium.

Prisoners' dilemma: a game in which the players make their choices independent of each other, and the players are worse off than if they had cooperated with each other. The outcome generally is a Nash equilibrium. An oligopoly forming a cartel faces a prisoners' dilemma situation, since each firm has an incentive to cheat regardless if other firms cheat or not.

14.3 The prisoners' dilemma tends to apply in single-period games. However, it can often be avoided in repeated games, i.e., games in which decisions have to be made over time. In repeated games players have an opportunity to learn about the behavior of each other, and to punish those who refuse to cooperate. The likelihood of a cartel's success is much greater in repeated games, although success is still not certain. Keep in mind that these games do not take into consideration entry of new firms, so that strategies that work for a fixed number of players may not work when entry takes place.

14.4-14.5 The models utilized to this point have assumed that market participants possess information concerning price, location of buyers and sellers, quality, and all other factors necessary to make decisions in the marketplace. However; it is obvious that consumers often do not know the identity of the seller with the lowest price or the quality of the commodity sold by a particular seller, and sellers often do not know the prices charged by other sellers. Like all goods, information is scarce and resources must be used to obtain better information. **Imperfect information** implies that we must alter some of our analysis if we are to explain many real-world phenomena.

An important information problem is **asymmetric information,** which occurs when one party in a transaction has information the other party does not have. Asymmetric information characterizes most market transactions to some degree. The seller of a commodity or service generally has better information about the quality than the buyer. For example, the seller of a used car knows more about the quality of the car for sale than the buyer knows. If someone is selling a relatively new used car, it is not unreasonable to think there must be something wrong with the car. Consequently prospective buyers will not be willing to pay top dollar for the car. This implies that sellers who have high quality cars will not be able to get the price they want, and the quantity supplied of high quality cars will fall. On the other hand, the quantity supplied of low quality cars will increase, and the market for used cars will contain a high proportion of low quality cars. Both buyers and sellers realize the problem caused by asymmetric information, and have incentive to find solutions to these problems.

In some markets, the consumer has better information than the seller. For example consumers of insurance generally have better information about their health or life styles than the insurance company has. The result is called **adverse selection**--consumers more likely to suffer the risk being insured are more likely to purchase insurance than consumers who are lower risks. For example, someone living on low land near a river is more likely to want flood insurance than someone living on a hill. While the insurance company may be able to identify the high risk person in this case the company may not be able to identify the person with a high risk of heart disease or being in an auto accident. The greater proportion of high risk consumers the greater the cost to the insurance company and the higher the premiums. Again, market participants have developed methods to reduce the cost associated with adverse selection, such as gathering more information.

Moral hazard is another informational problem common to insurance markets. For many undesirable events the behavior of the insured individual can affect the probability that the event takes place. It is more likely that one's car will be stolen if the owner leaves the keys in the ignition. If the person is fully insured, he or she will be indifferent whether the event occurs or not. In such cases the individual has no incentive to behave in a way that reduces the likelihood of the event. This implies that the undesirable event is more likely to occur, raising costs to the insurance company. Hence, insurance companies generally do not fully insure events where the behavior of the consumer affects the probability of the event taking place.

14.6-14.7 Consumers often do not know where they can obtain the lowest price for a good. It is reasonable to expect they will engage in some search before purchasing a good. But search is costly. The consumer spends gasoline in driving from one store to another, and the opportunity cost of the consumers time is a relevant cost.

Theory predicts that consumers will engage in search until the expected marginal benefit from additional search equals the expected marginal cost of the additional search. Theory also predicts that a single, competitive price will exist in a market even when some consumers are ignorant of the price so long as a high enough proportion of consumers are well informed.

Advertising is an important source of information in many markets. We learn about new products, where commodities can be sold, sales, price, and other information through advertising. Firms advertise in order to lower the search costs of consumers. But, firms also advertise in order to persuade consumers to purchase their products. Economists have long noted the dual nature of advertising-it is informative but also persuasive. As information, advertising aids the functioning of markets, but-as persuasion, some feel it distorts the functioning of markets.

ILLUSTRATIONS

Cournot and Game Theory

The Cournot model often is criticized for unrealistic behavior since firms never learn the true behavioral response of their rivals. The assumption that each firm believes its rival will continue to produce its current rate of output is ad hoc. Game theory can be used to generate the same equilibrium. The demonstration relies on the idea of infinite regress, which is of the nature, "I know that you know that I know that you know that I know that you know, etc."

Firm A chooses its optimal rate of output subject to its model of Firm B's strategy. Firm A's model of B's strategy is subject to B's model of A's strategy, and so on. Based on this type of infinite regress reasoning, Andrew Daughety has shown that the output selected by each firm is the Cournot equilibrium. The solution does not depend on myopic behavior.

[See Andrew F. Daughety, "Reconsidering Cournot: The Cournot Equilibrium is Consistent," *The Rand Journal of Economics,* 16 (Autumn 1985), pp. 368-379.]

Advertising and Contractual Performance

How can a firm inform consumers that its claims about the quality of its product are true when consumers have a hard time determining quality without consuming the good? Benjamin Klein and Keith Leffler examine this question, and argue that advertising expenditures provide one method. They argue that a firm will keep its promises about quality if it can charge a high enough price above costs so that the loss of future business would cause a large reduction in wealth of the owners of the firm. If the firm cheats and consumers are disappointed, they will no longer purchase from the firm. Thus, the loss of future sales is the threat to firms to keep them honest. Still, how can consumers know that some firms are high quality and some are not? If the high quality firm makes investments that cannot be recouped if the firm goes out of business, then it has an incentive to stay in business and not to cheat by reducing the level of quality. Since advertising expenditures cannot be recouped if the firm goes out of business, they are a signal to consumers that the firm will continue to produce its promised level of quality. In this model the message of the ads are not what matters, but merely the existence of the ads.

[See Benjamin Klein and Keith B. Leffler, "The Role of Market Forces in Assuring Contractual Performance," *Journal of Political Economy, 89* (August 1981), pp. 615-641.1

KEY CONCEPTS

game theory
players
strategies
payoffs
payoff matrix
dominant firm
Nash equilibrium

prisoners' dilemma
repeated game model
tit-for-tat strategy
       asymmetric information
adverse selection
strategy   moral hazard
     price dispersion
search costs
artificial product differentiation
full price

REVIEW QUESTIONS

True/False

____ 1. Game theory can be used to analyze any type of strategic interaction.

____ 2. In a game, a particular strategy uniquely determines the profit (payoff) of the firm.

____ 3. A dominant strategy is one that allows one firm to make more profits than the other firm(s) in the industry.

_____ 4. All Nash equilibria are also dominant strategy equilibriums.

_____ 5. The Cournot equilibrium is a Nash equilibrium.

_____ 6. The prisoners' dilemma model generates an equilibrium that is inferior for both players even though each pursues his or her own self-interest.

_____ 7. The prisoners' dilemma model can show why firms have an incentive to cheat on a collusive agreement.

_____ 8. The repeated prisoners' dilemma game generates the same equilibrium as the single-period prisoners' dilemma game.

_____ 9. Asymmetric information is a characteristic of all markets.

_____ 10. If half the used cars are high quality and worth $10,000 and half are low quality and worth $5000, the equilibrium price will be $7500.

_____ 11. In question 10, if the buyers knew which cars were high quality and which were low quality the equilibrium price would be $7500.

_____ 12. All real world markets are inefficient because all markets have some type of information problem.

_____ 13. Adverse selection in insurance markets leads to a larger proportion of high-risk customers than would be the case in a full-information world.

_____ 14. Adverse selection is a problem when firms provide group health insurance to all employees.

_____ 15. Moral hazard is a problem in insurance markets when the individual's behavior is likely to change as a result of having insurance.

_____ 16. Theory suggests that the price dispersion of lower-priced goods will be less than the price dispersion of higher-priced goods.

_____ 17. Consumers obtain useful information from advertising only when advertising is informative.

_____ 18. Advertising can lower the full price of a commodity by reducing search costs of customers.

Multiple Choice/Short Answer

1. In an oligopolistic game, strategies involve
    a. prices.
    b. output.
    c. advertising budgets.
    d. all of the above are possible.

2. Figure 14-1 presents a payoff matrix for a duopoly faced with choices between complying with a collusive agreement or cheating on the agreement. The payoff matrix is an illustration of

3. a. a dominant strategy equilibrium.
    b. a Nash equilibrium.
    c. a prisoners' dilemma.
    d. all of the above.

3. In Figure 14-1, the probable equilibrium is that
    a. Cournot Enterprises cheats and Stackelberg, Inc. complies.
    b. Cournot Enterprises complies and Stackelberg, Inc. cheats.
    c. both Cournot Enterprises and Stackelberg, Inc. cheat.
    d. both Cournot Enterprises and Stackelberg, Inc. comply.

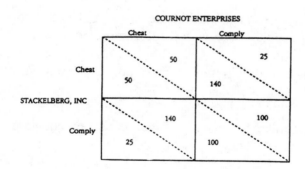

Figure 14-1

Questions 4 through 7 use information in Figure 14-2.

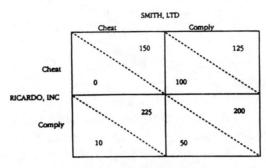

Figure 14-2

4. The dominant strategy for Smith, Ltd. is
   a. cheat.
   b. comply.
   c. cheat if Ricardo, Inc. cheats and comply if Ricardo, Inc. complies.
   d. comply if Ricardo, Inc. cheats and cheat if Ricardo, Inc. complies.

5. The best strategy for Ricardo, Inc. is
   a. cheat.
   b. comply.
   c. cheat if Smith, Ltd. cheats and comply if Smith, Ltd. complies.
   d. cheat if Smith, Ltd. complies and comply if Smith, Ltd. cheats.

6. The probable equilibrium is
   a. both cheat.
   b. both comply.
   c. Smith, Ltd. cheats and Ricardo, Inc. complies.
   d. Smith, Ltd. complies and Ricardo, Inc. cheats.

7. The probable equilibrium is called
   a. a dominant strategy equilibrium.
   b. a Nash equilibrium.
   c. a prisoners' dilemma.
   d. all of the above.

8. The prisoners' dilemma applied to oligopolistic firms trying to form a cartel implies that
   a. cartels will never be formed.
   b. cartels will be formed but not be successful
   c. there are incentives to cheat but a cartel can be successful if a method of enforcement can be found.
   d. cartels will be formed and the firms will easily find ways to enforce the collusive agreement.

9. Cartels are more difficult to form when there are more firms in an industry because
   a. each firm wants to be a leader.
   b. the demand curve faced by a cheater is more inelastic
   c. cheating is harder to detect when there are more firms
   d. none of the above. Cartels are easier to form when there are more firms.

10. Cartels are more likely to be effective in a repeated game situation because
   a. it is easier to determine if someone is cheating.
   b. a cheater can be punished in future time periods.
   c. the potential rewards to cheating are less.
   d. none of the above. Cartels are less effective in a repeated game situation.

11. The assumption of perfect information that is used in many market models means that
   a. all market participants know all information in the world.
   b. all market participants know the relevant information about prices, technology, outputs, etc. to make good decisions.
   c. the models are useless since such information does not exist in any real world markets.
   d. market participants know what all other participants are planning to do.

12. A market is characterized by asymmetric information when
   a. no one has information about the characteristics of a commodity.
   b. the quality of a good is not known for sure by any of the market participants.
   c. the quality of a good can be determined by examining it.
   d. one side of the market knows more about the good than the other side.

13. If half of the used cars sold are high quality and worth $10000 and half are low quality and worth $6000, the market price with asymmetric information will be
   a. $8000.
   b. $6000.
   c. $10000.
   d. Cannot tell without knowing the reaction of the sellers.

14. Using the information if question 13, if the buyers could easily identify the high quality cars; the market price would be
   a. $8000.
   b. $6000.
   c. $10000 for the high quality cars and $6000 for the low quality cars.
   d. uncertain without more information.

15. Consumers do not collect all possible information about a good because
   a. it is too costly.
   b. they are not small enough to understand it.
   c. the information does not exist.
   d. the seller won't provide the information.

16. Suppose a study is performed that determines that the average person who applies for a medical insurance policy supplemental to medicare is more likely to be hospitalized in the next year than those who did not apply for the insurance. This finding is an example of
   a. moral hazard.
   b. symmetric information.
   c. adverse selection.
   d. prisoners' dilemma.

17. Universal medical insurance provided by the government and paid out of tax revenues would be a possible response to the problem of _____ but would increase the probability of _____.
   a. adverse selection; moral hazard.
   b. moral hazard; adverse selection.
   c. adverse selection; asymmetric information.
   d. asymmetric information; adverse selection.

18. If advertising is a source of information that is valuable to consumers, then
   a. the market price will tend to be lower with advertising than without advertising.
   b. the market price plus search costs will tend to be lower with advertising than without advertising.
   c. search costs will be greater for advertised goods than for unadvertised goods.
   d. the market price will be the same as the full price.

Discussion Questions and Problems

1. Using game theory explain why collusive agreements often break down under duopoly.

2. All dominant strategy equilibriums are Nash equilibriums but not all Nash equilibriums are dominant strategy equilibriums. Explain.

3. What is the prisoners' dilemma game? Why does it receive so much attention from economists?

4. How do single-period games differ from repeated games? Why does this difference lead to different expectations about the likelihood of cartels being successful? Why can't game theory be used to state with certainty whether a particular cartel will be successful or not?

5. Suppose there are 1000 used cars in a market, with 600 being poor quality and 400 high quality. The high quality cars are worth $10,000 and the low quality cars are worth $5000.

    a. If buyers can tell by observation whether a car is high quality or low quality, what will be the market equilibrium?

    b. If neither buyers nor sellers know the true quality of a car, what will be the market price for the cars?

    c. If asymmetric information applies what will happen?

6. Suppose the probability of hospitalization is 0.2, and there are 1000 people in the community. The cost of hospitalization is $10,000.

    a. What is the expected cost to the insurance company if it insures all 1000 people? What is the actuarially fair premium?

    b. Suppose the probability of hospitalization for blue-eyed people is .5 and 200 people are blue-eyed, while the probability for everyone else is 0.125. What premiums will be charged? Suppose that instead of blue-eyed people, the high-probability group were people whose favorite color was blue. How would the market respond?

7.	Explain the difference between adverse selection and moral hazard. How is asymmetric information inherent in both?

8.	Why do we expect the price dispersion on automobiles to be less than the price dispersion on refrigerators?

9.	For many years, professional associations of lawyers and physicians prohibited members from advertising. However, the Federal Trade Commission has challenged these prohibitions? What would be the economic reason for outlawing these advertising prohibitions?

10.	There are examples where advertising has led to lower prices and other examples where advertising has led to higher prices. Explain how advertising may still be beneficial even when prices are higher for advertised products than for unadvertised products.

ANSWERS

Review Questions

True/False

1. True
2. False
3. False
4. False
5. True
6. True
7. True
8. False
9. False
10. False
11. False. The equilibrium price for high quality would $10,000 and for low quality $5000.
12. False. Information is costly so it is efficient for consumers to be less than fully informed.
13. True
14. False
15. True
16. False
17. False
18. True

Multiple Choice/Short Answer

1.	d	10.	b
2.	d	11.	b
3.	c	12.	d
4.	a	13.	d
5.	d	14.	c
6.	c	15.	a
7.	b	16.	c
8.	c	17.	a
9.	c	18.	b

Discussion Questions and Problems

1. Table 14-3 provides a payoff matrix that shows this. Joint profits are maximized if both firms comply with the collusive agreement (lower right comer of the matrix). However, if Firm A complies and B cheats, B's profits are greater than if both comply. The reverse is true if B complies and A cheats. If both cheat, profits are lower for both. Firm A looks at the table and determines that it does better by cheating regardless if B cheats or complies. Therefore, A will cheat. Similarly, B arrives at the same conclusion so they both cheat and the collusive agreement breaks down.

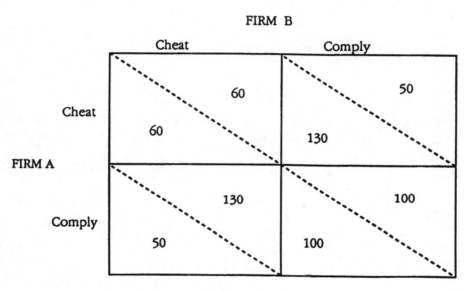

Figure 14-3

2. A Nash equilibrium exists when each player's choice is the best one possible given the strategy chosen by the other player. A dominant strategy exists when a player will select the same strategy regardless of the strategy selected by the other player. A dominant strategy equilibrium occurs when both firms have a dominant strategy. Hence, each player's choice is the best one possible given the strategy of the other, which is the definition of a Nash equilibrium. However, a Nash equilibrium can occur when one firm's optimal strategy differs, depending on what strategy the other player selects. As long as the firm can determine what the other player's best strategy is, it will select the optimal strategy for itself. Such an equilibrium is a Nash equilibrium but not a dominant strategy equilibrium.

3. The problem in the first discussion question is an example of the prisoners' dilemma. Each firm selects a strategy that is the best for itself yet is inferior to the strategy that would maximize joint profits. This model is used in economics because it seems applicable to many situations faced in economics, especially situations involving oligopoly.

4. A single-period game is one that happens only once, while a repeated game occurs many times over a period of time. That is, the repeated game allows firms to adjust their actions in the future in response to changes in behavior of the other firms. Since the incentive to cheat is so high in a single-period game, it seems reasonable to conclude that firms will cheat. However, in a repeated game the cheater can be punished. The threat of punishment may increase the likelihood that each firm will refrain from cheating. The cost of cheating is greater in a repeated game than in a single-period game. Game theory cannot predict what will happen in a specific industry because so many things are important to the success of a real-world cartel that game theory cannot model well. For example, game theory ignores entry and technological change.

5. a. The high quality cars will sell for $10,000 each and the low quality cars will sell for $5000 each.
    b. The market price will be the weighted average of the high quality and the low quality prices. That is, the price will be $10000 x 0.6 + $5000 x 0.4 = $6000 + $2000 = $8000.
    c. If we start at a price of $8000, it is clear that sellers with high quality cars will not offer their cars for sale because they will not get what the car is worth. On the other hand the owners of low quality cars will be eager to sell their cars for $8000. Consequently, the actual cars in the market will be made up of low quality cars. Since buyers can anticipate this response, they will not be willing to pay $8000 for a car. They will presume that the cars offered for sale are low quality cars. Under asymmetric information, the low quality products tend to drive out high quality products.

6. a. The expected cost to the insurance company is $2,000,000 ($10,000 x 1000 x 0.2). The actuarially fair premium is $2000 if all 1000 people get insurance.
    b. The company could identify the blue-eyed people by observation, so they can charge them a higher premium. The premium for the blue-eyed people would be large enough to cover the expected costs, which would be 0.5 x 200 x $1000 = $1,000,000. The premium would then be $1,000,000/200 = $5000. The expected costs for the other people would be equal to 0.125 x 800x $10,000 =$1,000,000, and the premium would be $1,000,000/800 = $1250. In the case of people whose favorite color is blue, the insurance company would not be able to distinguish them from the low-risk consumers, so they would want to charge a premium of $2000 (like in part a). However, at such a premium, the less risk averse of the low-risk consumers would

not pay the premium. This means that the premium would have to be higher which would drive out more of the low-risk consumers. This is the adverse selection problem, and the high risk consumers would drive the low-risk consumers out of the market.

7.   Adverse selection deals with the situation when the desirable consumers choose not to buy insurance while undesirable consumers are more likely to buy insurance. Moral hazard deals with the situation where the behavior of the insured can affect whether the event insured against will take place. Asymmetric information is involved in both. The consumer knows more about his or her potential for using the insurance in the case of adverse selection and the insurance company has difficulty determining whether the occurrence of the event was due to the behavior of the insured individual or not.

8.   There are costs to searching for lower prices on any commodity. The major cost is the opportunity cost of one's time. Since this cost is similar regardless of the good, one will spend more time and effort in search the more costly the product. The expected benefit from additional search when buying an auto is greater than when buying a refrigerator, so people will spend more time searching when buying an automobile. The greater search effort implies that more people will find relatively lower prices in the case of autos than in the case of refrigerators, so the price dispersion will be less in the case of autos.

9.   The Federal Trade Commission must be arguing that advertising provides information that is valuable to consumers and provides a cheap substitute for search on the part of consumers. The advertising reduces the monopoly power of the associations.

10.   The full price of the product equals the money price good plus the search costs. If advertising lowers search costs by more than it raises the money price, then consumers are still better off with advertising.

CHAPTER 15 *Using Noncompetitive Market Models*

CHAPTER ANALYSIS

In this chapter models that utilize a degree of market power are used to analyze several important issues. When you read the examples, note how the result differs from the perfectly competitive result. Also, try to identify the source of monopoly power in the examples.

ILLUSTRATIONS

Ramsey Prices

When price exceeds marginal cost, consumers value additional units of output at more than the unit's cost to produce, and consumers' welfare will increase if output expands until price equals marginal cost. For this reason, marginal cost pricing is one goal of regulating a natural monopoly. However, if the firm is truly a natural monopoly, marginal cost lies below average cost, and the firm would incur long-run losses if forced to charge marginal cost. Hence, other types of pricing arrangements are made.

One solution to the problem caused by natural monopoly is to have the monopoly charge Ramsey prices, which are a form of price discrimination. If the natural monopoly has several classes of customers with different demand elasticities and the different markets can be kept separated, then the monopolist should charge prices to the different groups that are inversely proportional to the elasticities of demand of the groups. That is, if one group of customers has a more elastic demand than another group, then the group with the more elastic demand should be charged a lower price than the other group. Prices set in this way are Ramsey prices.

The way Ramsey prices are set is similar to the way a nonregulated monopolist sets prices if it price-discriminates. Ramsey prices are recommended by many economists because they result in an increase in the total consumption of the good, which in turn results in a more efficient output. Similarly, price discrimination by nonregulated monopolists often results in greater output, which reduces the welfare loss of monopoly. For example, quantity discounts result in an increase in the total consumption of the good.

[Ramsey prices are derived in F. P. Ramsey, "A Contribution to the Theory of Taxation," *Economic Journal* 37 (March 1927): 27-61.]

KEY CONCEPTS

deadweight loss of monopoly   natural monopoly

REVIEW QUESTIONS

Multiple Choice/Short Answer

1. Estimates of the deadweight loss of monopoly in the United States have been relatively low because
    a. there are few instances of pure monopoly in the United States.
    b. the estimates are relative to the whole economy.
    c. the economy is reasonably competitive.
    d. all of the above.

2. Estimates of the deadweight loss of monopoly may be underestimated because
    a. some firms have monopoly power that economists do not recognize.
    b. monopolist's actually produce on the inelastic portion of their demand curves.
    c. the estimates exclude costs the firm incurs in acquiring or maintaining its monopoly.
    d. all of the above.

3. Since profits can be increased by marketing a worthwhile invention, monopolists have no incentive to suppress a worthwhile invention.   True   False

Questions 4 to 7 use information in Figure 15-1 about a monopolist producer of light bulbs.

4. One bulb provides 1000 hours, or 1 kilohour, of lighting. It costs the firm 60 cents to make a bulb and it charges 80 cents per bulb. Suppose the firm develops a new light bulb that will burn 6000 hours and cost twice as much to make as the current bulb. The new price per kilohour will be
    a. 60 cents.
    b. 40 cents.
    c. 30 cents.
    d. 20 cents.

5. How many of the new bulbs will the firm sell?
    a. 400
    b. 200
    c. 66.67
    d. 50

6.　What price does the monopolist charge for the new bulbs?
　　a. 60 cents
　　b. $1.20
　　c. $2.40
　　d. $3.60

7.　What are the increases in profits available to the monopolist by selling the new light bulb?
　　a. zero
　　b. $120
　　c. $160
　　d. $200

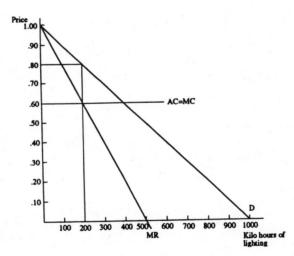

Figure 15-1

8.　If the long-run average cost curve is still declining when it intersects the total market demand curve, what do we have?

Questions 9 and 10 refer to Figure 15-2.

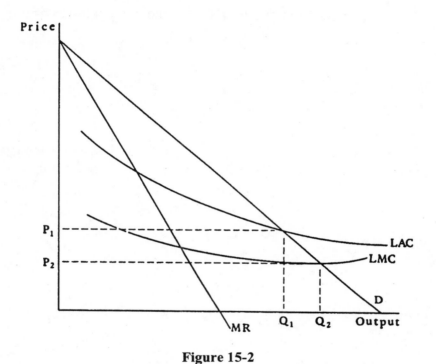

Figure 15-2

9.   If the regulatory commission sets price P_1, it is (average/marginal) cost-pricing, while if it sets P_2 it is (average/ marginal) cost-pricing.

10.   If price P_2 is set by the regulatory agency, the firm will
   a. produce Q_2 units of output.
   b. produce Q_2, units in the short run and Q_1 in the long run.
   c. make zero economic profits.
   d. make economic losses and go out of business.

11.   A regulated firm has a strong incentive to keep costs down.   True   False

306

12. Government-established cartels have fewer problems compared to other cartels because
    a. they produce necessities rather than luxuries.
    b. entry can be limited by the government.
    c. they have less elastic demand curves.
    d. there is no incentive to cheat on the cartel agreement.

13. British Columbia's Egg Marketing Board has raised the price of eggs above the cost of production. Which of the following *best* supports this statement?
    a. Egg prices are higher in British Columbia than in the United States.
    b. People in British Columbia consume fewer eggs per capita than people in the United States.
    c. The market value of a quota is above zero.
    d. None of the above.

14. The study on the effects of the British Columbia Egg Marketing Board found the costs due to higher production costs exceeded the welfare costs of the higher prices.

    True   False

15. To find a Nash equilibrium when there are no dominant strategies, one can rely on the concept of iterated dominance. Iterated dominance involves
    a. committing to a certain course of action.
    b. always choosing the high-price strategy.
    c. ruling out any strategy that is dominated by another strategy.
    d. all of the above.

16. For a commitment to be effective it must
    a. be the most profitable action for all parties.
    b. generate the greatest losses on other firms.
    c. be legal.
    d. be credible.

Discussion Questions and Problems

1. Some economists maintain that competition for monopoly increases the deadweight loss of monopoly. What do they mean by this?

2. Monopolies are often accused of laxity in keeping costs down. Suppose a monopolist knows of a production technique that will produce its product at a lower cost. Using a graph, show that the profits of the monopolist will be greater using the lower-cost method. *(Hint:* Use horizontal marginal cost curve.)

3. Would you think the deadweight loss of monopoly in the American auto industry is more or less today than 30 years ago? Why?

4. Figure 15-3 reproduces Figure 15-1 used in multiple choice problems 4 - 7. From the information in problem, draw the new MC/AC curve and show the new equilibrium output and price.

5. Using Figure 15-3, show the new equilibrium if the new bulbs had the same marginal (average) cost as the old, 1000 hour bulbs.

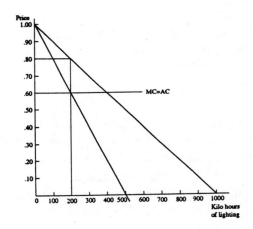

Figure 15-3

6. When P = MC, the cost of producing one more unit equals the value of an additional unit to consumers. Hence the efficient price is obtained when P = MC. What are the effects of setting P = MC for a natural monopoly?

7. The text states that a monopoly will not suppress inventions and will try to keep costs down but that a regulated monopolist may suppress or slow down the introduction of inventions and not hold down costs. How can these apparently contradictory statements be resolved?

8. Government support of farmers takes many forms. All programs, though, seek to raise farmers' incomes, which can be accomplished only by raising the prices of agricultural products.

   a. What is the result of programs to artificially raise price, and what problem does this pose for the government?

   b. In this chapter we saw how the British Columbia Egg Marketing Board operates. The U.S. government provides price supports for farmers by guaranteeing specific prices that usually are above the market price. How do these two methods of raising farm prices differ and how are they similar? Figure 15-4 is available for use. (Hint: Analyze one industry under both types of programs. Assume the long-run supply curve is upward-sloping and that there are no imports.)

   c. Suppose the government sets quotas on production, but it sets a maximum price below the equilibrium price associated with the quota. What are the effects?

9. Figure 15-5 is the payoff matrix for Quality Motors and A-1 Motors—the only car dealers in a town. Use the concept of iterated dominance to find a Nash equilibrium.

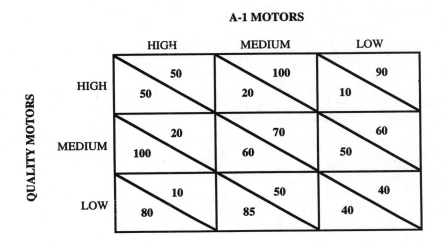

Figure 15-5

10. Explain how a commitment strategy works. Why does the commitment have to be "credible"?

ANSWERS

Review Questions

Multiple Choice/Short Answer

1. d
2. c
3. True
4. a
5. c
6. d
7. b
8. natural monopoly
9. average; marginal
10. d
11. False
12. b
13. c
14. True
15. c
16. d

Discussion Questions and Problems

1. If a firm can obtain a monopoly, it can earn monopoly profits. These monopoly profits encourage firms to try to become monopolies, which may result in competition for the first monopoly. For example, to protect itself from competition, a monopoly might lobby the government to impose tariffs or licensing requirements, or it might try to buy up all sources of a key input. Any of these actions would involve additional welfare costs.

2. Figure 15-6 illustrates. When marginal costs (and average costs) are MC_1, the monopolist produces Q_1 units and charges a price of P_1. Profits are the area of the rectangle P_1BEC_1. If costs fall to MC_2, output expands to Q_2 and price falls to P_2. New profits are $P_2BE'C_2$, which are greater than the profits when costs were higher.

3. I would think the deadweight loss of monopoly in the auto industry today is less than 30 years ago because of the increased competition from Japan and other producers.

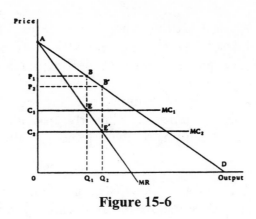

Figure 15-6

4. In Figure 15-7, the new marginal cost curve is MC', generating an output rate of 400 kilohours and a price of 60 cents per kilohour.

5. In Figure 15-7, the relevant marginal cost curve is MC'', generating an output rate of 450 kilohours and a price of 55 cents per kilohour.

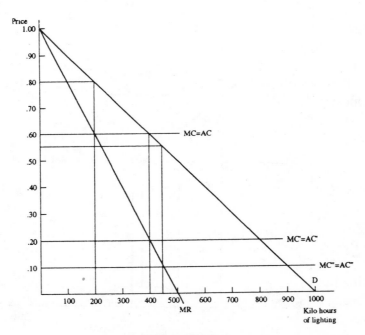

Figure 15-7

313

6. A natural monopoly has a declining average cost curve. Since the average cost is declining, the marginal cost curve must lie below the average cost curve. Hence if P = MC, P < AC and the firm is making losses. In the long run, it will go out of business.

7. A regulated monopolist receives a certain rate of return regardless of its costs. Hence it has little incentive to keep costs down. Similarly, new innovations will not generate extra profits for the regulated firm, so there is no incentive for them to implement innovations rapidly.

8. a. An excess supply of the food develops when government programs artificially raise prices. The government must remove the excess supply in some way.

    b. See Figure 15-8. The equilibrium price and output are P_e and Q_e. If the government promises to buy at a higher price (P_s) then quantity supplied increases to Q_s and quantity demanded falls to Q_d. There is an excess supply of $Q_s - Q_d$ units. The British Columbia Egg Marketing Board uses a quota system. If the government restricted production to Q_d units, price would rise to P_s, but there would not be an excess supply for the government to purchase. The price support system used in the U.S. means the government must buy and store the excess supply. The quota system is cheaper for the government than the price-support system.

    c. Refer to Figure 15-8. If the government places a quota of Q_d units and a maximum price of P_m then there is an excess demand of $Q_m - Qd$ units.

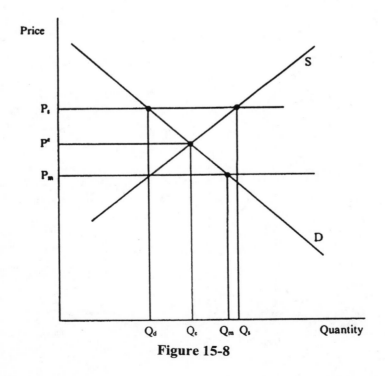

Figure 15-8

314

9. For Quality Motors the medium price strategy always dominates the high-price strategy, so the high-price strategy can be eliminated from consideration. Similarly for A-1. The resulting 2x2 payoff matrix is the four squares left after eliminating the top row and the left-column. If A-1 goes medium, Quality goes low and if A-1 goes low, Quality goes medium. If Quality goes medium, A-1 goes medium and if Quality goes low A-1 goes medium. So, A-1 will always go medium, making Quality's best strategy the low price. This is the Nash equilibrium.

10. A commitment strategy involves making a commitment to a particular action regardless of what the other party does. A party constrains its own choice of strategies, usually to influence the behavior of the other parties. However, a commitment must be credible to be effective. For example, a cartel's "commitment" to run a cheater out of business by pricing below cost indefinitely would not be credible since it would also drive many of the members out of business too.

CHAPTER 16 *Employment and Pricing of Inputs*

CHAPTER ANALYSIS

Our emphasis shifts from analyzing the markets of final goods and services to analyzing the markets for the inputs that are used to produce goods. In Chapter 16, the general analysis of input markets is developed. In Chapter 17 this analysis is used to examine specific markets to see how wages, profits, interest and rent are determined. Chapter 18 contains several examples that apply the tools developed in Chapters 16 and 17.

16.1 Firms employ inputs to produce the goods and services they sell. An input will be hired as long as its contribution to total revenues is at least as great as its contribution to total costs. For a competitive firm, an input's contribution to total revenues equals the extra output that it produces times the price of the good produced. The input's contribution to total costs is determined by the price of the input.

When all other inputs are held fixed, the demand curve for a given input is directly related to the marginal product curve for the input. The marginal product of an input measures the additional output produced when one more unit of the input is hired. For instance, 99 workers are able to produce 200 units of output, and 100 workers are able to produce 210 units, the marginal product of labor is 10. The additional 10 units of output can be sold at the price that prevails in the competitive market. If the price is $5, then the additional 10 units generate an additional $50 of total revenue. This $50 is called the **marginal value product of labor** (MVP_L) and measures the extra revenue the competitive firm can receive by selling the additional output produced when an additional unit of the input is employed. When all other inputs are fixed, the marginal value product curve of an input is the competitive firm's demand curve for the input. The short-run demand curve for an input slopes downward because the law of diminishing marginal returns applies in the short run.

When all inputs are variable, the MVP_L curve is *not* the demand curve for the input because the firm will change its employment of all inputs in response to a change in the price of one input. However, the demand curve still slopes down no matter whether the inputs are complements or substitutes. Review Figure 16.2 in the text.

The adjustment of a firm to a change in the price of an input can be separated into a **substitution effect** and an **output effect**. If the price of labor falls, more labor and less capital will be used to produce the same rate of output because isoquants are convex. This is the substitution effect and is analogous to the substitution effect when moving along an indifference curve. A change in the price of an input also shifts the firm's marginal cost curve. A lower price for labor shifts the marginal cost curve to the right, and the firm will expand production. The output effect is the increase in the quantity of labor employed when output increases. A lower wage rate will induce greater employment of labor because of both the substitution and the output effects.

16.2-16.6 We have seen that there is a substitution effect and an output effect when the price of an input changes. If the price change of an input affects all firms, the combined output effects will cause industry output to change, which results in a change in the price of the good produced. Since the marginal value product of an input depends partially on the price of the good produced, the MVP curve will shift. For example, if the price of labor falls, each firm will increase its output, which causes the price of the good to fall. The fall in the price of the good causes the MVP curve to shift to the left. Review Figure 16.4 in the text to make sure you understand completely the derivation of the industry demand curve for an input.

The **price elasticity of demand for an input**, which is defined as the percentage change in the quantity of the input employed divided by the percentage change in the price of the input, is relevant to analysis of input markets. There are four major factors that affect the elasticity of demand for an input. The elasticity of demand for an input will be more elastic

1. The more elastic the demand for the product produced
2. The easier it is to substitute one input for another in production
3. The more elastic the supply curve of other inputs
4. The longer the time allowed for adjustment

It is important to distinguish between the supply of an input to a specific industry and the supply of an input in existence in the economy at a given time. The short-run supply curve of engineers may be inelastic, for example, while the short-run supply curve of engineers to the aerospace industry is very elastic. This is so because the aerospace industry employs only a small fraction of all engineers, and the engineers can seek employment in other industries.

16.5 Once we have derived the industry demand and supply curves for an input, it is easy to find the equilibrium price and employment of the input. The intersection of the industry demand and supply curves determines the equilibrium price of the input, and the competitive firm can hire as many units of the input as it wishes at that price, that is, the supply curve of the input to the firm is horizontal at the market price of the input.

Competition among industries for inputs will result in identical inputs receiving the same price regardless of what industry employs them, other things being equal. If the wage earned by electricians employed in the computer industry exceeds the wage earned by electricians in the communications industry, electricians will leave the communications industry and enter the computer industry until the wages are equalized. This analysis applies to different regions in the

United States as well as different industries.

16.7 A monopoly will hire additional units of an input as long as the additional units' contribution to revenues exceeds their contribution to cost. For a monopolist, one more unit of an input expands the output that can be sold. For a monopoly to sell more units of its output, however, the price of the output must fall. The addition to revenues, then, will not equal $(P_x)x(MP)$, as is true for perfect competition, but will equal $(MR_x)x(MP)$. This is known as the **marginal revenue product** (MRP) of an input. A monopolist in the output market will hire additional units of an input until the price of the input equals the marginal revenue product of the input. Since the MRP curve will lie below the MVP curve, the monopolist will employ fewer units of an input than would be hired by a competitive industry.

16.8 A **monopsony** is a firm that is the single buyer of an input. A monopsony faces the market supply curve of the input, which generally slopes upward. It can hire additional units of the input only by raising the price paid to all units of the input it employs. As a result, the marginal cost of hiring an additional unit of the input is greater than the price of the input because the monopsonist must raise the price paid to all the units it already employs. Figure 16.10 in the text illustrates the hiring decision of a monopsonist The wage rate and the employment rate under monopsony are below the wage rate and employment rate under perfect competition. The workers also make a wage that is less than their marginal value product.

ILLUSTRATIONS

Further Evidence of the North-South Wage Differential

According to economic theory, real wages will be equalized across industries and regions. This process can come about from labor migrating to the higher wage region until wages are equalized or from industry moving to the lower wage region until wages are equalized. As indicated in the text, the North-South wage differential tends to disappear when adjusted for cost-of-living differences. Another factor that has tended to equalize wages has been the migration of industry from the North to the South.

Robert Newman found that industry migration to the South is the result of three factors: (1) the lowering of state corporate income taxes in the South relative to the North, (2) less unionization in the South, and (3) a more favorable business climate in the South. As industry moves South, the demand for labor in the South increases. The result is higher wages in the South than before and the elimination of any regional wage differential.

[See Robert J. Newman, "Industry Migration and Growth in the South," *Review of Economics and Statistics* 65 (February 1983): 76-86.1

Baseball Player's Market

For many years, the professional baseball player's market was a monopsony. The device used by the owners to maintain their monopsony position was the reserve clause, which prohibited a player from negotiating with other teams. The team that first signed a player had the rights to the player as long as he played professional baseball or until the team traded him to another team. When he was traded, the player's contract was owned by the new team. A player could quit playing baseball but could not sell his services to the highest bidder within baseball.

Under the reserve clause a player could negotiate with only one buyer--the team that owned his contract. Hence the team had monopsony power. We would expect the player to earn less than his marginal value product under these circumstances. In 1976, the Supreme Court ruled that the reserve clause was unconstitutional. A player may now sell his services to the highest bidder once his contract runs out. As a result, players' salaries have risen considerably, which suggests that under the reserve clause, they were earning less than their marginal value product.

The average salary of a baseball player in 1967 was less than $50,000. In 1976, the year the reserve clause was declared unconstitutional, the average salary had risen to approximately $75,000. According to the Associated Press, the 2001 average salary was $2,264,403.

KEY CONCEPTS

marginal value product
derived demand
substitution effect
output effect

marginal revenue product
monopsony
marginal input cost
average input cost

REVIEW QUESTIONS

True/False

_____ 1. A firm's short-run demand curve for labor has the same shape as the marginal physical product curve for labor.

_____ 2. The marginal value product of labor curve is the firm's demand curve for labor.

_____ 3. When all inputs are variable, the firm's demand curve for labor slopes downward if labor and capital are complements but slopes upward if labor and capital are substitutes.

_____ 4. The substitution effect of a change in the wage rate is illustrated by a movement along an isoquant.

_____ 5. The competitive firm's demand curve for labor assumes a given product price.

_____ 6. The movement along an industry demand curve for labor causes the competitive firm's demand curve for labor to shift.

_____ 7. The competitive industry's demand curve for labor is found by horizontally adding up all the firm's demand curves for labor.

_____ 8. The input demand curve is more elastic the greater the elasticity of demand for the good produced.

_____ 9. The supply curve of labor to a competitive firm slopes upward due to the law of diminishing marginal returns.

_____ 10. In the long run, we expect labor to receive the same wage regardless of which industry employs them.

_____ 11. A firm with monopoly power in the product market will also have monopoly power in input markets.

_____ 12. A monopoly would hire more workers if it set its product price equal to marginal cost rather than setting $MR = MC$.

_____ 13. A monopsony hires fewer workers than a competitive industry but pays a higher wage.

Multiple Choice/Short Answer

1. Profits will be increased by hiring additional workers as long as
    a. the marginal product of labor times the price of the good produced exceeds the wages that must be paid.
    b. the marginal product of labor exceeds the wages that must be paid.
    c. the marginal value product is less than the wages paid.
    d. the marginal revenue product exceeds the marginal value produce.

2. In the short run, marginal value product slopes downward because
    a. product price falls as the competitive firm produces more output.
    b. of the law of diminishing marginal returns.
    c. of decreasing returns to scale.
    d. the marginal revenue curve slopes downward.

3. The competitive firm's short-run demand curve for labor is
    a. the marginal physical product curve.
    b. the marginal value product curve.
    c. the marginal revenue curve.
    d. None of the above.

4. If the product price increases as a result of an increase in demand,
    a. the firm moves down its marginal value product curve.
    b. the firm moves up its marginal value product curve.
    c. the marginal value product curve shifts to the left.
    d. the marginal value product curve shifts to the right.

5. When all inputs are variable, an increase in labor employed causes the marginal value product curve of capital to shift, which
    a. causes further movement along the MVP_L curve.
    b. causes the wage rate to increase.
    c. causes the firm's long-run demand curve for labor to shift.
    d. causes the MVP_L curve to shift.

6. If labor and capital are complements and the amount of capital increases, then the MVP_L curve shifts to the _____; if labor and capital are substitutes and the amount of capital increases, then the MVP_L curve shifts to the _____.
    a. right; left
    b. right; right
    c. left; right
    d. left; left

7.	If the price of labor falls, the movement along an isoquant is called the _____ effect.

8.	To derive the industry demand curve for an input we must take into account
	a. that increased output will affect the price of the product.
	b. the substitutability or complementarity of the input.
	c. whether or not the input is a normal input.
	d. that a competitive firm's demand curve is horizontal.

9.	The demand for an input is a _____ demand.

10.	The input demand curve will be more elastic the
	a. less elastic the demand for the product being produced.
	b. more difficult it is to substitute one input for another.
	c. more elastic the supply curve of other inputs.
	d. shorter the time allowed for adjustment.

11.	Under perfect competition, the market-determined input price equals
	a. marginal revenue.
	b. marginal product.
	c. average revenue product.
	d. marginal value product.

12.	In the long run, identical inputs receive the same wages regardless of which industry employs them because
	a. its the law.
	b. firms will pay only the lowest wage workers are receiving anywhere else.
	c. workers will move to higher-paying industries until wages are equalized.
	d. None of the above. Wages are not always equalized across industries.

13.	If there are two industries that hire labor and the demand for labor increases in one industry, the quantity demanded of labor in the other industry will
	a. be unchanged.
	b. increase.
	c. decrease.
	d. Can't tell from the information.

14.	Other things equal, a monopolist will hire (more/less) than would be hired by a competitive industry.

15. In the short run, the monopolist's demand curve for the variable input is its
    a. marginal product curve.
    b. marginal value product curve.
    c. marginal revenue curve.
    d. marginal revenue product curve.

16. A monopolist pays a wage that is
    a. higher than would be paid by a competitive industry.
    b. lower than would be paid by a competitive industry.
    c. the same as would be paid by a competitive industry.
    d. Any of the above are possible.

17. The difference between a monopsonist and competitive firms is that
    a. the monopsonist faces a downward sloping demand curve for the input.
    b. the monopsonist must reduce wages in order to hire more workers.
    c. the monopsonist must raise wages in order to hire more workers.
    d. the monopsonist's marginal revenue curve differs from its demand curve.

18. Other things equal, a monopsonist pays a wage rate that is
    a. lower than would be paid by a monopolist.
    b. higher than would be paid by a monopolist.
    c. the same as would be paid by a monopolist.
    d. any of the above are possible.

Discussion Questions and Problems

Questions 1 and 2 use the following information.

Number of workers	Output	MP_L	Price of good	MVP_L
100	1000		$10	
110	1200		10	
120	1350		10	
130	1460		10	
140	1540		10	
150	1600		10	
160	1640		10	
170	1660		10	
180	1670		10	
190	1675		10	
200	1676		10	

1.   Fill in the blanks in the table.

2.   a. If wages are $40 a day, how many workers will be hired?

 b. If wages are $80 a day, how many workers will be hired?

 c. If the price of the good produced increases to $15 and wages are $60 a day, how many workers will be hired?

 d. If wages are $40/ day and product price falls to $5, how many workers will be hired?

3.   When is the MVP curve the demand curve for an input? Why does it slope down?

4. Assume that capital and labor are complements in production and that both can vary. What are the effects to a competitive firm of an increase in the price of labor?

5. Using Figure 16-1, derive a competitive firm's long-run demand curve for labor when labor and capital are complements and when labor and capital are substitutes. Explain the graph.

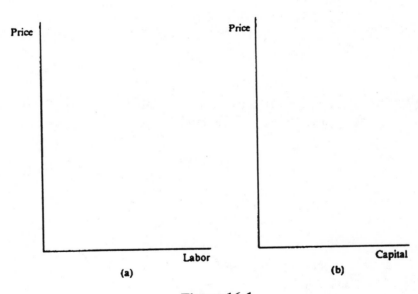

Figure 16-1

6. Using Figure 16-2, explain how an industry demand curve for labor is found. (Let the price of labor increase in your discussion.)

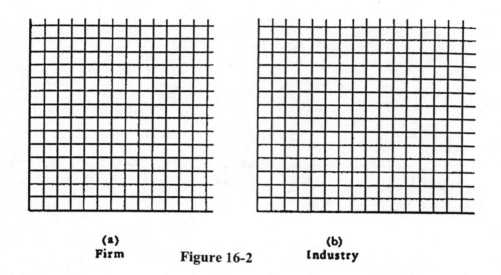

(a)
Firm   Figure 16-2   (b)
Industry

7. What are the four factors that affect the price elasticity of demand for an input? State why each affects the price elasticity of demand for an input as it does.

8. If an input is highly specialized and used in one industry only, will the supply curve be relatively elastic or inelastic? Why?

9. Suppose computer programmers work in two industries-the computer industry and the machine tool industry. The supply curve of computer programmers is upward sloping. What are the effects of each of the following on the employment of computer programmers in each industry and the wages of each?

   a. The demand for computers falls.

   b. There is an influx of computer programmers from abroad.

   c. A third industry starts using computer programmers.

   d. Firms in the machine tool industry increase their purchases of capital equipment.

   e. One-third of the computer programmers are drafted into the Air Force.

10. Suppose real wages differ between the North and the South even though labor is identical and that labor cannot move from one part of the country to the other. Would it be possible to get equalized wage rates across regions in this case? Explain.

11. Suppose the demand for automobiles increases. What are the effects on the price of inputs and the employment of inputs in the automobile industry, and on the employment of inputs in other industries?

12. Robots are being introduced into American manufacturing to perform routine, repetitive tasks previously performed by some types of labor. Suppose there are two types of labor, L_A and L_B, such that L_A and robots are substitutes while robots and L_B are complements. What will be the effects on the wages and employment of the two types of labor?

13. Why does a monopoly producer hire less labor than would be hired if perfect competition prevailed?

14. Since a monopoly charges a higher price than a competitive industry, a worker would rather be employed by a monopolist. Do you agree or disagree? Why?

15. A monopsonist hires less labor and pays a lower wage than prevails under competition. How can this be when the demand curve for labor slopes downward? Illustrate your answer with a graph.

16. Use Figure 16-3.   What is the wage and employment level under the following conditions?
    a. Perfect competition

    b. Monopoly

    c. Monopsony

    d. A firm that is a monopoly in its product market and a monopsony.

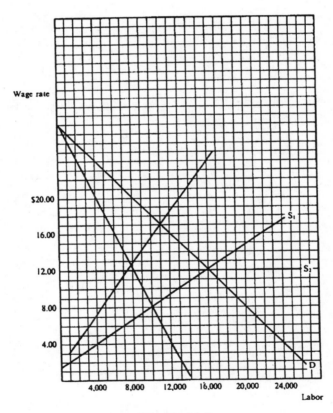

Figure 16-3

The following questions relate to the material in the mathematical appendix.

17. a. Show that a competitive firm hires an input to the point where its marginal value product equals the wage.

b. Why does the competitive firm hire more labor if the wage rate falls?

18. Show formally that a monopolist's demand curve for labor differs from the demand curve for labor of a competitive firm.

ANSWERS

Review Questions

True/False

1. True
2. False. The statement is true when all other inputs are held constant.
3. False
4. True
5. True
6. True
7. False
8. True
9. False. It is horizontal. The law of diminishing marginal returns affects the demand curve for labor.
10. True
11. False
12. True
13. False. It pays a lower wage.

Multiple Choice/Short Answer

1. a
2. b
3. b
4. d
5. d
6. a
7. substitution
8. a
9. derived
10. c
11. d
12. c
13. c
14. less
15. d
16. c
17. c
18. a

Discussion Questions and Problems

Number of workers	Output	MP_L	Price of good	MVP_L
100	1000		$10	
110	1200	20	10	200
120	1350	15	10	150
130	1460	11	10	110
140	1540	8	10	80
150	1600	6	10	60
160	1640	4	10	40
170	1660	2	10	20
180	1670	1	10	10
190	1675	.5	10	5
200	1676	.1	10	1

2. a. 160
    b. 140
    c. 160
    d. 140

3. The MVP curve is the demand curve for an input when the firm is competitive and all other inputs are held constant. Since MVP = (P_x)x(MP), it slopes downward because of the law of diminishing marginal returns.

4. An increase in the price of labor causes a movement along the firm's demand curve for labor. However, the demand curve is not the MVP_L curve. As the price of labor goes up, the firm will reduce the quantity demanded for labor. Since labor and capital are complements, less capital will be used, too, which causes the MVP_L curve to shift to the left. The result is less labor and capital employed by the firm as it produces fewer units of output.

5. See Figure 16-4. The initial equilibrium is at A in panel a and D in panel b. If wages fall to P_{L2} the firm moves to B, and more labor is hired. More labor means that capital is now more productive (labor and capital are complements), so the marginal value product of capital shifts to MVP_K'. More capital is hired (K_2), so the marginal value product of labor shifts to MVP_L'. At a price of P_{L2}, L_3 workers are hired. The long-run demand for labor (d_L) connects points A and C. If labor and capital are substitutes, the move from A to B causes the MVP_K curve to shift to MVP_K'' and less capital is hired ($K_3<K_1<K_2$). Less capital makes labor more productive, so MVP_L shifts to MVP_L'. Again, we get the long-run demand curve for labor of d_L.

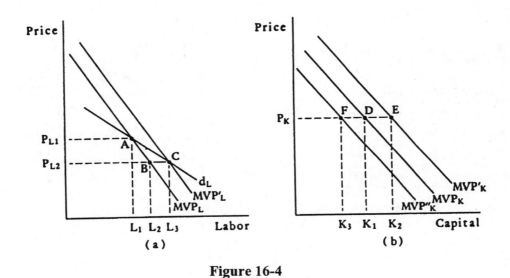

Figure 16-4

6. Refer to Figure 16-5. Let the original wage rate be W_1, so the firm hires l_1, workers and the industry L_1 workers. When the wage rate increases to W_2 the firm moves up its demand curve to point B, where it wishes to hire l_2 workers. But, as each firm does this, industry output falls, which causes product price to increase from P_1 to P_2. The higher product price shifts the firm's demand curve to d', and the firm hires l_3 workers. The summation of the firm's new demand curve is shown as $\Sigma d'(P = P_2)$ on the right-hand graph. The industry does not move to B', but to C', hiring L_3 workers. Hence, the industry demand curve D_L, goes through points A' and C'.

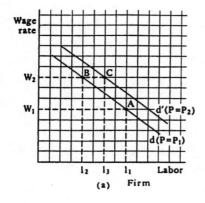
(a)   Firm

Figure 16-5

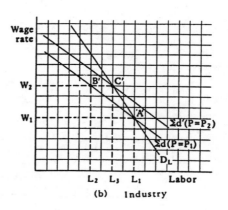
(b)   Industry

7. The input demand curve will be more elastic: (1) the more elastic the demand for the product produced, because the output effect of an input price change will be greater, (2) the easier it is to substitute one input for another, because the substitution effect will be greater, that is, the firm will substitute more of the relatively cheaper input for the relatively more expensive input; (3) the more elastic the supply curves of the other inputs, because the prices of the other inputs will not change as much when the firm alters its purchases of them; (4) the longer the time period allowed for adjustment, because firms can make more complete adjustments in the long run. All long-run demand curves are more elastic than short-run demand curves.

8. Inelastic. The input would not have other industries in which to find employment so the supply curve of the input to the economy and the supply curve of the input to the industry are the same.

9. a. The price of computers falls when the demand for computers falls, which shifts the demand curve for computer programmers in the computer industry to the left. This generates a leftward shift of the total demand for computer programmers and a decline in the wage rate. Some programmers leave the market, while others leave the computer industry and go to the machine tool industry. The final result is that fewer programmers in the entire market fewer programmers in the computer industry, and more in the machine tool industry, with all making lower wages.

    b. The total supply curve of programmers shifts outward, reducing the wage rate in both industries. More programmers are hired in both industries at the lower wage.

    c. Total demand for programmers increases and wages increase. Some programmers move from the computer and machine tool industries to the new industry, and some people enter the market as programmers who had not been working as programmers before.

    d. Assume capital and labor are complements. Increased capital in the machine tool industry makes labor in the industry more productive. The demand curve for labor in the machine tool industry shifts to the right. The rest of the analysis is identical to that in Figure 15.8 in the text, with the machine tool industry as Industry B.

    e. Opposite of part b.

10. If real wages are higher in the North, then the price of capital must be lower in the North than in the South. Capital would move from the North to the South until the price of capital was equalized across the regions. More capital in the South makes southern labor more productive and raises wages. Less capital in the North makes northern labor less productive and reduces wages in the North. The wage rates move toward each other and should equalize.

11.   An increase in the demand for automobiles will lead to an increase in the employment of the inputs used to produce automobiles. Since some inputs are supplied by firms in other industries (such as tires), employment of inputs in those industries will increase too. The increased price for automobiles (due to the increased demand) leads to higher prices paid to inputs in the industry. The higher prices for the inputs will cause other industries to cut back output and employ less of the inputs. Then, inputs will flow into the auto industry, and the industries that supply parts to the auto industry, from the other industries in the economy.

12.   Less L_A will be used in the industries that begin to use robots. This results in wages for L_A falling. L_B is complementary to robots, so the introduction of robots shifts the marginal product curves of L_B outward. This results in higher wages for L_B. Robots must be produced, so the effect on L_A will be attenuated if the robot manufacturers use L_A in the production process. If they use L_B too, wages will increase even more for these workers.

13.   A monopolist can sell additional output only by lowering price. Hence revenues do not increase by the price at which additional output is sold, but by marginal revenue. The contribution to revenues from employing one more unit of the input equals marginal revenue product rather than marginal value product. Since the marginal revenue product curve lies to the left of the marginal value product curve, the monopolist hires less of the input.

14.   Disagree. The worker would not care whether a monopoly or competitive firm hired him or her as long as the supply curve of labor to either was horizontal. The worker's wages will be the same in either case.

15.   Figure 16-6 shows how this happens. The demand curve for labor slopes downward and the supply curve slopes upward. Under competition, L_c units of labor will be hired at a wage of W_c. For the monopsonist, the MC_L curve is relevant because the monopsonist can hire more workers only by raising wages to all workers. The monopsonist sets $MC_L = D_L$ and hires L_m workers, but L_m workers will accept a wage of W_m ($W_m < W_c$).

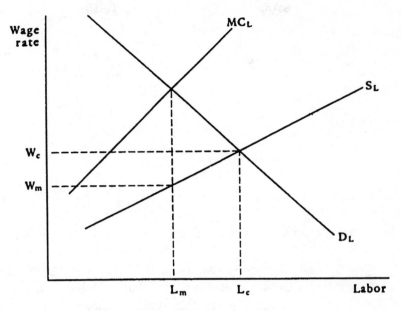

Figure 16-6

16. a. W = $12.00; L = 16,000
     b. W = $12.00; L = 8,000
     c. W = $8.75; L = 11,000
     d. W = $6.75; L = 7,750

17. a. $\pi = P \bullet Q(L,K) - w \bullet L - r \bullet k$ (1)

$\partial\pi/\partial L = P \bullet \partial Q/\partial L - w = O$ (2)

$\partial\pi/\partial K = P \bullet \partial Q/\partial K - r = O$ (3)

Therefore,

$P \bullet \partial Q/\partial L = w$ (4)

$P \bullet \partial Q/\partial K = r$ (5)

$P \bullet \partial Q/\partial L$ is the marginal value product of labor, and is equal to the wage rate.

b. Given (4), a reduction in the wage implies that $P \bullet \partial Q/\partial L$ must decrease. The price of the good is constant, so $\partial Q/\partial L$, the marginal product of labor, must decrease. It will decrease when more labor is used, so the firm will hire more labor at a lower wage.

18. In general, the profit equation is:

$\pi = P(Q) \bullet Q(L,K) - wL - rK$ (6)

The first-order conditions is:

$\partial\pi/\partial L = P \bullet \partial Q/\partial L + (\partial P/\partial Q)(\partial Q/\partial L)Q - w = O$ (7)

This can be rearranged,

$[P + Q(\partial P/\partial Q)]\partial Q/\partial L = w$ (8)

That is, the wage equals marginal revenue product. However, for a competitive firm, $\partial P/\partial Q = 0$ and (8) reduces to

$P \bullet \partial Q/\partial L = w$ (9)

The difference is due to the competitive firm having no effect on price while a monopolist affects price.

CHAPTER 17 *Wages, Rent, Interest, and Profit*

CHAPTER ANALYSIS

The tools developed in the last chapter are used to analyze specific input markets in this chapter. Although the emphasis is on the labor market because labor earnings account for the bulk of national income, the determination of rent, interest, and profits is also analyzed.

17.1-17.2 To derive a worker's supply curve for labor services, we must consider the element of time. Since time is in fixed supply (24 hours a day), the time spent working cannot be used to consume goods or services, sleep, or just relax. We lump all nonwork activities together and label it **leisure**. The 24 hours in a day can be divided into time spent working and time in leisure. A worker who spends one more hour in leisure must spend one less hour in work. If the wage rate is $10 an hour, the worker gives up $810in order to spend one more hour in leisure, that is, the price of an hour of leisure is $10--the wages lost from not working that hour. A change in the wage rate will cause the price of leisure to change in the same direction.

Individuals work to have money to purchase goods and services. The wage rate and the number of hours worked determine a worker's income. The greater the income, the more goods and services the worker can buy. But time is required to enjoy the goods that are bought, so as a person's income increases he or she will want more leisure time. A change in the wage rate will also change the income of the worker and the number of leisure hours the worker wishes to enjoy.

There are two effects of a change in the wage rate, and these effects are in opposition to each other. An increase in the wage rate increases the price of leisure, so the worker will use less hours in leisure (and work more hours). This is the **substitution effect** of an increase in the wage rate. An increase in the wage rate also increases the income of the worker for a given number of hours worked, which enables the worker to purchase more goods and services. However, the worker will also want to increase the time spent in leisure since time is required to enjoy the goods and services. To put this differently, leisure is a normal good, and consumption of leisure increases with income. Thus the increase in the wage rate leads to increased consumption of leisure (fewer hours worked) because of the **income effect**.

If the substitution effect is stronger than the income effect, a worker will work more hours if the wage rate increases. If the income effect is stronger than the substitution effect, the worker will work fewer hours. Figure 17-1 illustrates the case when the worker supplies fewer hours after a wage rate increase. The initial equilibrium is point E and the individual consumes L_1 hours of leisure per week (or 168--L_1 hours of work). If the wage rate increases, the budget line shifts to A'B and the new equilibrium is point E'.

The substitution effect is found by shifting A'B back such that it is tangent to the original indifference curve. The worker reduces consumption of leisure from L_1 to L_2, which is the substitution effect. The income effect is measured by the shift from E" to E', or from L_2 hours of leisure to L_3 hours. In this case, the income effect is greater than the substitution effect, so total time spent on leisure activities increases from L_1 to L_3. If leisure time increases, hours worked falls as a result of a wage increase. Most economists believe an individual's supply curve slopes upward at lower wage rates and bends backward at higher wage rates. (Review Figure 17.3 in the text for further elaboration.)

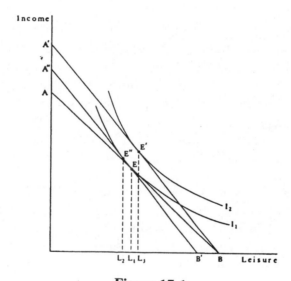

Figure 17-1

The market supply curve for labor can slope upward or bend backward just like the individual's supply curve of labor. The market supply curve of labor is the horizontal summation of individuals' supply curves. For specific industries, the supply curve of labor will be upward sloping and very elastic because workers can move into the industry from other industries in response to higher wages.

17.3-17.4 The determination of the general level of wage rates for the economy as a whole is analyzed by using aggregate demand and supply curves for labor. The aggregate demand curve slopes downward because of the law of diminishing marginal returns. The aggregate supply curve is upward sloping since higher real wages will attract new entrants into the labor market. The interaction of the aggregate demand curve and the aggregate supply curve yields the equilibrium average real wage and the level of employment Over time, demand and supply tend to increase, so whether real wages increase over time depends on whether demand increases faster than supply.

Everyone does not receive the same wage rates. There are three reasons for equilibrium differences in wage rates. First, nonpecuniary characteristics of jobs (such as security, comfort, location, and so on) differ such that some jobs are less desirable than others, *ceteris paribus*. A second reason for wage differentials across jobs is that some jobs require more training than others. The third reason for differences in wage rates is that human beings differ in ability.

17.5 The supplier of an input receives **economic rent** if he or she would be willing to retain the input in its present use for a lower payment. The difference between the payment received and the minimum amount the input supplier must receive to retain the input in its present use is defined as economic rent. For example, if a baseball player making $2,500,000 a year would be willing to play ball for anything more than $100,000 a year, he is receiving $2,400,000 in economic rent. Rents measure the extent to which input owners gain from selling their inputs in a particular market over other market for the input.

17.6 **Unions** are difficult for economists to analyze because there is not a clear-cut goal for the union as there is for consumers (utility maximization) or producers (profit maximization). One possible goal for unions is to maximize the economic rent of the members. Take the case of autoworkers. The demand curve for autoworkers is the sum of all firms that produce autos and car parts. The union representing auto workers then faces this market demand curve for its members. Since it is the monopolist-supplier of autoworkers, it has a marginal revenue curve. As a monopolist producer maximizes profits by equating marginal revenue and marginal cost, so the union can maximize economic rent by equating its "marginal revenue" with the opportunity cost of labor, found on the supply curve. Review Figure 17.8 in the text to make sure you understand this analysis.

17.7-17.10 Review of Sections 5.4 and 5.5 in the text, the background for this material, would be useful. Some people borrow funds in order to spend more today than their current income allows, while others save in order to increase consumption in the future. The demand curve for funds slopes downward just as the demand curve for goods slopes downward. The supply curve for funds slopes upward initially but may bend backward if the income effect of an increase in the interest rate dominates the substitution effect.

Firms borrow funds to enlarge their capital stock and expand production in the future. The **rate of return on an investment** in capital is found by

$$C = R_1/(1+g) + R_2/(1+g)^2 + R_3/(1+g)^3 + \bullet\bullet\bullet + R_n/(1+g)^n$$

where C is the initial cost of the capital equipment, R is the resulting addition to output, n is the number of years the capital equipment is expected to last, and g is the rate of return of the investment (or the **net productivity of an investment**).

Suppose a firm has five investment projects that it can undertake. How will it decide which investments to make and which not to make? As long as the rate of return of an investment is greater than or equal to the rate at which it can borrow funds, the firm will make the investment. If investment A yields a rate of return of 20 percent, B a rate of return of 18 percent, C a rate of return of 16 percent, D a rate of return of 12 percent, and E a rate of return of 7 percent, and the interest rate is 10 percent, then the firm will undertake investments A, B, C, and D. If the interest rate is 15 percent, project D is no longer profitable and the firm will borrow fewer funds.

Thus the firm's demand for investment dollars is inversely related to the interest rate, and the investment demand curve slopes downward. Review Figure 17.9 in the text and make sure that you understand how the equilibrium levels of saving, investment, and the interest rate are determined.

Economic profits are a signal to investors that profitable opportunities exist in the industry. As capital flows to the industry, output expands and the economic profits dissipate. As long as entry into an industry is not blocked, we would expect rates of return to tend toward equality across industries. There is considerable evidence that market forces tend to equalize rates of return across industries.

ILLUSTRATIONS

Baseball Players and Rent

Imagine the career of a superstar baseball player--Johnny Longball. Johnny begins playing baseball for $200,000 a year. If he weren't a baseball player, he would make $30,000 a year working in a gas station. He rapidly becomes a superstar and his salary increases to $8 million. Being handsome and famous, Johnny is given a small part in a movie and does well. A few years later, he is making $8 million a year playing baseball, but he could make $8 million a year making movies. He quits baseball to concentrate on a movie career. He makes $12 million a year in movies, but could make $4 million playing baseball. Finally, he is too old to play baseball, and he would make $100,000 a year coaching baseball if he wasn't making movies.

The portion of Johnny's salary that is rent at various stages in his career is calculated below:

Job	*Salary*	*Next-Best Alternative*	*Salary*	*Rent*
Baseball	$ 200,000	Gas station attendant	$ 30,000	$ 170,000
Baseball	8,000,000	Gas station attendant	30,000	7,970,000
Baseball	8,000,000	Actor	8,000,000	0
Actor	12,000,000	Baseball	4,000,000	8,000,000
Actor	12,000,000	Coach	100,000	11,900,000

Rent is the difference between the return the input owner receives and the return that would have been earned if the input was used differently.

The Intertemporal Behavior of Economic Profits

Economic profits provide a signal to entrepreneurs that encourages them to pull resources out of less profitable or unprofitable uses and put those resources to a more profitable use. If this process continues, the rate of return on investment tends toward equality and economic profits disappear. If there are barriers to entry, this process will not work well and we would not observe rates of return converging toward a normal level.

Connolly and Schwartz studied economic profits to see whether they tend to persist (indicating the existence of barriers to entry) or dissipate over time (indicating that resources are reallocated toward profitable activities). They examined 699 firms between 1961 and 1980 and found that high profits dissipated over time. That is, profits tended to converge to normal levels over time, indicating that market forces tend to work as our theory predicts.

[See Robert A. Connolly and Steven Schwartz, "The Intertemporal Behavior of Economic Profits," *International Journal of Industrial Organization,* 3 (December 1985): 379-400.]

KEY CONCEPTS

leisure
compensating wage differentials
human capital investment
economic rent
interest rate
gross marginal productivity of capital
net marginal productivity of capital
investment demand curve
nominal interest rate
real interest rate
present discounted value
net present value

REVIEW QUESTIONS

True/False

_____ 1. In the income-leisure model, painting one's house is considered labor.

_____ 2. An increase in the wage rate makes leisure more expensive.

_____ 3. People work more hours when the wage rate increases.

_____ 4. The aggregate supply curve of labor is inelastic.

_____ 5. Anything that increases the marginal productivity of labor tends to increase real wages.

_____ 6. In long-run equilibrium, all wage rates are equal.

_____ 7. If the supply curve of an input is perfectly inelastic, the entire return to the input is considered economic rent.

_____ 8. The income effect of a higher interest rate is the same for borrowers and lenders.

_____ 9. Investing more today means that future incomes will be greater.

_____ 10. Since the rates of return are never equal for all industries, there is no tendency for rates of return to equalize.

Multiple Choice/Short Answer

Questions 1 to 3 refer to Figure 17-2.

1. The slope of line AB measures
   a. income.
   b. the wage rate.
   c. hours worked.
   d. hours of leisure.

2. Are there more or fewer hours worked at point F than point E?

3. If the wage rate changes such that the budget line shifts from AB to A'B, does the wage rate increase or decrease?

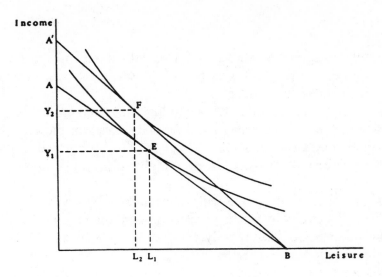

Figure 17-2

4. Which of following statements is correct?
   a. The substitution effect of a higher wage encourages less work, and the income effect encourages less work.
   b. The substitution effect of a higher wage encourages more work, and the income effect encourages more work.
   c. The substitution effect of a higher wage encourages less work, and the income effect encourages more work.
   d. The substitution effect of a higher wage encourages more work, and the income effect encourages less work.

5. An individual's supply curve of labor will bend backwards when
   a. the income effect of a higher wage is greater than the substitution effect.
   b. the substitution effect of a higher wage is greater than the income effect.
   c. the income and substitution effects of a higher wage reinforce each other.
   d. leisure is a Giffen good.

345

6. Which of the following are true statements? (More than one may be correct.)
   a. High wages in the United States makes it impossible for U.S. firms to compete with foreign firms that use cheap labor.
   b. High wages in the United States are due to high marginal productivity of labor.
   c. High wages in the United States are due to increases in the labor force that bring skilled workers into the work force.
   d. Wages in the United States would be even higher if immigration was prohibited.

7. One of the major causes of declining real wages in the 1970s was that
   a. the labor force increased by a much greater amount than usual.
   b. imports from Japan increased rapidly.
   c. the demand for labor increased greatly.
   d. energy prices increased sharply.

8. List the three factors that cause equilibrium differences in wage rates.

9. In Figure 17-3, which supply curve generates the least amount of rent?
   a. I
   b. II
   c. III
   d. IV

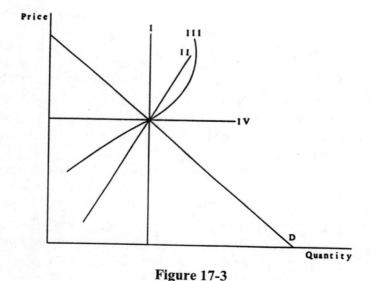

Figure 17-3

346

10. If a union raises the prevailing wage rate by restricting the number of workers, it also
    a. creates a deadweight cost.
    b. maximizes its profits.
    c. maximizes its rent.
    d. none of the above.

11. An increase in the interest rate causes
    a. the income of borrowers to rise and the income of lenders to rise.
    b. the income of borrowers to rise and the income of lenders to fall.
    c. the income of borrowers to fall and the income of lenders to rise.
    d. the income of borrowers to fall and the income of lenders to fall.

12. Firms will invest in capital as long as
    a. the gross marginal productivity of capital exceeds zero.
    b. the rate of return exceeds the cost of borrowed funds.
    c. the rate of return is positive.
    d. they have funds to invest.

13. Greater investment in the present
    a. reduces current consumption and reduces the capacity to produce goods in the future.
    b. increases current consumption and increases the capacity to produce goods in the future.
    c. reduces current consumption and increases the capacity to produce goods in the future.
    d. increases current consumption and reduces the capacity to produce goods in the future.

14. If the demand for investment funds increases, the interest rate on consumer loans will
    a. increase.
    b. decrease.
    c. remain the same.
    d. Can't tell without more information.

15. Interest rates tend to be greater
    a. the lower the risk.
    b. the shorter the duration of the loan.
    c. the greater the costs of administering the loan.
    d. for local governments than for private firms.

Discussion Questions and Problems

1. In Figure 17-4, draw a budget line when the wage rate is (a) $8 an hour; (b) $4 an hour, (c) $12 an hour; (d) $8 an hour for 40 hours of work and time-and-a-half for overtime.

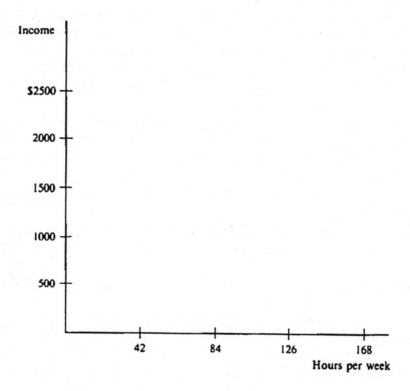

Figure 17-4

2. At $8 an hour, Bill earns $352 a week. How many hours does he spend in leisure activity? At $9 an hour, he earns $387 a week. How many hours does he spend in leisure activity? Is Bill's income or substitution effect stronger at these wage rates? How do you know?

3. You have the following information about Carol's earnings. In Figure 17-5 draw her supply curve for labor.

Wage Rate	Weekly Income
$7.00	$273
7.50	315
8.00	352
8.50	391
9.00	423
9.50	456
10.00	470
10.50	472.50
11.00	462

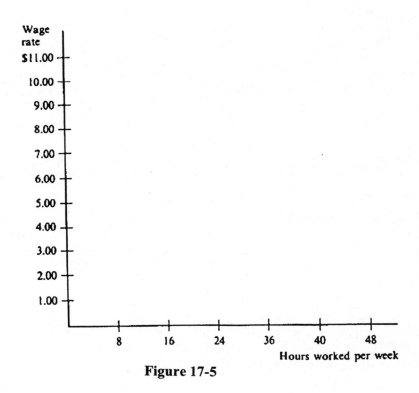

Figure 17-5

4. In Figure 17-6, derive an individual's supply curve of labor such that it bends backward at $10 an hour. Use wage rates $5, $8, $10, $12, and $15.

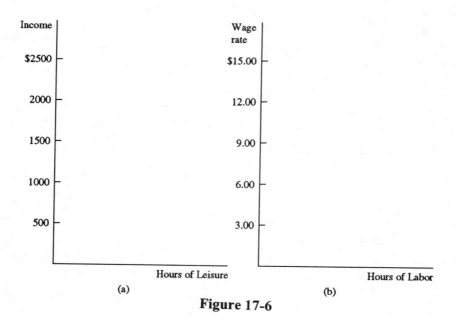

Figure 17-6

5. Explain how an individual worker can have a backward-bending labor supply curve.

6. If a worker likes to work, he or she will not have a backward-bending labor supply curve. Do you agree or disagree? Why?

7.   Use a graph of the income-leisure model to explain why firms often pay time-and-a-half for overtime work. *(Hint:* Think how the budget line is affected.)

8.   Why are real wages higher in the United States than in less developed countries?

9.   Explain why wage differentials can persist over time with the labor markets in equilibrium.

10. What is economic rent, and how is it related to the elasticity of supply of an input?

11.   Use a graph to show that rent to the owner of an input is analogous to consumer surplus for a consumer.

12.   Suppose a union want to maximize rent of its members. What should it do?

13.   How is the supply curve of loanable funds analogous to the supply curve of labor?

14.   Suppose the interest rate is 10 percent and the expected rate of return on an investment is 8 percent. Should the firm make the investment if it has to borrow the funds to make the investment? Why or why not? Should the firm make the investment if it does not have to borrow the funds but can use current profits to make the investment? Why or why not?

15.   There is a tendency for rates of return on investments to equalize. Would this be true of rates of return on investments in education? That is, would we expect the rate of return to an accountant and the rate of return to a historian to equalize over time? Explain.

16.   If interest rates are higher when the duration of a loan is longer, why are mortgage rates lower than the interest rates on short-term consumer loans?

ANSWERS

Review Questions

True/False

1. False
2. True
3. False
4. True
5. True
6. False
7. True
8. False
9. True
10. False. Demand and supply conditions change often, so the differences indicate a disequilibrium. Over time, the rates of return tend toward equalization.

Multiple Choice/Short Answer

1. b
2. more
3. Increase
4. d
5. a
6. b, d
7. a
8. Variations in the innate attractiveness of jobs; differences in human capital investment; differences in ability
9. d. There is no rent if the supply curve is perfectly elastic.
10. a. The union would not be maximizing its economic rent, but the economic rent of its members. We also cannot be sure that this would be its goal or not.
11. c
12. b
13. c
14. a
15. c

Discussion Questions and Problems

1. See Figure 17-7.
   a. Budget line AB
   b. Budget line AC
   c. Budget line AD
   d. Budget line AEF

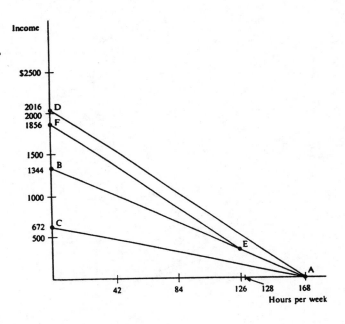

Figure 17-7

2. 124 hours of leisure. 125 hours of leisure. Bill's income effect is greater than his substitution effect because he consumes more leisure at the higher wage rate.

3. See Figure 17-8.

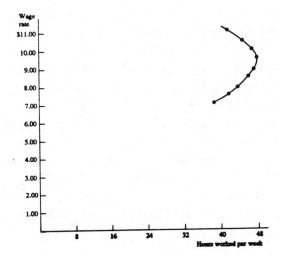

Figure 17-8

4.   See Figure 17-9.

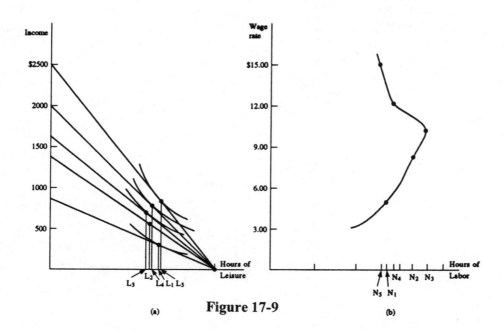

Figure 17-9

5.   An increase in the wage rate has two effects--a substitution effect and an income effect. The higher wage makes leisure more costly, so the worker will consume less leisure. The substitution effect causes the worker to work more hours. Leisure is a normal good, so the worker at a higher wage will want to consume more leisure.   The income effect causes the worker to work fewer hours.   The worker's labor supply curve will be backward-bending if the substitution effect is greater than the income effect at lower wage rates, but the income effect is greater than the substitution effect at higher wages.

6.   Disagree. As long as leisure is a normal good, the income effect of a higher wage will be to work fewer hours. If the worker likes to work, his or her supply curve may not bend backwards as soon as it would if he didn't like to work, but it will still bend backward eventually. (No one can work 24 hours a day.)

7. In Figure 17-10, AB is the budget line facing the worker if there is no overtime. The worker's equilibrium position is point E, where he or she consumes L_1 hours of leisure (works 168 - L_1 hours a week). Line CD has a steeper slope than AB, indicating the time-and-a-half wages for overtime. The new equilibrium is point F, where the worker consumes less leisure and works more hours. Offering time and a half for overtime raises the price of leisure, which tends to increase the importance of the substitution effect.

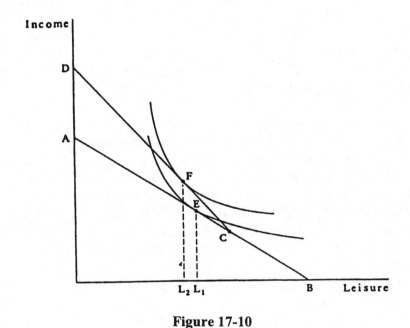

Figure 17-10

8. The marginal productivity of labor is greater in the United States than in the less developed countries. In the United States, labor works with more capital than labor in the less developed countries, which makes U.S. labor more productive. Further, U.S. labor is better educated (more human capital), is healthier, and has access to greater technological knowledge.

357

9.   There are three factors that can cause wage differentials to persist. First, the innate attractiveness of jobs differs. People take into consideration the work environment as well as the salary when looking for a job. Second, people's productivity depends partially on their training and education, so those with more human capital earn a higher wage. Third, people differ with respect to ability. Those with abilities that are scarce relative to demand earn a higher wage.

10.   Economic rent is the portion of the payment to the supplier of an input that is in excess of the minimum amount necessary to retain the input in its present use. If the supply curve is perfectly elastic, there is no rent since all inputs would change jobs if any firm tried to reduce its payments to the inputs. When a supply curve is perfectly inelastic, the entire payment to the input is rent because the same quantity would be available at a zero price. The more inelastic the supply curve of the input, the greater the portion of the input's remuneration is rent.

11.   Consumer surplus and rent are illustrated in Figure 17-11. Initially, let the demand curve be the demand curve for a good. Consumer surplus is measured by the area of the triangle ABP_c. For any quantity less than Q_c consumers would be willing to pay more than P_c. Since they have to pay only P_c, they are receiving more value than they are paying for. Now let the supply curve be the supply curve for labor. Rent is measured by the triangle W_cBC. Many workers would be willing to work for less than W_c, but they don't have to. They receive more pay than the minimum necessary to work in their present place of employment. In both cases, the benefits received by people exceeds their costs.

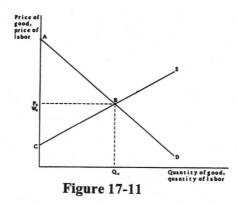

Figure 17-11

358

12. The union takes the market demand curve for labor as the demand curve it faces. It is downward-sloping, so the union can also calculate a marginal revenue curve. By equating marginal revenue and the marginal opportunity cost, which is the supply curve of labor, the union finds the amount of workers and wage that maximizes the economic rent of the workers.

13. Both supply curves can be backward bending. The income effect of a higher wage encourages greater consumption of leisure or fewer hours worked. Similarly, the income effect of a higher interest rate on a saver encourages more present consumption or less saving.

14. The firm should not make the investment in either case. Clearly the firm would not want to borrow money at 10 percent if it will make a return of only 8 percent. It will not want to use its profits to make the investment either, because it could make 10 percent by loaning the money to others who have investment opportunities that generate at least a 10 percent rate of return.

15. Yes, we would expect them to move toward equality. If the return for an accountant exceeded that of a historian, more students would become accounting majors and fewer would major in history. This would continue until the rates of return moved closer together.

16. Mortgages are secured by the house, so the risk to the lender is not as great as with a loan with no collateral.

CHAPTER 18 *Using Input Market Analysis*

CHAPTER ANALYSIS

This chapter presents applications that use the tools developed in Chapters 16 and 17. In order to analyze real-world labor markets, the correct labor supply curve must be used because of the differences in the elasticity of supply of the aggregate supply curve and industry supply curves. Note which supply curve is used in the applications, when it is appropriate to use supply and demand analysis, and when it is appropriate to use the income-leisure model.

ILLUSTRATIONS

Markets and the Jim Crow Laws

The Jim Crow era in the South is identified with the period from the late nineteenth century to the middle of the twentieth century when a legally enforced system of racial segregation existed. There is a growing literature documenting the effects of market forces on economic discrimination prior to the Jim Crow era. This literature shows that market forces often did not generate segregation, and that the white majority responded by enacting legislation that mandated segregation. These laws were passed because the marketplace did not generate the results that the politically powerful wanted.

Studies have found that segregation of streetcars was fought by the streetcar companies,[1] that railroads were integrated prior to legislation that prohibited the practice,[2] and that competitive pressure in southern labor markets tended to equalize equal payments for equal work.[3] Jennifer Roback concludes, "The evidence indicates that the law, not the market, was the chief oppressor of blacks in the Jim Crow era."[4]

---

[1] Jennifer Roback, "The Political Economy of Segregation: The Case of Segregated Streetcars," *Journal of Economic History*, 46 (1986): 893-917.

[2] Charles Lofgren, *The Plessy Case: A Legal-Historical Interpretation*. (New York: Oxford University Press, 1987).

[3] Rober Higgs, "Firm-Specific Evidence on Racial Wage Differentials and Workforce Segregation," *American Economic Review*, 67 (March 1977): 236-245.

[4] Jennifer Roback, "Southern Labor Law in the Jim Crow Era: Exploitative or Competitive?" *University of Chicago Law Review*, 51 (Fall 1984): 1161-1192.

Who's Discriminated Against the Most

In a study concerning discrimination against minority- and women-owned firms in the Louisiana construction industry, owners were asked whether they thought the contracting system used by the state discriminated against various groups. The groups were blacks, French-Acadiens, women, and Other, which included Hispanics, Asians, and Native Americans. Each targeted group perceived that discrimination against their group was greater than discrimination against any other group. That is, more blacks believed firms owned by blacks faced discrimination than believed that firms owned by women, or by members of other racial or ethnic groups faced discrimination. Similarly, more women believed firms owned by women faced discrimination than believed firms owned by blacks faced discrimination, and so on. While each group perceived discrimination against themselves to be greater than against any other group, clearly each group cannot be correct.

[See John Lunn and Huey L. Perry, "Justifying Affirmative Action: Highway Construction in Louisiana," *Industrial and Labor Relations Review*, 46 (April 1993): 464-479.

KEY CONCEPTS

disemployment effect

efficiency wage

crowding-out effect

REVIEW QUESTIONS

Multiple Choice/Short Answer

1. Use Figure 18-1 in answering questions a to e.
    a. How many unskilled laborers will be hired if there is no minimum wage?
    b. How many unskilled laborers will be hired if the minimum wage is $5.00?
    c. At a minimum wage of $5.00, how many workers will want jobs?
    d. How many unskilled workers are disemployed as a result of the minimum wage?
    e. How many unskilled workers are unemployed as a result of the minimum wage?

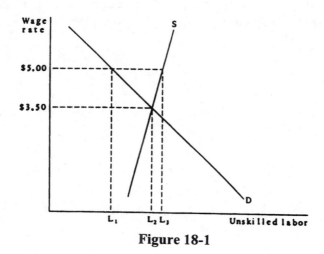

Figure 18-1

2. Among unskilled workers, the most productive workers will be most likely to lose their jobs as a result of the minimum wage.   True   False

3. An efficiency wage is
    a. another term for the prevailing market wage rate.
    b. a wage higher than the prevailing market wage that increases firms' profits.
    c. a wage lower than the prevailing market wage that decreases firms' profits.
    c. the wage rate at which the unemployment rate is minimized.

4. As the minimum wage has risen over time and the share of industries covered by the minimum wage has expanded,
   a. the unemployment rate of minority teenagers has risen relative to the unemployment rate of white teenagers.
   b. the share of the workers who receive minimum wage that are in poor households has increased.
   c. the poverty rate has fallen.
   d. All of the above.

5. If the aggregate supply curve of labor is very inelastic, the burden of the Social Security tax
   a. falls mostly on consumers because the price of goods increases.
   b. falls mostly on the firms.
   c. falls mostly on the workers.
   d. depends on how much of the tax is collected from employees and how much from employers.

6. The long-run effects of a rise in the Social Security tax is that
   a. wage rates will rise.
   b. wage rates will fall.
   c. wage rates will stay the same.
   d. wage rates will fall initially but return to their previous level in long-run equilibrium.

7. One way to make the burden of the social security tax more equitable between employers and employees would be to
   a. increase the share of the tax paid by employers.
   b. increase the share of the tax paid by employees.
   c. raise the social security tax rate.
   d. None of the above.

8. A cartel of buyers reduces the wage rate paid to workers by
   a. increasing employment and moving down the labor-demand curve.
   b. replacing skilled labor with unskilled labor and capital.
   c. lowering the product price, which lowers the value of the marginal product of labor.
   d. restricting employment collectively.

9. A cartel of employers is
   a. common since the cartel lowers labor costs and increases profits.
   b. common because there are no laws against such cartels.
   c. rare because unions have the power to prevent the formation of the cartels.
   d. rare because so many firms in different industries would have to coordinate their activities.

10. Which of the following is evidence that the NCAA has established a monopsony-like result for college athletics?
    a. Not all athletes graduate from college.
    b. Many schools offer illegal inducements to athletes.
    c. Revenues for college athletes has increased due to television.
    d. All of the above.

11. Who is harmed by the NCAA rules?
    a. Sports fans.
    b. Athletes in non-revenue generating sports.
    c. Administrators of small private colleges.
    d. Athletes in revenue generating sports.

12. If some, but not all, employers discriminate against blacks, then we would observe
    a. segregated employment patterns but not wage rate differentials.
    b. segregated employment patterns and wage rate differentials.
    c. wage rate differentials but not segregated employment patterns.
    d. neither wage rate differentials nor segregated employment patterns.

13. Racial or sexual discrimination is more likely in nonprofit organizations than in profit-making organizations.
    True   False

14. Which of the following explain part of the gap between the wages received by African-Americans and whites in the United States? (More than one answer may be correct.)
    a. The median age of African Americans is higher than the median age of whites.
    b. On average, whites have more schooling than African-Americans.
    c. The percentage of whites that are married is greater than the percentage of African-Americans who are married.
    d. A higher percentage of African-Americans than whites live in urban areas.

15. Which of the following explain part of the gap between the wages received by women and the wages received by men? (More than one answer may be correct.)
    a. Men work more hours per week than women.
    b. On average, men have more schooling than women.
    c. Women tend to choose lower-paying majors.
    d. The median age of men is higher than the median age of women.

Discussion Questions and Problems

1. Use a two-part graph to show that the effect of the minimum wage on unemployment depends on the elasticity of demand for labor and the elasticity of supply of labor.

2. Some areas have a lower minimum wage for teenagers than for adults. Can you offer any reasons for such a system?

3.   There are people who want a "living wage" law passed, which would require all jobs to provide enough income that a family of four could live on it. What would be the economic effects of such a law?

4.   People who are self-employed have to pay the entire Social Security tax themselves. Does this mean that self-employed people bear a larger share of the Social Security tax than workers who are not self-employed? Explain.

5.   Analyze the effects of a national health insurance program financed by payroll taxes on workers and employers paid entirely by employers.

6.   Explain why the correct answer to Multiple Choice question #7 is d.

7.   Explain how the NCAA is able to keep wages for college athletes below the marginal value product of the athletes. Is the wage below MVP for all college athletes? Explain.

8. Who is harmed by the NCAA's cartel-like behavior? Who benefits?

9. Explain why it is difficult for an input cartel to be successful. If this is so, why is the cartel involving college athletes so successful?

10. What factors other than discrimination might explain the gap between the average wage for women and the average wage for men?

11. Explain why firms that want larger profits are less likely to discriminate when hiring workers.

12. Suppose a study finds that 80 percent of the gap in the wages received by men and women is due to factors such as majors selected, work experience, and hours worked. Does this imply that the remaining gap is due to discrimination? Explain.

ANSWERS

Review Questions

Multiple Choice/Short Answer

1. a. L_2 b. L_1 c. L_3 d. L_2-L_1 e. L_3-L_1
2. False
3. b
4. a
5. c
6. b
7. d
8. d
9. d
10. b. (a) is not evidence since not all students graduated and (c) provides an incentive to colleges to operate sports programs like a business but not evidence of monopsony power.
11. d
12. a
13. True
14. b, c
15. a, c

Discussion Questions and Review

1. The minimum wage will lead to more unemployment the more elastic the demand for unskilled labor and the more elastic the supply of unskilled labor. In Figure 18-2, the supply curve for unskilled labor is vertical, and two demand curves are shown—D_2 is more elastic than D_1. The disemployment effect of the minimum wage is greater for D_2 (L_1-L_3) than for D_1 (L_1-L_2). In Figure 18-3, the demand curve is vertical and S_2 is the more elastic of the supply curves. Again, unemployment is greater after the minimum wage is established for the more elastic supply curve.

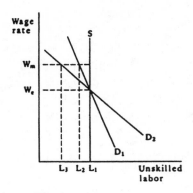

Figure 18-2

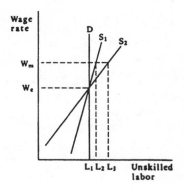

Figure 18-3

2. The minimum wage hurts the least productive workers the most. Teenagers are not very productive generally, so the minimum wage affects teenagers more than adults. The unemployment rate is higher among the teenagers, especially black teenagers, so a lower minimum wage would permit more teenagers to find jobs. The jobs provide opportunities for the teenagers to increase their productivity through work experience, which will increase their earning capabilities when they are older.

3. The "living wage" would have similar effects to the minimum wage. Assuming the living wage would be higher than the minimum wage, the impact on unemployment among unskilled workers would likely increase.

4. The burden of the Social Security tax that is borne by workers does not depend on how the tax is collected. Figure 18.3 in the text shows that the worker bears the entire burden of the tax when the supply curve of labor is vertical. If the supply curve of labor is not vertical, the employer bears some of the burden of the tax. Hence, the self-employed person does bear a larger share of the burden of the tax (all of it) than workers that are not self-employed, as long as the supply of labor is not perfectly inelastic.

5.   Figure 18-4 illustrates the effects of the tax. The demand for labor shifts downward by an amount equal to the payroll tax when the employer has to pay the tax. The new demand curve, D', intersects the supply curve at point B, so the workers receive a wage of W_A. The tax rate is W_B-W_A, so the firm pays this amount to the government. The firm's total expenditure on a worker is W_B. (Note that the effects are identical to those of the Social Security tax. Compare Figure 18-4 to Figure 18.2 in the text.)

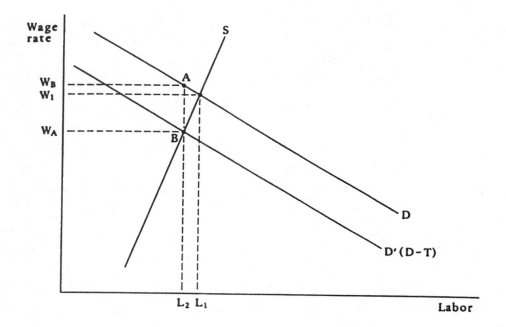

Figure 18-4

6.   The share of the burden of the tax does not depend on who pays the tax. Instead, the share depends on the elasticities of demand and supply of labor. Altering the share of the tax paid will not affect the actual burden of the tax. Raising the social security tax would not affect the distribution of the burden of the tax.

7.   The NCAA determines the maximum financial rewards student athletes can receive and the maximum number of athletes that can receive the awards. By doing so, the NCAA restricts employment of student-athletes, causing a movement down the supply curve of labor and a lower wage. Colleges that offer athletes more than what is allowed and are caught, are punished financially. The wage may not be below MVP for all athletes, especially those in sports that do not generate much revenue.

370

8. The athletes who earn less than their MVP are harmed. Beneficiaries include athletes in non-revenue generating sports who are subsidized by athletes in revenue generating sports, and coaches who have a comparative advantage in recruiting.

9. An input cartel faces more difficulties than an industrial cartel because specific inputs tend to he hired by firms in many industries. For such a cartel to work, many firms in different industries would have to coordinate their actions with respect to the input owners. The costs of doing so would be enormous. Further, like any type of cartel, cheating and new entry would prevent the cartel's success.

10. If wages are determined by productivity, a wage differential between men and women may be due to productivity differences. Many factors affect productivity--age, education, experience, and turnover, to name a few. If these factors differ by sex, productivity can differ and the wage differential would not necessarily be the result only of discrimination.

11. If minorities or women are making lower wages because of discrimination, an employer can increase profits by hiring members of the group(s) facing discrimination. Given that labor costs account for about 70 percent of production costs for American firms, a relatively small decrease in labor costs can have a large impact of the firm's rate of profit.

12. No. Other important factors may have been left out.

CHAPTER 19 *General Equilibrium Analysis and Economic Efficiency*

CHAPTER ANALYSIS

This chapter is concerned with the way various economic arrangements affect the welfare of the members of society. We also recognize that markets are interrelated, and develop a general competitive equilibrium. It is then shown that the general competitive equilibrium is efficient. Chapter 20 introduces and discusses some situations for which a competitive market will not generate efficient outcomes.

19.1 **Partial equilibrium analysis** focuses on individual markets and the characteristics of an equilibrium in those markets. When we use partial equilibrium analysis, we assume that some things, such as the prices of other goods, are held constant when in fact they may change. The *ceteris paribus* assumption of partial equilibrium analysis permits us to focus on the factors most important in determining an equilibrium price and quantity in a given market.

General equilibrium analysis recognizes the interrelationships among markets and focuses on the characteristics of an equilibrium in *each* market simultaneously. All prices are permitted to vary. Although we have considered market interrelationships in studying goods that are complements or substitutes and in studying cross-price elasticity, these analyses do not take into account the interrelationships that exist among all markets. For example, a change in demand for automobiles will affect the demand for tires, a complementary good. But it can also affect the price of cooking utensils by affecting the demand for steel, which affects the price of aluminum, which affects the price of all products made with aluminum, including cooking utensils. Such **spillover effects** into other markets are ignored by partial equilibrium analysis. Further, the spillover effects in one market may also induce changes in that market and have a **feedback effect** on the original market. For example, a change in the demand for automobiles may cause a disequilibrium in the market for motorcycles (spillover effect), but as the market for motorcycles adjusts toward a new equilibrium, it may affect the automobile market (feedback effect). As these examples show, markets are mutually interdependent, a fact that is taken into account in general equilibrium analysis.

Economists use both partial equilibrium and general equilibrium analyses, depending on the problem under consideration. An important area in which general equilibrium analysis has been used successfully is international trade.

18.2 Economists are unwilling to make interpersonal comparisons of utility (or well-being) because an individual's well-being is subjective and personal. Instead, economists attempt to identify **efficient**, or **Pareto optimal**, outcomes. An allocation of resources is efficient (Pareto optimal) if it is impossible, through any feasible change in resource allocation, to make one person better off without making another person worse off. The assessments of being better or worse off are made by the individuals themselves. Any allocation of resources for which it is possible to make at least one person better off without making another person worse off is inefficient.

There is more than one efficient allocation of resources. Figure 19.2 in the text illustrates a welfare frontier, which shows how any allocation of resources affects two individuals. Any point on the welfare frontier is efficient, while any point inside the welfare frontier is inefficient. There is no way to identify the "best" point on the frontier, since interpersonal comparisons of utility would involve value judgements.

19.3　Any economy must find a way to determine how much of each good to produce, how much of each input to use in the production of each good, and how to distribute the goods among consumers. It is desirable that these three tasks are performed in an efficient manner.

In Chapter 6 we examined the distribution of goods among consumers, using the Edgeworth exchange box diagram to illustrate exchange between two consumers. Recall that the contract curve was the locus of points where the consumers' indifference curves were tangent to each other, indicating that the marginal rate of substitution for one consumer equaled the marginal rate of substitution for the other. The equality of the marginal rates of substitution is the necessary condition for consumption to be efficient. The concept was extended to many consumers; in general, an efficient distribution of goods requires the marginal rates of substitution between any two goods are equal for all consumers: $MRS^1 = MRS^2 = \ldots = MRS^i$.

19.4-19.5　Efficiency in production can be analyzed in a similar fashion to efficiency in consumption. An **Edgeworth production box** identifies all the ways that the inputs (labor and land in our example) can be allocated between the production of the two goods. The Edgeworth production box is analogous to the Edgeworth exchange box presented in Chapter 6.

An Edgeworth production box is derived and used in Figures 19.3 and 19.4 in the text. Make sure you understand these graphs. The contract curve is the locus of points at which an isoquant for food is tangent to an isoquant for clothing, and any point on the contract curve is a possible equilibrium point because the condition of cost minimization is met: $w/\upsilon = MP_L/MP_A = MRTS_{LA}$. Just as the contract curve in an Edgeworth exchange box with indifference curves is the locus of equilibria that are efficient distribution of goods, so is the contract curve in an Edgeworth production box with isoquants the locus of equilibria that are efficient allocations of inputs. At every point on the contract curve, the **marginal rate of technical substitution** for the production of one good equals the marginal rate of technical substitution for the production of the other good.

Figure 19-1 provides a contract curve for the production of wine and corn. Each point on the contract curve corresponds to a specific rate of wine and corn production that uses all the available land and labor. Figure 19-2 presents a production possibility frontier, which shows the alternative combinations of wine and corn that can be produced with the available land and labor. Each point on the contract curve corresponds to a point on the **production possibility frontier**. That is, point A in Figure 19-1 corresponds to point A in Figure 19-2, B to B, and so on. The slope of the production possibility frontier is called the **marginal rate of transformation** (MRT); it measures the marginal cost of one good in terms of the other. Efficient production implies that we are on the production possibility frontier.

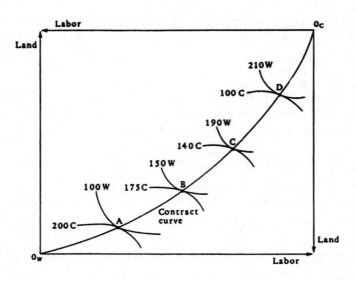

Figure 19-1

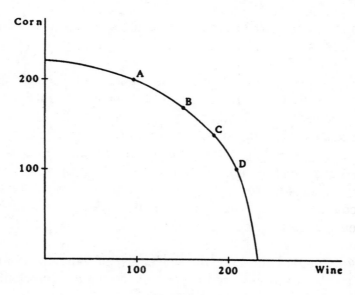

Figure 19-2

374

To produce an efficient output requires that the subjective preferences of consumers be balanced with the objective conditions of production. This condition is met when the slope of the production possibility frontier equals the marginal rates of substitution between the products. Since the marginal rates of substitution equal the price ratio, the marginal rate of transformation also equals the price ratio, MRS=MRT. (Review Figure 19.6 in the text if needed.)

Price equals marginal cost in a competitive industry, so we know that $P_c = MC_c$, $P_w = MC_w$, and $MC_w/MC_c = P_w/P_c$. That is, the ratio of each product's marginal cost equals the ratio of prices. The ratio of monetary marginal costs is the slope of the production possibility frontier and the ratio of prices is the slope of the consumer budget line. Since consumers equate their MRS_{wc} to the price ratio, the MRS of a consumer equals the MRT. When the total quantities of wine and corn demanded by all consumers equal the quantities produced, at the prevailing prices, the product markets are in equilibrium.

19.6 It is now easy to show that perfect competition is efficient. Since each consumer equates his or her MRS with the price ratio and the price ratio is the same for everyone, the MRSs of everyone will be equal. Thus there is an efficient distribution of goods among consumers.

Similarly, when each firm minimizes cost, it equates the marginal rate of technical substitution between the inputs to the input price ratio. Under competition, all firms face the same input prices, so the MRTS is the same for all firms. This is the condition for efficiency in production. Finally, perfectly competitive firms equate price and marginal cost. The ratio of prices equals MRS and the ratio of marginal costs equals MRT, so MRS=MRT. Thus efficient output is achieved, and perfect competition is efficient.

The chart below summarizes the conditions and criteria necessary for economic efficiency.

Efficiency Conditions	Criteria
1. Distribution of products among consumers must be efficient.	$MRS^H_{wc} = MRS^S_{wc}$
2. Allocation of inputs must be efficient.	$MRTS^C_{LA} = MRTS^W_{LA}$
3. The output mix must be efficient.	$MRS_{wc} = MRT_{wc}$

19.7 While perfect competition is efficient, monopoly is not. A monopoly maximizes profits by equating marginal revenue and marginal costs. The result is that P>MC in monopoly, which violates the condition for an efficient output. If there are two goods, x and y, and one is monopolized (x), then $P_x/P_y > MC_x/MC_y$. Consumers equate their MRSs to the price ratio, so $MRS_{yx} = P_x/P_y$. The ratio of the marginal costs equals the MRT. Thus $MRS_{yx} > MRT_{yx}$. Labor unions also cause a misallocation of resources

There are other conditions that prevent an economic equilibrium from being efficient--imperfect information and the presence of externalities and public goods. The latter two situations are discussed in Chapter 20.

ILLUSTRATIONS

Ecology and Economics

Ecology is a branch of biology that deals with the relationships of organisms to their environment and to other organisms. An equilibrium will exist when the populations of the various organisms are constant over time. When this balance of nature is disrupted, the effects can be great.

Suppose, for example, there are farmers and sheep ranchers near a wilderness area. Coyotes occasionally raid the flocks of sheep and kill off some of the sheep. The shepherds may seek to eliminate the coyote population. If they use a partial equilibrium analysis, they may conclude that eliminating the coyotes will save the lives of sheep but have no other effects. A general equilibrium approach recognizes that there are other effects. Coyotes also feed on rabbits and rodents. Extermination of coyotes will result in an increase in the population of rabbits and rodents, which may increase the rate at which crops are destroyed. Rodents carry diseases that may ultimately infect the sheep and reduce the size of the flocks. Given the interrelationship of the organisms in the environment, policies that are designed to affect one organism only will likely affect many other organisms as well. Similarly, policies designed to affect one economic market are likely to affect many other markets as well.

Consumer Sovereignty

The notion of consumer sovereignty is that a competitive market economy produces the goods and services that consumers want. Of course, this does not imply that each and every consumer is able to buy every type of good they want. Some things are too costly to produce--vacations to the moon for example. Markets generally do not produce goods that only a few people want; again, the cost of production would be too high.

There are critics of market organization who claim that the market fails to produce what people "really" want, or need. Instead, the market provides things people really don't want but are persuaded to buy through heavy advertising. Technically, the model of perfect competition assumes perfect information so there is no role for advertising in competitive markets. However, the real world is characterized by imperfect information and advertising provides a useful role. There are numerous examples of heavily-advertised products that failed to garner a market. A prominent example was the Edsel, introduced by Ford a number of years ago. A more recent example is the XFL. The football league was sponsored by a successful wrestling company, shown on two networks, and heavily advertised. After obtaining decent ratings at first, the ratings steadily declined as consumers decided in large numbers that they didn't want the XFL. Consequently, the XFL failed in spite of heavy advertising.

KEY CONCEPTS

general equilibrium analysis
partial equilibrium analysis
spillover effect
feedback effect
Pareto optimality
Efficient
inefficient
welfare frontier
Edgeworth production box
production possibility frontier
marginal rate of transformation

REVIEW QUESTIONS

True/False

_____ 1. The difference between general equilibrium analysis and partial equilibrium analysis is the extent to which market interrelationships are considered.

_____ 2. If we are interested in only one market, then spillover effects are important only if they generate feedback effects.

_____ 3. Every point on the welfare frontier is efficient.

_____ 4. The midpoint on the welfare frontier is the most efficient point.

_____ 5. Every point in an Edgeworth production box corresponds to a point on the production possibility frontier.

_____ 6. The marginal rate of transformation is measured by the slope of the production possibility frontier.

_____ 7. If $MRS_{xy} = 3x/1y$ and $MRT_{xy} = 1x/1y$, then consumers can be made better off by producing more y and less x.

_____ 8. When perfectly competitive markets are in equilibrium, the three conditions for economic efficiency are satisfied.

_____ 9. In a general equilibrium, the rate at which one good can be substituted for another good is equal to the rate at which any consumer would be willing to exchange one good for another good.

_____ 10. Prices serve a rationing function in determining how much of available supplies each person will get .

_____ 11. Under monopoly the marginal rate of substitution is greater than the marginal rate of transformation.

_____ 12. Even though the market power of unions leads to inefficiency, society is still on the production possibilities frontier.

Multiple Choice/Short Answer

1. If steel and aluminum are substitutes and the demand for steel increases, which of the following would be true of the aluminum market?
   a. The supply of aluminum will increase.
   b. The quantity supplied of aluminum will decrease.
   c. The quantity demanded of aluminum will increase.
   d. The demand for aluminum will increase.

2. Assume the change in Question 1 has taken place. Which of the following describes the feedback effect in the steel market?
   a. The supply of steel will increase.
   b. The quantity supplied of steel will decrease.
   c. The demand for steel will increase.
   d. The demand for steel will decrease.

3. If it is possible to make someone better off without making someone else worse off, then the situation is
   a. efficient.
   b. Pareto optimal.
   c. optimal.
   d. inefficient.

Questions 4 through 6 refer to Figure 19-3.

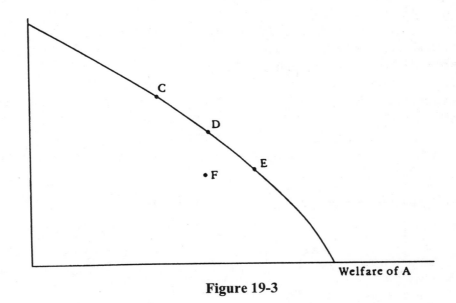

Figure 19-3

4. Points C, D, and E are on the _____.

5. Indicate which of the following statements are true and which are false.
    a. Points C, D, and E are efficient while F is inefficient. True False
    b. Point D is preferred to C.   True False
    c. Point D is preferred to F.   True False
    d. Point C is preferred to F.   True False

6. The movement from F to C
    a. is not an efficient move because C is not an efficient point.
    b. is not an efficient move because it makes A worse off.
    c. is an efficient move because C is an efficient point.
    d. is an efficient move because it makes B better off without harming A.

7. Efficiency in the distribution of products among consumers occurs when
    a. marginal rates of technical substitution are equated.
    b. P=MC.
    c. $P_x = MU_x$.
    d. consumers' marginal rates of substitution are equal.

8. The dimensions of an Edgeworth production box are determined by
    a. the total quantities of the products.
    b. the total quantities of the inputs.
    c. the contract curve.
    d. the tastes of consumers.

Questions 9 and 10 refer to Figure 19-4.

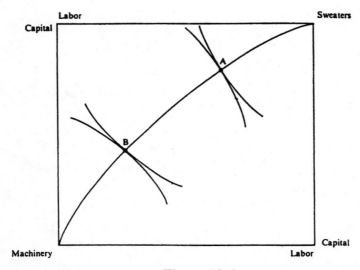

Figure 19-4

9. a. Which good uses relatively more labor than capital?
    b. Which good uses relatively more capital than labor?
    c. The curve connecting the origins is called a _____ curve.

10. Which of the following is a true statement?
    a. The price of labor to price of capital ratio is greater at B than at A.
    b. The price of labor used to produce sweaters is greater than the price of labor used to produce machinery.
    c. The price of labor to price of capital ratio is greater at A than at B.
    d. The price of labor to price of capital ratio is the same at A and B, since the same amount of labor and capital exists at both points.

11. If the contract curve is a straight line connecting the two origins, then the production possibility frontier is
    a. bowed out.
    b. bowed in.
    c. a straight line.
    d. Can't tell without more information.

12. The slope of the production possibility frontier measures
    a. the marginal cost of one good in terms of the other.
    b. the marginal cost of substitution.
    c. the marginal rate of technical substitution.
    d. the input price ratio.

13. In Figure 19-5, which output is efficient?
    a. A.
    b. B.
    c. C.
    d. D.

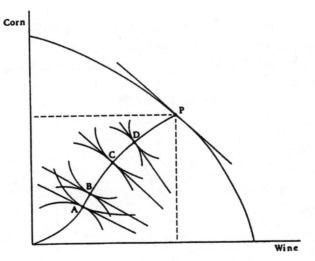

Figure 19-5

14. Efficiency in output occurs when
    a. marginal rates of substitution are equal.
    b. MRS=MRT.
    c. $P_x = MU_x$.
    d. marginal rates of technical substitution are equal.

15. A perfectly competitive economy results in an efficient distribution of products among consumers because
    a. firms maximize profits by equating price and marginal cost.
    b. firms minimize costs.
    c. all consumers face the same prices.
    d. P=MC.

16. Monopoly is inefficient because it does not satisfy which condition for efficiency?
    a. Distribution of goods among consumers.
    b. Allocation of inputs among firms.
    c. Output mix.
    d. Monopoly does not satisfy any of the conditions.

17. An important function of price is to
    a. ration existing supplies among consumers.
    b. distribute goods fairly to the consumers who need them most.
    c. Both of the above.
    d. None of the above.

18. General equilibrium analysis should be used instead of partial equilibrium analysis when
    a. a change in conditions affects primarily one market.
    b. a change in conditions affects many markets but the quantitative effects are small.
    c. a change in condition affects many markets at the same time or to the same degree.
    d. a change in conditions has no feedback effects. An important function of price is to

Discussion Questions and Problems

1. What are the primary differences between partial equilibrium analysis and general equilibrium analysis?

2.   The spillover and feedback effects of a tax on margarine are discussed in the text. What other markets would be affected by a tax on margarine? What would be the spillover and feedback effects?

3.   How is it determined whether an allocation of resources is efficient or inefficient?

4.   Any point on the welfare frontier is preferred to any point inside the frontier. Do you agree or disagree? Why?

5.   Redistributing income from the rich to the poor generally is efficient. Do you agree or disagree? Why?

6. Explain how the contract curve in an Edgeworth production box is found and why a general equilibrium must lie on the contract curve.

7. Explain how a production possibility frontier is derived.

8. What does the slope of the production possibility frontier measure? How is this slope related to the general competitive equilibrium of consumers?

9. Suppose the production possibility frontier between corn and wine is a straight line with a slope of - 1.

   a. What do we know about the competitive general equilibrium?

   b. Suppose the demand for corn increases. What effects will there be?

10. State the three conditions for economic efficiency and provide an intuitive explanation of each.

11. Explain why perfect competition is Pareto optimal.

12. Assume we are initially at point A on the production possibility frontier shown in Figure 19-6. Bearing in mind that cotton production is more labor-intensive than automobile production, describe the effects of a change in demand that moved society to point B on the production possibility frontier.

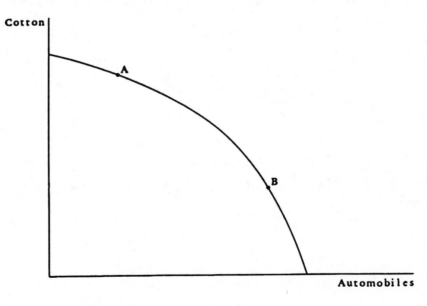

Figure 19-6

13. Under monopoly, society is not on the welfare frontier. Do you agree or disagree? Explain.

14. Can you offer an explanation for trade between nations?

15. a. Suppose there are two industries—wine and corn. What are the welfare effects of an excise tax on wine? (Assume that the government makes a lump-sum payment to individuals to keep their wealth at the pre-tax level.)

    b. How do the effects differ if the government does not make a lump-sum payment to taxpayers?

ANSWERS

Review Questions

True/False

1. True
2. True
3. True
4. False
5. False. Every point on the contract curve corresponds to a point on the production possibility frontier.
6. True
7. True
8. True
9. True
10. True
11. True
12. False

Multiple Choice/Short Answer

1. d
2. c
3. d
4. welfare frontier
5.
   a. True
   b. False
   c. True
   d. False. C is not preferred to F for person A.
6. b
7. d
8. b
9.
   a. sweaters
   b. machinery
   c. contract

10. c
11. c
12. a
13. c
14. b
15. c
16. c
17. a
18. c

Discussion Questions and Problems

1. General equilibrium analysis takes into consideration more of the interrelationships in the economy than partial equilibrium, but still does not include all the interrelationships among all markets. In either case, we try to focus on the important interrelationships and factors and ignore the trivial ones.

2. There is no single correct answer to this question. Many markets could be affected by a tax on margarine: bread, jelly, muffins, cheese, milk, cattle, feed for cattle, farm laborers, and factory workers, to name just a few. The spillover and feedback effects would be numerous. For example, the tax on margarine may affect the demand for jelly, which could affect the demand for margarine in return. The tax on margarine increases the demand for butter, and milk is used in the processing of butter. Hence, the demand for milk may increase, which may induce an increase in the demand for dairy cows, which increases the demand for cattle feed, etc. The above answer mentions only a few markets.

3. If there is any way that the allocation of resources can be changed that permits someone to be better off without making someone else worse off, then the allocation of resources is inefficient. If this cannot be done, it is efficient.

4. Disagree. Figure 19.2 in the text illustrates. Point D is inside the welfare frontier. Any points on the welfare frontier between B and C are preferred to D since either Tiny Tim or Scrooge (or both) can be made better off without the other being made worse off. However, a move to A required that Scrooge be made worse off, so we cannot conclude that A is preferred to D.

5. Disagree. For a move to be efficient, it must be the case that no one is harmed. Taking money from the rich harms the rich, so would not be efficient. Of course, societies do make such changes since efficiency is not the only goal a society has.

6. The contract curve is found by connecting all the points of tangency between the isoquants of the two goods. When isoquants of the two goods are tangent to each other, the ratios of marginal products for both goods are equal to each other and equal to the ratio of input prices. When this occurs, firms in both industries are minimizing costs. Hence a general equilibrium must be on the contract curve.

7. Every point on the contract curve identifies a combination of the two goods that can be produced with the available supply of inputs when firms minimize costs. The production possibility frontier plots these various combinations of output directly. (Review Figures 19-1 and 19-2 in this guide.)

8. The slope of the production possibility frontier measures the amount of one good that must be given up to produce one more unit of the other good. In other words, it measures the ratio of the monetary marginal costs of the two goods. Since P=MC in perfect competition, the slope also measures the price ratio of the goods. Consumers equate their MRS with the price ratio, so the slope of the production possibility frontier equals the slope of the consumer's indifference curve at equilibrium.

9. a. The $MRTS_{cw} = -1$. We know that $MRT = MC_w/MC_c = P_w/P_c$, so all these ratios must also equal 1. The production possibility frontier must have been derived from a contract curve that is the diagonal of the Edgeworth production box, since the constant MRT implies that the inputs that leave one industry go into the second industry at a constant rate. Thus input prices are constant too.

   b. The increase in the demand for corn causes the price of corn to increase relative to the price of wine. Some resources shift from producing wine to producing corn. But the constant MRT implies that the new long-run equilibrium must have the same price ratio as the original equilibrium. Input prices also will not change, although more land and labor will be employed in the production of corn than before.

10. Efficiency in the distribution of products among consumers requires that the marginal rates of substitution are the some for all consumers. When this condition holds, all consumers value an additional unit of a product, in terms of the other product, equally. Hence there are no further gains from trade. Efficiency in the allocation of inputs requires that the marginal rates of technical substitution are equal in the production of all goods. When this condition holds, there is no way to increase production by rearranging the allocation of the inputs. Efficiency in output requires that MRT=MRS. When this occurs, consumers value an additional unit of a good, in terms of the other good, in the same proportion for which it is possible to produce one more unit of the good. The marginal benefit to consumers of one more unit equals the marginal cost of producing it.

11. Perfect competition fulfills the three conditions for Pareto optimality: (1) There is an efficient distribution of products among consumers under perfect competition. Each individual chooses his consumption bundle by setting $MRS_{xy} = P_x/P_y$. Since prices are the same for everyone, $MRS^A_{xy} = MRS^B_{xy}$, where A and B represent any two consumers. (2) Inputs are allocated efficiently in perfect competition. Each firm minimizes costs by employing units such that $P_L/P_K = MRTS_{LK}$. All firms face the same prices for labor and capital, so $MRTS^X_{LK} = MRTS^Y_{LK}$. (3) In a perfectly competitive economy, firms maximize profits by setting $P = MC$. Thus, $P_x = MC_x$, $P_y = MC_y$, and $P_x/P_y = MC_x/MC_y$. Further, $MRT_{xy} = MC_x/MC_y$, and $MRS_{xy} = P_x/P_y$. Therefore, $MRS_{xy} = MRT_{xy}$. When perfectly competitive markets are in equilibrium, all three conditions for Pareto optimality we satisfied.

12. A movement from A to B causes the price ratio to change such that the price of automobiles rises relative to the price of cotton. Resources leave the cotton industry and flow to the automobile industry. Since automobile production is more capital-intensive than cotton production, capital becomes scarcer relative to consumers' demands. The price on capital rises and the wage rate falls, so capital owners are wealthier than before, while wage earners are poorer. The change in demand affects the prices of the goods, the prices of inputs, and the income distribution.

13. Agree. Price is greater than marginal cost under monopoly, so we know that MRS>MRT. Hence we know that it is possible to change the output mix and make both consumers better off. Since both can be made better off, we must not be on the welfare frontier.

14. Trade between nations exists because the total amounts of different goods differ between nations. This results in consumers in different countries having different marginal rates of substitution. Exchange between nations, just like exchange between individuals, makes the parties to the exchange better off.

15. a. See Figure 19-7. Production moves from E to M as less wine and more corn is produced. The price of wine consumers pay (P^c_w) is greater than the price of wine received by producers (P^p_w). Hence $P^c_w/P_c) > (P^p_w/P_c) = MC_w/MC_c$; therefore, MRS>MRT, and the output is inefficient.

   b. Consumers have less money to spend, so they consume less wine and less corn. Society moves inside the production-possibility frontier to F.

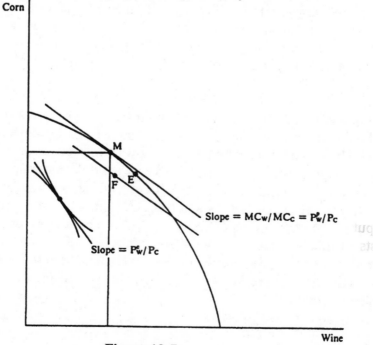

Figure 19-7

390

CHAPTER 20 *Public Goods and Externalities*

CHAPTER ANALYSIS

In Chapter 19 we saw that perfect competition efficiently produces the goods people want. In this chapter two situations are discussed for which perfect competition does not provide an efficient outcome. When public goods or externalities exist, perfect competition is not efficient, and it is possible for government to intervene and correct the situation.

20.1-20.2 There are two important characteristics of a **public good—nonrival consumption** and **nonexclusion**. If one person's consumption of a good does not diminish the quantity consumed by another person, there is nonrival consumption. A private good is characterized by rival consumption. Suppose there are two people, A and B, and two goods, X and Y. Good X is a private good and good Y is a public good. We can characterize the private good in this way:

$$X_T = X_A + X_B \text{ or } X_A = X_T - X_A$$

The total amount of X (X_T) is divided between the amount A consumes (X_A) and the amount B consumes (X_B). If X_T is fixed, the only way A can increase consumption of X is if B consumes less. The public good can be characterized:

$$Y_T = Y_A = Y_B$$

The total amount of Y (Y_T) can be consumed by A (Y_A) and by B (Y_B). One person's consumption of a public good does not affect another person's consumption of it.

The nonexclusion characteristic of a public good means that it is impossible (or too costly) to exclude those who don't pay for the good from receiving the benefits of it. People can be free riders when they know they can receive the benefits of a good whether they pay for it or not. If everyone, or a large segment of the population, tries to be a free rider, competitive markets will not supply the public good efficiently. In such cases, the government often provides the good and forces people to pay for it by taxing them.

The efficient output of a public good is found by equating the marginal benefits of the good with the marginal costs of producing the good. When there is nonrival consumption, the marginal benefit of the good is found by adding together the marginal benefits of all consumers. The demand curve for a public good is found by vertically summing individual demand curves. (Contrast this method with the horizontal summation of a private good described in Section 4.4 of the text).

Review Figure 20.1 in the text to make sure you understand how individual demand curves are summed vertically to obtain the social demand curve.

20.3 **Externalities** exist when side effects are borne by people who are not directly involved in the market exchange. Individuals and firms make decisions on the basis of private costs and benefits and do not consider **external costs and benefits**. As a result, goods that generate external costs are produced in too great a quantity while goods that generate external benefits are produced in too small a quantity. The government can use taxes to force individuals to consider the external costs when making decisions and subsidies to encourage people to consider the external benefits.

The case of external benefits and subsidies is illustrated in Figure 20-1. The market output and price are found by the intersection of the demand curve (D) and the supply curve (S). Q_1 units will be produced and sold at a price of P_1. The MEB curve measures marginal external benefits of the good. Vertically adding the MEB curve to the demand curve yields the social demand curve (D_S). (Note the similarity to the social demand curve for a public good.) The efficient output is found by the intersection of the social demand curve and the supply curve. The efficient output is Q_E. The government can generate the efficient output by subsidizing production of the good. The subsidy shifts the supply curve down by an amount equal to the subsidy. The subsidized supply curve (S') intersects the private demand curve (D) at an output of Q_E units.

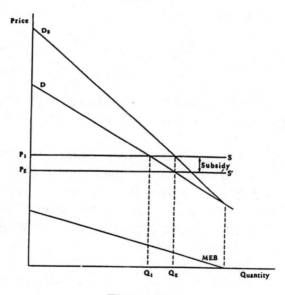

Figure 20-1

20.4 Externalities exist because property rights are not well defined in some areas. A person who owns land can legally prevent others from dumping garbage on it, but cannot legally prevent others from polluting the air over it. Property rights are well defined on land but not in the air. One way to solve the problem of externalities is to have well defined property rights. The problem that remains is that defining property rights on some goods is very difficult (for example, air, fish in the ocean, and space on a freeway during rush hour).

Ronald Coase demonstrated that there are no externalities when property rights are well defined and enforced.[1] This is due to the fact that the costs or benefits are no longer external. Suppose a laundromat and a factory are close to each other. Pollution from the factory raises the laundry's cleaning costs by $100. If the laundry has the legal right to be compensated, then the factory has to pay the laundry $100 compensation. The external cost is no longer external.

If it is legal for the factory to pollute, the laundry might be willing to pay the factory to stop polluting; for example, they might offer it $100. In this situation, the factory would not accept the payment because the $100 would not compensate them for all their costs incurred in stopping the pollution. The factory still bears a cost of $100--the $100 offer it turned down. In either case, the factory bears the cost of the pollution, so there is no longer an externality.

20.5 Pollution is a prime example of negative externalities caused by poorly defined property rights. For example, a steel firm may emit pollutants into the atmosphere as part of their production process. The production costs of the steel are less than they would be if the firm had to clean up their emissions. The government has regulated air pollution for a number of years. Recently, they have begun to utilize more **"market-based"** programs to create better incentives for firms to clean up. Market-based programs are more efficient than a command and control approach.

ILLUSTRATIONS

The Fable of the Bees

A popular example of external benefits involves honey producers and orchard owners. Bees feed on flower blossoms, so honey production increases if there are flower-producing plants nearby. Bees aid in the pollination of plants, so farmers benefit when bees are nearby. If beekeepers do not consider the external benefits that bees' activities provide to farmers, they will not provide as many bees as society would like. Similarly, if the farmers do not consider the external benefits to the beekeepers, they will not provide as many crops as is socially optimal.

---

[1]Ronald H. Coase, "The Problem of Social Cost," *The Journal of Law and Economics*, 3 (October 1960): 1-45.

Steven Cheung hypothesized that beekeepers and farmers would realize the existence of these external benefits and negotiate contracts that would internalize the external benefits. He found that such contracts were well developed and took into consideration the benefits that various crops provided beekeepers and the benefits bees provided farmers in pollinating their crops. For example, beekeepers paid rent to farmers for the right to place hives on their land when the crop was one that has high honey yields (such as alfalfa), while farmers paid beekeepers to place hives on their land when the crop had low honey yields. Economic incentives provided a way to internalize the external benefits.

[See Steven N. S. Cheung, "The Fable of the Bees: An Economic Investigation," *Journal of Law and Economics* 16 (April 1973) 11-33.]

The Development of Property Rights and Externalities

The illustration of the beekeepers and farmers indicates that contractual arrangements often evolve to internalize external benefits and costs. Harold Demsetz argues that property rights will evolve when the cost of an externality becomes greater than the cost of internalizing the externality. He cites as an example the development of property rights by Native Americans on the East Coast after the arrival of Europeans. The hunting activity of one Native American would have external effects on others to the extent that there were fewer animals for others to kill and fewer animals for procreation. Before the arrival of Europeans, the external costs were low. After the arrival of Europeans, the demand for fur increased sharply. As a result, hunting activity increased and many animals were overhunted. In response, the Native Americans developed a private property arrangement of the hunting land. Now each hunter had an incentive to manage his resources in a way that ensured there would be a continuous supply of fur-bearing animals in the future. The external costs were eliminated by the development of a private property system.

[See Harold Demsetz "Toward a Theory of Property Rights," *American Economic Review, Papers and Proceedings 57* (May 1967): 347-359.]

KEY CONCEPTS

public good
externality
nonrival in consumption
nonexclusion
free rider

social marginal benefit curve
vertical summation of demand curves
external benefits
external costs
Coase theorem

REVIEW QUESTIONS

True/False

____ 1. Nonrival consumption involves goods that people like to consume as a group.

____ 2. Nonexclusion means that it is prohibitively costly to prevent anyone from receiving the benefits of the good.

____ 3. Free-rider behavior is rational in the case of public goods.

____ 4. Free-rider behavior is more likely in a large group than in a small group.

____ 5. The total demand curve for a public good is found by horizontally adding up the individual demand curves.

____ 6. The biggest problem associated with public goods is the rationing problem.

____ 7. In the presence of external costs, competitive production leads to an output that is larger than the efficient output.

____ 8. Externalities are connected with the way property rights are defined.

____ 9. The Coase theorem states that assigning property rights will not generate an efficient pattern of resource use because there are distributional effects.

____ 10. Assigning property rights will always solve externalities.

Multiple Choice/Short Answer

1. Indicate whether the following goods are characterized by nonrival consumption (yes) or not (no).
   a. Post office   Yes No
   b. National defense   Yes No
   c. Flood control   Yes No
   d. Social security   Yes No
   e. Books in public libraries   Yes No
   f. TV programs   Yes No
   g. A beautiful sunset   Yes No

2. Which of the preceding goods are characterized by nonexclusion?

3.   A free rider is one who
      a. tries to consume more of a public good than others.
      b. tries to convince others not to consume a public good.
      c. pays no taxes by taking advantage of tax loopholes.
      d. understates the value of a public good in order to secure the good at a lower cost.

4.   Competitive markets cannot supply public goods efficiently because
      a. public goods are more expensive than private firms can afford.
      b. not everyone desires the same amount of public goods.
      c. of the free-rider problem.
      d. it is the government's job to provide public goods.

5.   The social demand curve for a public good is found by
      a. vertically summing the consumers' demand curves.
      b. horizontally summing the consumers' demand curves.
      c. using the demand curve of the consumer who values the public good the most.
      d. the demand curve of the president.

6.   When a good provides nonrival benefits but exclusion is possible,
      a. it is efficient to exclude some from consuming the good.
      b. it is efficient to exclude only those people who benefit from the good the least.
      c. it is inefficient to exclude anyone because they still have to pay for the good.
      d. it is inefficient to exclude anyone because their consumption of the good harms no
         one.

7.   Patents encourage a greater, more efficient output of new knowledge, but
      a. inefficiently restrict the consumption of the product.
      b. encourage too many resources to be devoted to research and development.
      c. cannot solve the nonexclusion characteristic of new knowledge.
      d. only do so for 17 years.

8.   Externalities are likely to lead to an inefficient allocation of resources because
      a. they create benefits or costs not borne by anyone.
      b. they are associated with monopoly.
      c. they involve fixed costs that are not a part of marginal cost.
      d. market demands and supplies will not reflect the external benefits or costs.

9.   With external costs, is the competitive output too large or too small?

10.   With external benefits, is the competitive output too large or too small?

11. With external benefits, the government can correct the inefficiency by choosing an appropriate (subsidy/tax). (Circle the correct answer.)

12. Externalities tend to occur when
    a. people behave selfishly.
    b. property rights are not well defined.
    c. people take nature for granted.
    d. people act irrationally.

13. Coase argued that
    a. the free-rider problem will prevent an efficient allocation of resources even when property rights are assigned.
    b. an efficient allocation of resources is independent of who is initially assigned property rights.
    c. the government should use taxes and subsidies to correct externalities.
    d. the distribution of income is the same regardless of who is assigned property rights.

14. If the tax per unit of pollution increases, the rate of pollution abatement for a firm will
    a. increase.
    b. decrease.
    c. remain the same.
    d. can't tell without more information.

15. Market-based pollution control mechanisms such as tradable emissions permits
    a. ensure that society attains efficiency of output.
    b. cost society more for pollution abatement than command and control systems.
    c. ensure that the amount of abatement produced by an industry is produced at the lowest possible cost.
    d. ensure that pollution abatement will be less than under a command and control system.

Discussion Questions and Problems

1. Distinguish between nonrival consumption and nonexclusion.

2. What is a free rider? How are free riders associated with public goods?

3.   Why is government involvement of public goods often necessary?

4.   Is a national park (such as Yellowstone) a public good? Explain.

5.   Explain how the social demand curve for a public good is derived.

6.   Why is there no rationing problem with a public good?

7.   During the Vietnam War, some people would withhold a portion of their taxes equal to the portion of the government's budget for the war because of their opposition of the war. The government would then take the people to court and force them to pay the extra taxes. Why wouldn't the government allow people to not pay taxes for something the people considered to be morally wrong?

8.   We have the following data concerning the true value and the stated value of a good characterized by nonrivalrous consumption and nonexclusion:

Person/Unit	True Value		Stated Value	
	1	2	1	2
A	$100	$ 75	$ 20	$ 10
B	150	75	100	50
C	50	25	10	5
D	200	100	125	75
E	200	100	75	25
F	75	50	50	25
G	125	100	40	20
H	50	25	20	10
I	40	20	10	5
J	10	5	5	0

a.   In Figure 20-2, draw the individual demand curves for persons A, B, and C and the summed demand curve for A, B, and C.

b.   Suppose it costs a firm $900 to build one unit and a total of $1200 to build two units of this good. How many units will be built? Explain.

c.   Suppose the government comes in and does a cost-benefit analysis. How many units of the good will be built? Explain.

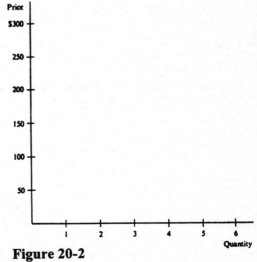

Figure 20-2

399

9. The private supply curve, private demand curve, and marginal external cost curve of a good are provided in Figure 20-3. Find the market equilibrium output and label it Q_1. Find the efficient output and label it Q_E. Show and explain how the government can intervene so that the efficient output is produced.

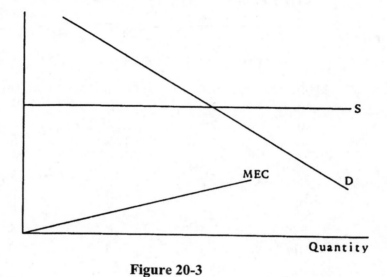

Figure 20-3

10. Explain why externalities are likely to lead to an inefficient allocation of resources.

11. Buffalo and cattle provide similar products to society. Why did the buffalo almost become extinct while cattle have never been in danger of extinction?

12. Suppose there is a farm and a ranch adjacent to each other and that the cost of a fence is prohibitive. The rancher is contemplating the purchase of an additional head of cattle. The net benefits to the rancher of the extra head of cattle are $75, but the extra head will trample $50 worth of crops that belong to the farmer.

    a. If the farmer can legally prevent the rancher from buying the extra head of cattle, will the cattle be purchased? Explain.

    b. If the farmer cannot legally prevent the purchase, will the extra head of cattle be purchased? Explain.

    c. Is society better off if the cattle is purchased or not?

    d. What is the cost to the rancher in part a? In part b?

    e. What is the value of the externality?

    f. Suppose the rancher and farmer cannot negotiate for some reason. Will the head of cattle be purchased under the conditions in part a? In part b? Explain.

13. Explain why True/False Question #10 is false.

14. Explain why market-based pollution control mechanisms promote efficiency in production but not necessarily efficiency in output.

ANSWERS

Review Questions

True/False

1. False
2. True
3. True
4. True
5. False. The demand curves are summed vertically.
6. False. There is no rationing problem with a public good.
7. True
8. True
9. False
10. False

Multiple Choice/Short Answer

1. a. No
   b. Yes
   c. Yes
   d. No
   e. No
   f. Yes
   g. Yes
2. National defense, flood control, a beautiful sunset.
3. d
4. c
5. a
6. d
7. a
8. d
9. Large
10. Small
11. Subsidy
12. b
13. b
14. a
15. c

Discussion Questions and Problems

1. Nonrival consumption means that consumption by one person does not have to diminish the quantity consumed by others. Nonexclusion means that once a good is produced, it is prohibitively costly to exclude anyone from consuming the good. It is possible to exclude people from consuming some goods even though the good is characterized by nonrival consumption.

2. A free rider is one who receives the benefits of a good without paying for it. Free riders are associated with public goods because of the nonexclusive nature of most public goods. Individuals who didn't contribute to the payment of a public good cannot be excluded from consumption of the public good. They can consume for free the good paid for by others.

3. Government involvement in the provision of public goods is generally necessary because of the free-rider problem. People have an incentive to understate the value of a public good in an effort to be a free rider. If enough people behave as free riders, the good either will not be produced or will be provided in a suboptimal quantity by competitive markets.

4. No. A natural park is characterized by nonrival consumption only to a point, for if the park is very congested, the consumption of individuals interferes with others' consumption. Further, nonpayers can be excluded from national parks.

5. The social demand curve for a public good is found by vertically summing all individuals' demand curves for the public good. Vertical summation is employed because of the characteristic of nonrival consumption. The height of an individual's demand curve indicates the marginal benefit of another unit of the good. To find society's marginal benefit of another unit we must add the marginal benefits of another unit for all individuals.

6. Since public goods are characterized by nonrival consumption, a good doesn't have to be rationed among consumers. All consumers can consume as much of the good as exists.

7. People have a tendency to understate the value of a public good in order to pay less for it. To prevent this free-rider problem, the government forces all to pay for these goods by paying taxes. To permit some to not pay a portion of their taxes because of objections to public policy would open the door for many to reduce their tax bill by claiming opposition to the policy. It would be impossible for the government to distinguish genuine opposition to a policy from freerider behavior.

8.   a. See Figure 20-4.

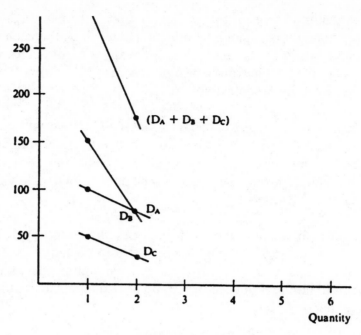

Figure 20-4

b. Zero units will be built because the stated value of the good to the people is below the cost of producing it.

c. Zero units if the government uses the stated values in the calculation of benefits. If the government could determine the true value of the good, then it would build two units.

9. See Figure 20-5. The social marginal cost curve (S_s) is found by adding vertically the MEC curve to the private supply curve. The intersection of S_s and the demand curve identifies Q_E. The government can set a tax of T dollars per unit produced to generate the efficient output. The tax shifts the private supply curve up to S', which intersects the demand curve at Q_E.

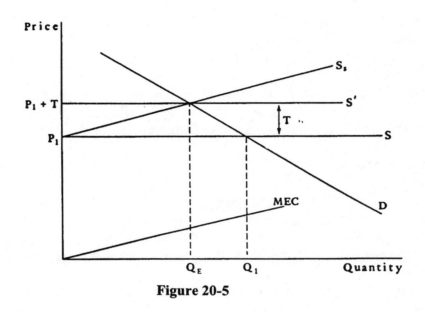

Figure 20-5

10. Individuals make decisions on the basis of private marginal benefits and costs and do not take into consideration the benefits and costs that fall on others. As a result, the true benefits or costs are not used in making decisions, so the output chosen is likely to be inefficient.

11. Buffalo were wild, whereas cattle have always been privately owned. Hence property rights have been well defined on cattle for centuries but were not well defined on buffalo in the nineteenth century. A person obtained property rights on a buffalo by killing it, so there was an incentive to overkill buffalo. Since individuals owned cattle, they had an incentive to keep enough cattle for procreation to ensure future supplies of cattle. No such incentive existed for buffalo, so they came close to extinction. They were saved from extinction by the government's establishing property rights on them.

12.   a. Yes. The rancher will pay the farmer $50 to allow him to purchase the extra head of cattle.
       b. Yes. The farmer will offer to pay the rancher up to $50 to not buy the cattle, but the rancher will turn down the offer, since the cattle is worth more than $50.
       c. Society is better off if the cattle is purchased and the crops destroyed, since the value of the cattle is $75 and the value of the crops is $50.
       d. $50. $50.
       e. Zero. The rancher bears the cost of $50 regardless of who has the legal property rights.
       f. No. Yes. The rancher is unable to offer $50 to the farmer, so the farmer will exercise his legal rights and prevent the extra head from being bought. In the second case, the rancher will buy the extra head, since the farmer cannot legally prevent him from doing so. In this case, the allocation of resources between beef and crops differs with different assignments of property rights.

13.   The Coase theorem states that bargaining between individuals will achieve an efficient pattern of resource use when property rights are clearly defined and enforced. In such cases, there are no externalities because market participants bear all costs and benefits. However, many externalities involve large numbers of people, which makes negotiations among all people involved prohibitively costly. When this is true, the negotiations will not take place and the externality will persist.

14.   Efficiency in production requires firms to have equal marginal costs at the outputs produced. A control-based pollution abatement system is likely to require all firms to reduce pollution by some fixed amount. As long as different firms have different costs of pollution abatement, the control-based system is inefficient--different firms will have different marginal costs of abatement. A market-based mechanism generates equal marginal costs of abatement across firms, so production efficiency is achieved. However, the correct amount of abatement is not necessarily achieved by either market-based or control-based systems.